Common Sense in Business Writing

Common Sense in Business Writing

RICHARD J. LONDO
St. Norbert College

MACMILLAN PUBLISHING CO., INC.
New York

COLLIER MACMILLAN PUBLISHERS
London

Macmillan Publishing Co., Inc.
866 Third Avenue, New York, New York 10022

Collier Macmillan Canada, Ltd.

Library of Congress Cataloging in Publication Data

Londo, Richard J.
  Common sense in business writing.

  Includes index.
  1. Commercial correspondence. 2. Business report
writing. 3. Communication in management. I. Title.
HF5721.L65   808'.066651021   81–5964
ISBN 0–02–371740–8   AACR2

Printing: 1 2 3 4 5 6 7 8 9   Year: 2 3 4 5 6 7 8 9

for Barb

Preface and Acknowledgments

The approach this text takes to business writing is unusual enough to require some explanation. So is the content. Both are the result of practical experience in teaching college students how to write effective letters and reports and in tutoring middle-management employees of large companies in these same skills.

Part III (Business Letters) and Part V (Reports) are the heart of the text, of course; and they are not very unusual. They cover the standard types of messages most people in business need to write. The focus in these parts of the book is on the basics of organization and strategy, rather than on the wide variety of business forms and situations that the student can quickly and easily learn when on the job. In my experience, students who have a solid foundation in logic and organization have little trouble writing whatever kinds of business messages their jobs demand.

There may be some surprises in the other parts of the book, however. An entire chapter on avoiding noun clutter, another on using transitive active verbs, and some of the others on reducing language fog may seem more appropriate for a freshman composition textbook than for one in business writing. Yet, I have found that these are precisely the things students need to learn in order to improve their proficiency as writers of reports or business letters. In fact, these same chapters have proved very successful in helping managers and engineers, some of them with master's degrees in their fields, to write much clearer, much more readable reports than they thought they were capable of. I am *not* suggesting that English composition courses fail in their responsibility; I *am* suggesting that the clearest, most concise expository prose is not always the object of those courses; nor should it be. This book, then, aims at helping the student adapt previous writing instruction to the specific needs of business writing. The business context imposes its own demands on the writer, and that is why the grammar and rhetoric I include in this text are quite different from the material found in any freshman composition text. Certainly the *emphasis* is far different.

I have also tried to make the text useful to the student who has had very little instruction in grammar or writing skills. That is why some of the chapters may seem overexplained. But even the student who already knows the content of the chapters may well find that developing a writing style which incorporates that content is challenge enough.

Often during my courses for managers and engineers, after I have suggested changing transitive passive verbs to transitive active, a student, surprised at the improvement this one technique can produce, would ask why textbooks do not stress that as a major lesson. Now there is one that does.

Concerning approach, this text presents a few surprises, too. First of all, it orients the entire writing process toward the reader. The first chapter explains why that is important.

Secondly, the writing style I use is rather informal for a college text. I use contractions and an occasional colloquialism, not because it is easier for me to write that way, but because I want the reader to feel as if I am *talking* to him or her. The student learns much more quickly from a *coach* than from a *judge*. I purposely keep the tone informal and unsophisticated so that the student will regard the text as the voice of a sympathetic friend. That is very close to the actual truth, anyway.

Finally, the structure of the chapters themselves needs some comment. The exercises woven into the text are not really programmed frames, but they are similar to them. The student should conscientiously write the answers in the book on the lines provided, even if the only change is to add a comma or an apostrophe. The mere practice of rewriting the entire sentence will help develop a feel for sentence structure and spelling.

The Test Yourself section of each chapter exactly parallels in form and difficulty the tests included in the *Instructor's Manual*. The student should try the Test Yourself section, check the answers at the end of the chapter, and restudy any troublesome areas before taking the test which the instructor may give for that chapter.

The text is flexible enough so that report writers and business-letter writers can use it for self-instruction while on the job. It should also work well for in-plant training programs. I have tried to apply common sense to the business-writing situation, and that approach has value for writers at any level.

RJL

Mr. David Morgan, Mr. Don Skupas, Mr. John Tessier, Mr. Bill Komsi, Dr. John Phythyon, and Mr. Cliff A. Bowers generously provided sample material for this text. Mrs. Billie Kontney, Mr. Harry O. Hoehne, and Dr. Kenneth Zahorski read sizable portions of the manuscript and offered valuable suggestions for improving it. Dr. Robert L. Horn, dean of St. Norbert College, provided encouragement and support. I am deeply grateful to all these kind friends.

I also wish to thank my editor, Mr. D. Anthony English, for often saving me from despair with his delightful wit, warm good humor, and extraordinary professional competence. His letters are always the quintessence of common sense in business writing.

Professor Stanley Matyshak deserves my very special thanks. As only a best friend would, he made me defend every word of the manuscript. Few are blessed with friends as talented and generous as this.

I am grateful to Mr. Lyle Lahey for his excellent cooperation in producing the cartoons sprinkled throughout the book.

But my deepest gratitude goes to my wife Barb and our children—Margie, Cathy, Tom, Mike, Ann, and Patrick—for their sacrifice, patience, understanding, and encouragement.

Contents

PART V: REPORTS

PART VI: REVIEW OF THE BASICS

Part I

Introduction

1

The Reader Comes First

Until a few years ago, most texts on business writing devoted several early chapters to giving students pep talks on why they should study the subject. Today such attempts to motivate would seem superfluous because help-wanted ads that plead for technical writers, and public lamentations by executives who need clear writing but are not getting it, have already convinced most people of the importance of good writing in the business world. Today's students know that, next to technical knowledge, the ability to communicate that knowledge on paper is the most important qualification a business person can have.

The question is no longer "Why should I study business writing?" The question today is "How can I improve my business-writing skills?" This book addresses itself to the second question only; you already know the answer to the first one.

The format of the text may seem strange to you at first. I place heavy emphasis on the dynamics of the sentence because no piece of business writing can be more clear and effective than the sentences that make it up, although it can be less so. I blend paragraphs of explanation with a quasi-programmed series of questions for you to answer right in the book because the best way for you to understand a principle fully is to apply it immediately. I have tried to see the subject from *your* point of view, tried to anticipate *your* needs in developing your business-writing skills; and that is why you will run into several topics in these chapters that may seem to you rather elementary for a text at this level—until you try to apply them. You may have studied grammar and sentence structure in earlier college courses or even in elementary school, but *not* in the context of a business-writing situation. It is one thing to define a transitive-active verb, for instance; but it is quite another thing to develop the habit of *using* transitive-active verbs in your business letters and reports. So be patient with the

3

text; there is nothing in it you don't need to know or to reapply in new ways in order to become a successful business writer.

Perhaps the most unusual aspect of this text is the approach it takes to the business-writing situation itself. The communication theory that underlies this approach is a very old one indeed, dating all the way back to Aristotle. But the interpretation of that theory, the parts emphasized, and the application of them are altogether new.

Aristotle rightly identified the three essential elements in any act of communication; but because he stressed oratory, he called those elements the speaker, the subject, and the hearer.[1] For our purposes, the speaker corresponds to the writer, the subject to the message, and the hearer to the reader. We can therefore translate Aristotle's concept into a diagram that looks like this:

If we regard the arrows as symbols of predication, we can get three statements from this diagram: (1) The writer has an effect on the message; (2) the message has an effect on the reader; and (3) the writer has an effect on the reader through the message.

We could hardly imagine a simpler model for communication than this one. In fact, at first glance it seems too simple to offer much help for improving business-writing skills. But if we use it as a heuristic device, we will see that isolating the subject, or message, both from the writer and the reader enables us to make some interesting observations about these three elements.

First of all, it becomes evident that the writer's intended meaning and the written message itself could be two different things. The same is true of the relationship between the message and the reader; what the message says and what the reader perceives it to say could also be very different things. There are many reasons for this. The writer may assume certain implications are clear when they are not, may be wrong about the meanings of some words chosen for the message, or may use inappropriate grammatical structures to encode the message into written English. At the other end of the process, decoding the message, the reader may have only a vague notion of the meanings of certain words in the message, may not recognize certain grammatical structures used, or may get inaccurate concepts of the relative importance of the various parts of the message.

Not even a single word means *precisely* the same thing to any two people; and when we consider the wide range of connotations most words, phrases, and statements are likely to have, we can see there is a problem indeed. We will call these difficulties language fog because they obscure the direct transmission of meaning from writer to reader. Adding this to our diagram, we get the following:

[1] W. Rhys Roberts, "Rhetoric," *Aristotle's Rhetoric and Poetics* (New York: Random House, Inc., The Modern Library, 1954), p. 32.

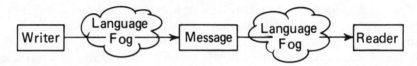

Fortunately, the less language fog there is between the writer and the message, the less there is likely to be between the message and the reader.

Many chapters in this text have the purpose of helping you to reduce language fog to the point where it can do little harm. Unless you work very hard to eliminate wordiness, dangling modifiers, noun clutter, passive-voice verbs, and the like, language fog will engulf your message and prevent you from ever becoming a successful business writer. Assuming you are willing to expend enough effort to minimize language fog, we will consider the little bit of it you cannot remove as inconsequential and leave it out of our future diagrams. But don't forget that some of that fog will always be there, no matter how hard you work at removing it.

The second observation we can make about Aristotle's concept is that the middle element, the message, is too general to be useful for our purposes. Does the term *message* mean the paper with the words on it or does it mean the subject, the meaning, of those words? We need to separate the two, and luckily someone has already done that for us. Meyer H. Abrams, in his excellent analysis of a specialized communication process, distinguishes four elements and arranges them this way:[2]

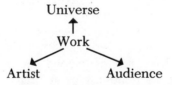

The arrows here mean "has a relationship to," so that if we are to analyze the "Work" we must take into account the "Universe," the "Artist," and the "Audience" because the "Work" has a relationship to all three.

Even though designed to explain certain aspects of literary criticism, Abrams's model has considerable usefulness as an explanation of what happens in business communications. For our purposes, we will translate the three terms *Universe, Artist,* and *Audience* into *Subject, Writer,* and *Reader,* respectively. We will use Abrams's term *Work* to represent the piece of business writing itself, whether letter or report. This gives us a more complex description than Aristotle's:

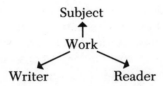

[2] Meyer H. Abrams, *The Mirror and the Lamp* (New York: W. W. Norton Co., 1958), p. 6.

This model begins to reveal relationships the other model hid. For instance, we must consider the relationship between the subject and the work itself; this has to do with the truth or accuracy of the piece of writing. The model also suggests that the work, being in the middle of the triangle, has some part to play in the interrelationships among the other three elements. Only the writer can insure that all these relationships remain intact.

The relationship between the writer and the work is important, of course, because the work can never be any clearer than the writer's own understanding of the subject. Strange as it may seem, some people think they will get lucky and write something that makes more sense to their readers than it does to themselves. But it never happens that way.

The relationship between the subject and the work is also important. For example, if the writer does not pay close attention to the subject, but instead includes only the information the reader will like to read, in a short time both the reader and the writer will be in serious trouble. The letter writer who promised a discount to a customer and later found the discount applied only to larger orders did not last very long, nor did the report writer who "invented" some of the data on a feasibility report that cost the company thousands of dollars. You must make sure your letters and reports tell the truth; your writing must explain your subject *accurately*.

The relationship between the work and the reader is perhaps the most important of all. The writer who concentrates so much on the subject that the report becomes nothing but a mass of undigested details, and the writer who sends a business letter containing everything about the subject except what the reader needs to know about it, are not communicating. Remember that every letter or report you write is useless unless your reader can make sense out of it.

Yet, the model we have just developed shows only half of the story. True, it reveals the proper relationships among the four elements; but it does not describe the *process* of successful business writing. It fails to take into account the sequence, the generation, the *dynamics* of writing in business.

J. Harold Janis, in his 1973 text, *Writing and Communicating in Business,* proposes the following model,[3] which takes into account the cyclical *process* of business communication:

The importance of this model is that it introduces the cardinal element *response* into our concept of business communication. It shows very clearly that the business writer must use feedback from the reader—or, generally, *any* available knowledge of the reader's needs—as a necessary factor in shaping the work, whether a letter or a report.

[3] Second edition (New York: Macmillan Publishing Co.), p. 22.

More recently, Ruth Mitchell and Mary Taylor, writing specialist at UCLA and researcher at The Rand Corporation, respectively, have developed a model that further emphasizes the importance of this feedback or response:

> Our model postulates that all writing is directed towards an audience and is to be regarded as the written medium of a transaction. Writing will therefore be classified according to its effects, not according to its conformity with extrinsic standards. Writing is a means of acting upon a receiver. Its success will be judged by the audience's reaction: "good" translates into "effective," "bad" into "ineffective." Instead of a product, we are studying an interaction, a dynamic relationship, with all the complexities that involves.[4]

[4] "The Integrating Perspective: An Audience-Response Model for Writing," *College English*, Vol. 41, No. 3 (November 1979), 250.

Their diagram resembles Janis's, except that it adds prominence to the *response* element, making it equal in importance to the piece of writing itself:

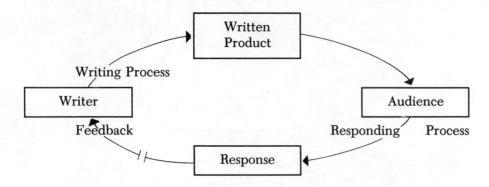

As the diagram shows, the feedback line between the response and the writer is not always complete; and when such a break occurs, the writer has very little hope of shaping the writing process so that the written product will be effective for the particular reader intended—except, of course, to follow the standard writing conventions *all* readers will understand. This is often the case when a writer constructs a formal report; there may be so many readers of the report that the only common denominator may well be standard writing conventions. But in any event, the writer must always employ the one ingredient that all readers are sure to respond to: common sense.

In explaining their communication model, Mitchell and Taylor emphasize the importance of the audience in any writing process:

> *The audience not only judges writing, it also motivates it. A writer answers a challenge, consciously or unconsciously. The conscious challenges are assignments, demands for reports, memos, proposals, letters. They may be requested by the audience directly, or for transmission to secondary audiences.*[5]

After declaring that it might seem best to consider the audience first in their audience-response model, they unfortunately begin with the writer in presenting the explanation. This is understandable; most people tend to think of the writing process as originating with the writer. But it really doesn't. In fact, we should have realized that long ago, for Aristotle hinted as much when, although discussing oratory, he said:

> *For the three elements in speech-making—speaker, subject, and person addressed—it is the last one, the hearer, that determines the speech's end and object.*[6]

[5] Mitchell and Taylor, pp. 250–251.
[6] Aristotle, p. 598.

And, of course, the end, object, or purpose must always be the *first* thing considered. Not only must we consider it first, but in a very real sense the *reader* of the business report or business letter is the *originator* of the whole writing process.

Here are a few examples to illustrate in what way the reader is the originator of the letter or report:

1. A manager finds he or she must decide whether or not to switch to a new accounting system, and this sets in motion a chain of activity that results in a recommendation report.
2. A customer wants an extension of credit, and this starts a process that ends in a letter granting or denying that extension.
3. A potential client could increase sales by hiring your advertising agency, but doesn't know it. When you write to that potential client and explain what your agency has to offer, you are trying to increase your own business, to be sure; but unless you focus your letter on possible benefits for your reader, you will not succeed. Like every other piece of business writing, your letter would have to start with your *reader's* need for information, even if your reader is unaware of that need.

We will need to modify Mitchell and Taylor's model to reflect this change of emphasis. Our model will look like this:

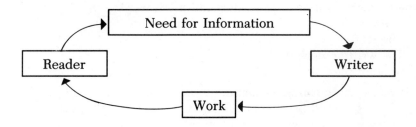

Once you, as the writer, recognize your reader's needs concerning a certain subject, you are ready to begin your writing process, but not before. Your first step must be to increase your understanding of that subject *and* of your reader's needs relative to it. Your *primary* purpose must be to satisfy your reader's needs concerning that subject. Hence, the first commandment of business writing:

Keep your reader in mind.

To familiarize yourself with the format used in all the chapters of this book, and also to find out how well you remember what you have learned so far and whether you can apply it, try answering these questions. The answers are on page 19.

CHOOSE ALL ANSWERS THAT APPLY

1. The main purpose of this text is to
(a) discuss communication theory.
(b) convince you that writing skills are important in business.
(c) help you improve your business-writing skills.
(d) help you get rid of semantic fog entirely.

2. The Aristotelian communication model suggests that
(a) the writer's intended meaning could be different from the actual message.
(b) the writer's intended meaning and the reader's interpretation will always be identical.
(c) the reader's interpretation could be different from the actual message.
(d) there is no difference between the actual work the writer produces and the subject of that work.

3. What element does Janis's model for business communication add to the Aristotelian model of communication?
(a) Language fog
(b) Subject of the message
(c) Writing process
(d) Response

4. According to Mitchell and Taylor's theory of communication, and also according to the model we ourselves have developed in this chapter, which of the following initiates, generates, and motivates the writing process?
(a) The writer
(b) The reader
(c) The written work itself
(d) None of the above

5. Because the business writer must keep the reader in mind, which of the following should be factors in shaping the letter or report?
(a) The reader's knowledge of technical terms
(b) Whether the recipient of the letter will regard the content of the letter as good news or bad news
(c) The sequence in which the writer gathered the information for the letter or report
(d) Whether the letter or report will be easy to read

The principle of keeping the reader in mind immediately raises two questions we need to consider in this chapter: (1) Should the writer try to use the same clichés, inflated language, and convoluted grammatical structures the reader has become familiar with in a particular trade or profession? (2) What are the best ways to minimize the semantic fog that prevents the reader from understanding the writer's intended message?

We will begin with the first question. Looking at our model for business communication, you might reasonably conclude that shaping your writing to satisfy your reader's need for information involves not only selecting and arranging the *content* of your letters and reports, but their *language* as well. If your reader habitually reads the vague abstractions that fog up many articles in certain types of journals, shouldn't you use fuzzy abstractions when writing a report or a business letter to that person? Or, if your reader has a steady diet of wordy reports to read, shouldn't you fill your letter or report with passive-voice verbs to make your writing look "scientific" or "objective" to that reader? Shouldn't you give your reader the kind of language your reader uses, even if it is hard to understand?

No.

A quarter-century's experience in teaching writing skills has taught me that, no matter what eccentric language habits might be popular in a particular reader's profession, that reader will nevertheless prefer to read clear, simple, effective sentences. Some readers don't realize how faulty their professional jargon is until they see it translated into plain, readable English. But most of them do realize the difference, and they heartily welcome reports and letters that make sense on the first reading.

Mitchell and Taylor, in discussing the implications of their audience-response model for writing, say just about the same thing:

> *Have we painted ourselves into a corner, so that the audience-response model must defend sociologese and its related styles? No. We defend only the right of audiences to set their own standards. . . . If bureaucrats and scientists are happy with the way they write, then no one should interfere.*
>
> *But evidence is accumulating that they are not happy. Our conference . . . heard complaint after complaint about student inadequacy in producing discipline-oriented writing. The federal government now hires experts to improve its writing for strictly economic reasons. . . . It is not English teachers who find the writing inadequate—the addressed audiences do.*[7]

As you grow in your profession, you are sure to acquire a professional jargon, words and expressions used only by people in your field. And there is nothing wrong with using that jargon when writing to someone you are sure will understand it exactly. But even then, keep your sentence structure simple and don't waste words. Don't try to write "business English," for there is really no such thing as business English, unless by that term you mean good, clear, forceful language that gets the job done. But then, that is the language of all good writing.

This is not to say that business writing is the same as any other kind; there is indeed a vast difference between a business letter or report on the one hand, and a poem, novel, or drama on the other. But it is not a difference in language. English grammar and sensible word choice are indispensable in every kind of writing, whether expository or creative. The difference is in what the writer is trying to do. In a business situation, you are always trying to convey information to your reader as efficiently as possible—within the bounds of courtesy and tact, of course.

Now try a few more exercises. The answers are on page 19.

---

[7] Mitchell and Taylor, p. 265.

TRUE OR FALSE

Indicate whether the following statements are true or false.

6. T F According to the audience-response theory of communication, a piece of writing is good if it is effective and bad if it is ineffective.

7. T F If someone sends you a letter you can barely understand, you should make sure your reply letter is just as hard to understand.

8. T F You should not try to write reports that are any clearer than the ones you have to read.

9. T F It is a good idea to write "at this point in time" instead of "now" because "now" doesn't sound very businesslike.

10. T F Writing a clear, specific statement requires more knowledge of the subject than writing a vague, general statement does.

Finally, we get to that other question: What are the best ways to minimize the language fog that prevents the reader from understanding the writer's intended message?

To help your reader understand your message, you must do two things: (1) Embody your meaning in grammatical sentences that your reader will recognize as complete statements; and (2) keep your words out of your reader's way.

Business writing demands complete statements; sentence fragments just will not do. A speaker can complete the meaning of a sentence fragment by using facial expressions and voice inflections. A speaker can also use gestures, if needed. But a writer does not have these aids; therefore, sentence grammar and punctuation are crucial to written communication. Part VI of this text explains how to avoid sentence fragments and how to use punctuation to make your meaning clear. If you are rusty in these matters, you should study Chapters 19 and 20 before starting Chapter 2.

There are eight things you can do to keep your words from calling attention to themselves and distracting your reader:

1. Avoid noun clutter.
2. Use the active voice.
3. Put modifiers where they belong.
4. Avoid sexist language.
5. Avoid wordiness.
6. Use precise language.
7. Use parallelism and balance.
8. Maintain continuity.

Part II covers the first four as preparation for the chapters on letter writing, and Part IV covers the last four as preparation for the chapters on report writing. But all eight of these chapters in Parts II and IV use illustrative material relating to both letters and reports; therefore, you can study them in any sequence that fits your needs. I told you I would try to anticipate your needs.

Finally, to get a little practice in recognizing language fog and in reducing it as much as possible, translate the following passages, most of them from government publications, into clear, concise English. The answers are on page 19.

11. By surveying correspondence periodically and finding where errors are being made, training needs and other actions to correct them can be determined to save time and produce high quality correspondence.

---

12. When reply is being made by form letter, the record copy should be omitted and a notation should be recorded on the incoming communication of the form letter and the date sent.

---

13. When a separate-page comment is being prepared, the reference symbol at the left margin should be typed on the eighth line from the top of the page using plain bond paper.

---

14. An employee suggestion, No. 12345, was forwarded to your office on 16 December 1977. In order that the suggester may be furnished an interim progress report, request appropriate date when the return of this suggestion may be expected.

_____

_____

_____

_____

15. Readers of this memorandum should consistently practice the procedure of extinguishing all electric illumination prior to making their departure for the day.

_____

_____

FOR CLASS DISCUSSION

Discuss the following statements:

A. "When I write a report, my first concern is to protect myself; I don't want to say anything that will make it look as if I haven't been doing my job."

B. "Business letters I write are always full of jargon and technical terms. I write that way to let my reader know I'm no dummy."

C. "I dont halfta rite good becuz Im so skiled at what I do I will have a secy. do my riting for me."

D. "After reading every report I receive, I make it a point to let the writer know what was good, bad, or indifferent about it."

E. "When I write a report, I include only the data that will make my boss happy. Why should I stir up trouble?"

F. "In my reports, I list information in the same order I happen to come across it. This makes report writing a lot easier."

G. "After I finish the draft of a letter, I read it through from the point of view of the person I'm writing to."

TEST YOURSELF

The answers are on page 20.

True or False

1. T F Because business English is so different from other kinds, the ordinary rules of grammar don't apply to it.

2. T F You should write letters and reports mainly from your reader's point of view.

3. T F Your primary purpose when writing a letter or report should be to satisfy your reader's needs concerning the subject you are writing about.

4. T F Aristotle's communication model suggests that the subject and the piece of writing can be very different things.

5. T F The careful writer can eliminate language fog entirely.

6. T F The communication model this book uses shows business writing as a cycle originating with the reader.

7. T F In the model of communication this book uses, the letter or report is the writer's response to the reader's need for information.

8. T F The first commandment of business writing is **Keep your reader in mind.**

9. T F The writer should try to keep the reader's attention on the subject, and not on the words.

10. T F Sentence fragments are often satisfactory in business writing.

APPLY YOURSELF

Assume that today you received two letters. The first letter is from Ms. Jane Wilkerson, personnel director of Accuwhiz Widget Company. You have recently applied at Accuwhiz for a summer job beginning next June. Ms. Wilkerson wants you to tell her what you have studied so far in your field. She needs enough detail to be able to decide whether you can do the job that will be available.

The other letter is from your nine-year-old nephew, who wants to know what you are studying to become and what you have to study in order to become that.

Write two paragraphs of 150 words each, one answering Ms. Wilkerson and one answering your nephew.

ANSWERS TO EXERCISES

1. c

2. a,c,d

3. d

4. b

5. a,b,d

6. T

7. F

8. F

9. F

10. T

11. Occasionally review your letters to find out what errors you need to correct.

12. Do not make file copies of form letters you send as replies; instead, record the form and date on the letter that you are answering.

13. Use plain bond paper for a separate-page comment and type the reference symbol at the left margin, eight lines from the top.

14. Please let me know when the employee who submitted suggestion No. 12345 on December 16, 1977, can expect your reply.

15. Turn out the lights when you leave.

ANSWERS TO TEST YOURSELF

1. F
2. T
3. T
4. F
5. F
6. T
7. T
8. T
9. T
10. F

Reducing Language Fog:
Fundamental Techniques

2

Avoid Noun Clutter

Suppose you are production supervisor of an electronics plant and one of your department managers sends you a report that begins like this:

> *Utilization of silicone adhesive in the attachment of speaker grilles to radio cabinets results in a .05% reduction in the cost of construction of radios.*

Such a sentence would only mildly irritate you. At any rate, you would be able to figure out the intended meaning without too much difficulty. But what would your attitude be if the rest of the report went on this way? For example:

> *This process involves the elimination of costly metal screws and the substitution of comparatively inexpensive silicone adhesive, which in turn effects the elimination of the requirement for holes in the grilles. By deletion of the automatic drills in the production line the achievement of a further reduction in costs results.*
>
> *Mr. McMaster made mention of the fact that the holes molded into the cabinets for the reception of the screws now have no function, so their elimination should also come under consideration. But the grilles provide for the concealment of these holes after installation. Therefore, no advantage would be the result of an alteration of the cabinet mold which would attain the elimination of these holes.*
>
> *Implementation of this new process requires the expenditure of $525 for the procurement and installation of adhesive dispensers and $750 for the modification of the production line to permit the accommodation of the new equipment. But the achievement of the reduction in costs by .05% makes possible the accomplishment of cost recovery by the expiration of . . .*

23

Had enough? What's going on here? Why is the report so hard to read? First of all, there seem to be too many nouns in most of the sentences. But the problem goes beyond that. It's the *kind* of noun the writer uses that causes most of the trouble.

Remember that nouns are names of persons, places, or things. Nouns that name specific objects or specific persons are easiest to understand because the reader can easily get mental pictures of what they represent. But abstract nouns like *happiness* and *loyalty* are hard to picture in the mind's eye, and nouns implying action, like *reception* and *concealment,* actually mislead the reader as to what's going on in the sentence. Nouns should *name; verbs* should show action. Let's take the report sample and revise it by converting as many action-implying nouns into verbs as we can:

> *Using silicone adhesive to attach speaker grilles to the radio cabinets reduces assembly costs by .05%. Substituting inexpensive adhesive for costly metal screws also permits removing automatic drills from the assembly line.*
>
> *Mr. McMaster mentioned that we ought to consider eliminating the screw holes molded into the cabinets, but the grilles conceal these holes anyway, so no change in the mold is necessary.*
>
> *Changing to the new process will cost $525 for buying and installing the adhesive dispensers and $750 for modifying the assembly line. But we can recover this cost by January 1, 19— because of the .05% saving.*

You should notice that, besides moving the action from nouns to verbs, the new version is only half as long as the first.

Learn to recognize nouns that hide action. One way is simply to underline all the nouns in your rough draft that do not name *persons* or *material things* and try to convert them into verbs or verbals.

Now don't let that term *verbal* throw you. It's a grammatical term that I will explain in a moment. The reason you need to know about verbals is that in this chapter we will consider them as verbs because they increase the readability of your sentences just about as much as action verbs do.

Verbals are certain verb forms used as nouns, adjectives, or adverbs. For instance, we could take the verb *make* and use it as an adjective if we add *-ing* to it:

> Anyone <u>making a mistake</u> will have to start over.

(Notice that verbals, like verbs, can take objects or have adverbs modifying them. The whole string of related words becomes a verbal phrase and serves as a single part of speech.)

Verbs turned into adjectives this way are participles. Actually, they are present participles; a past participle, the third principal part of a verb as listed in the dictionary, functions much the same way:

The report <u>written by the new office manager</u> clarified the issues.

Or, again by adding *-ing,* we could use it as a noun:

<u>Making a mistake here</u> is inexcusable.

Verbs turned into nouns this way are gerunds.

Or, we could put *to* in front of the verb and use it as a noun, as an adjective, or as an adverb:

<u>To make cloth</u> requires considerable skill. (noun)

In this case, *to make cloth* serves as the subject of the sentence. It therefore clearly is a noun.

The machine <u>to make cloth</u> is very expensive. (adjective)

In this sentence, *to make cloth* modifies the noun, *machine.* Only adjectives modify nouns, so the phrase is certainly an adjective.

Weavers worked around the clock <u>to make cloth</u>. (adverb)

Here *to make cloth* tells why the weavers worked; that is, it modifies the verb in the same way any other adverb would.

Verbs turned into other parts of speech by putting *to* in front of them this way are infinitives.

The important thing to remember is that although these verbals function as nouns, adjectives, or adverbs, they are still essentially verbs. That is, they show action, they can take direct objects, and they can have adverbs modifying them. This means that, like ordinary verbs, they powerfully suggest activity and call up in the reader's mind vivid mental pictures. Ordinary nouns do not have this power, and when they do hint at action they tend to mask it rather than help the reader to visualize it. For instance, notice how the following sentence masks the real action, *explain,* by hiding it in a noun form:

An <u>explanation</u> of the new process was given by Ms. Mapes.

Whether we put that action into a verb or a verbal, it suggests activity that is easy to visualize:

Ms. Mapes <u>explained</u> the new process.
Ms. Mapes <u>tried to explain</u> the new process.

Besides checking for nouns that do not name *persons* or *material objects,* another way to recognize those that hide action is to train your eye to recognize certain types of nouns, types that almost always derive from verbs

25

in the first place. Does it surprise you that some nouns are really "warmed-over" verbs? It shouldn't. Our language does a lot of that sort of thing.

The English language gets considerable mileage out of some of its words by making them serve as two, three, or even four parts of speech. Just by clapping a different ending on the noun *nation,* for instance, we can make it into an adjective: *national;* a verb: *nationalize;* and back into a noun again (this time with a different meaning from the one we started with): *nationalization.* And there are many other endings that can change verbs to nouns, nouns to adjectives, adjectives to adverbs, and so on. But what we are interested in here are two endings that turn verbs into nouns:

26

-tion and *-ment.* If you watch for them carefully and try to convert as many nouns as you can back into verbs, your writing will get livelier and begin to lose some of its heaviness.

Go back over the report sample at the beginning of this chapter and notice how many nouns ended in *-tion* or *-ment.* Now look again at the revision of the same report and notice how few such nouns there are. In revising your rough drafts you need to make the same kind of conversions of *-tion* and *-ment* nouns into verbs or verbals.

Of course, you cannot convert them all, nor would you want to. A sentence like "Manage*ment* chose the third op*tion*" delivers its message about as clearly and succinctly as one could wish. It is certainly preferable to "Those who *manage opted* for the third choice." If converting a *-tion* or *-ment* noun into a verb or verbal forces you into a clumsy expression, then don't convert it. But most of the time a *-tion* or *-ment* noun will hide action that really belongs in the verb. The idea is to reduce the number of such nouns to as few as you possibly can. Consider how heavy and clumsy the following sentence sounds:

Two electricians accomplished the calibration of the meters before noon, but a cessation of power caused a postponement of start-up time until they could find a solution to the problem.

If we convert the *-tion* and *-ment* nouns into their respective verbs, we get:

Two electricians calibrated the meters before noon, but a power failure postponed start-up time until they could solve the problem.

We could improve it further by subordinating the first clause to the second, but by just converting the *-tion* and *-ment* nouns to verbs and eliminating the one we couldn't convert *(cessation)* we have made it a whole lot better than it was.

You should also notice that usually when one of these *-tion* or *-ment* nouns has the preposition *of, by,* or *to* after it, the writer can profitably convert the noun to a verb or verbal.

Now let's try another sentence, this time watching for prepositions after the *-tion* or *-ment* nouns and converting those nouns into verbs or verbals.

In the preparation of his government report Mr. Girard made an examination of registration figures from the last election.

Here we have four *-tion* nouns and one *-ment* noun. But only two of them—*preparation* and *examination*—have a preposition after them. If we convert them to verbs or verbals, we get

In preparing his government report, Mr. Girard examined registration figures from the last election.

That's about as much as we can do for that sentence.

The next one is a little harder, and this time we will let you try it. See if you can convert one noun to a verb, one to a participle, one to an infinitive, and one to a gerund. There's no particular virtue in getting this kind of variety, but it's more fun that way and it will give you valuable practice in understanding verbals. The answer is on page 41.

1. The selection of personnel for the administration of the company's new retirement program was done by a committee under the supervision of Ms. Winlock after her consultation with the legal department.

_____

_____

_____

_____

Did supervision stump you? Yes, it's a *-tion* noun, too, even though it doesn't have *-tion* at the end. Decide on the basis of sound, not spelling (remember that in converting *make* to *making* we had to change the spelling somewhat); that will help you recognize other nouns—like *expansion, conversion, decision,* and the like—as possible candidates for your magic act of converting nouns into verbs or verbals.

There is one other little clue you can use to identify hidden action in nouns. You can generally cut out unnecessary words and at the same time give your reader a clearer mental picture of your meaning whenever you see the following construction in your rough draft:

the (noun) of (noun) . . . by (noun)

For example, suppose your original sentence came out like this:

The revision of the report was done by Mr. Jacobs.

You can easily convert this to the straightforward sentence:

Mr. Jacobs revised the report.

Let's try a few other examples of the same construction. It's your turn to try some. The answers are on page 41.

2. The completion of the program was desired by all the trainees.

_____

3. Ms. Stokes wanted the study of the guidelines to be done by Mr. Bradley.

_____

4. *The cancellation of the meeting was made by the department manager.*

---

5. *Although the curtailment of our employee services was brought about by budget cuts, the continuation of free coffee for our customers will be maintained by us.*

There is another clue for recognizing boring, turgid sentence structure in these last several frames. You should have noticed that in each of the sentences containing

the (noun) of (noun) . . . by (noun)

the main verb is rather flimsy and annoying to the reader. That is because in such a construction the verb will usually be in the passive voice. However, we will save our discussion of this clue and what to do about it for the next chapter. For the present it is enough to concentrate on nouns hiding action that belongs in the verb.

A word of caution: You can't *always* convert a *-tion* or *-ment* noun into a verb or verbal, even if it has a preposition after it. Some nouns with these endings are not former verbs at all. You will find out which ones are not when you try to change them. But try them all, anyway; it's instructive.

And one final note—Occasionally you will be able to convert a *-tion* or *-ment* noun into a verb or verbal even though the noun doesn't have a preposition after it. Consider the following sentence, for example:

The composition and the dictation of the letter took more than an hour.

You can convert both *-tion* nouns to gerunds, even though *composition* has no preposition immediately after it:

Composing and dictating the letter took more than an hour.

The same is true of *-ment* nouns:

Ms. Brandon will perform the establishment and enforcement of new security procedures.

Here both *-ment* nouns can become verbs, even though *establishment* has no preposition immediately after it:

Ms. Brandon will establish and enforce new security procedures.

Perhaps you do not usually clutter up your sentences with *-tion* and *-ment* nouns. You probably have never written sentences as atrocious as some of the examples in this chapter. Yet, you will be surprised how even your very good writing improves when you consciously search for hidden action in nouns and revise your rough drafts as suggested here.

So far we have discussed how to recognize nouns that hide action. But how about verbs? If our objective is to move the action from nouns to verbs, there must be something wrong with the original verbs in those clumsy sentences we have been revising. Here is a list of the main verbs in that original draft:

involves	have	would attain
effects	come	requires
results	provide	makes
made	would be	

Here is a list of the main verbs in our revision:

reduces	is
permits	will cost
mentioned	can recover

At first glance there doesn't seem to be much difference between the two sets. But if we read them in context and ask ourselves how much real action they make us see in our minds, we notice that the verbs in the first draft only *seem* to be describing action. Can you imagine Mr. McMaster *making* a mention, for instance? Hardly. Can you imagine him *mentioning* something? Easily.

The difference between an empty verb and one that shows real action becomes more noticeable when we read the sentence and pay attention to the mental pictures those verbs call up in the mind.

Whenever possible, then, choose nouns that give your reader clear mental pictures, and choose verbs that call up real actions in your reader's mind. The hidden action you take out of the noun will usually tell you what verb to choose.

REVIEW

Let's briefly go over what you've learned:

Use nouns that name persons or material objects, not actions or abstractions. Convert as many *-tion* and *-ment* nouns into verbs or verbals as you can.

Recognize weak noun constructions by looking for the prepositions *of, by,* and *to.*

Reconstruct the sentence if it contains *the (noun) of (noun)* . . . *by (noun).*

Check for empty verbs that only *seem* to show action.

Now let's practice applying these suggestions. The answers are on page 41.

6. Which of the following gives you the clearer mental picture?
   A. employment
   B. typewriter

_____

7. A. briefcase
   B. deferment

_____

8. A. Ms. Edwards
   B. consultation

_____

9. A. boxcar
   B. discussion

_____

10. Which of the following gives the clearer mental picture of action?
   A. The board held a discussion of employee benefits.
   B. The board discussed employee benefits.

_____

11. A. Mr. Sloan gave me some advisement about career planning.
    B. Mr. Sloan advised me about career planning.

_____

12. A. Ms. Dane instructed the managers in how to fill out accident forms.
    B. Ms. Dane gave the managers some instruction in how to fill out accident forms.

_____

13. A. Mr. Smith encouraged me to enroll in the first-aid course.
    B. Mr. Smith encouraged my enrollment in the first-aid course.

_____

14. A. The engineer made the suggestion that we recheck our figures.
   B. The engineer suggested that we recheck our figures.

In frames 15 through 21, convert the nouns into (a) verbs, (b) present participles, (c) past participles, (d) gerunds, and (e) infinitives.

15. selection

(a) _____   (b) _____   (c) _____

(d) _____   (e) _____

16. decision

(a) _____   (b) _____   (c) _____

(d) _____   (e) _____

17. requirement

(a) _____   (b) _____   (c) _____

(d) _____   (e) _____

18. consideration

(a) _____   (b) _____   (c) _____

(d) _____   (e) _____

19. explanation

(a) _____   (b) _____   (c) _____

(d) _____   (e) _____

20. assurance

(a) _____   (b) _____   (c) _____

(d) _____   (e) _____

21. development

(a) _____   (b) _____   (c) _____

(d) _____   (e) _____

22. Which noun hides action in the following sentence?
The revision of the proposal took two weeks.

_____

23. What is the verb form of *revision?*

_____

24. What is the gerund form of *revise?*

_____

25. In "the revision of the proposal took two weeks," substitute the gerund for "the revision of."

_____

26. Which noun hides action in the following sentence?
The crew achieved the completion of the project by the deadline.

_____

27. What is the verb form of *completion?*

_____

28. Revise the sentence, using the verb form of *completion.*

_____

29. Which noun hides action in the following sentence?
The attorney wanted the deferment of legal proceedings by us until the first of the year.

_____

30. What is the verb form of *deferment?*

_____

31. What is the infinitive form of *defer?*

_____

32. Revise the sentence, using the infinitive form of *defer.*

_____

_____

33. Which noun hides action in the following sentence?
The mechanic cut his finger during his installation of the safety shield.

_____

34. What is the verb form of *installation?*

_____

35. What is the present participle of *install?*

_____

36. Revise the sentence, using the present participle of *install.*

_____

_____

37. Which noun hides action in the following sentence? The cost study under the authorization of Ms. Grandis is a good one.

_____

38. What is the verb form of *authorization?*

_____

39. What is the past participle of *authorize?*

_____

40. Revise the sentence, using the part participle *authorized.*

_____

_____

41. Which noun hides action in the following sentence?
Ms. Grandis did the authorization of my cost study also.

_____

42. What is the verb form of *authorization?*

_____

43. Revise the sentence, using the verb *authorize.*

_____

44. Revise the following sentence if it needs it:
All members were in agreement that a meeting was necessary.

_____

45. Revise the following sentence if it needs it:
Both parties signed the agreement.

_____

So far we have concentrated on *-tion* and *-ment* nouns that hide action. These are just the most noticeable ones, however. There are other action-hiding nouns too, and although their endings don't help identify them we can look to their meanings as clues. They are usually the ones that do not name persons or material things. The remaining exercises will contain more and more of this type.

Revise the following sentences by changing the action-hiding nouns to verbs or verbals.

46. The rise of costs caused an increase in our budget this year.

_____

47. Ms. Jarvis gave her approval of my idea for the reduction of waste.

_____

48. The committee members were in agreement on giving help to Mr. Fain in making the decision on priorities.

_____

_____

49. The managers held a discussion on the recovery of overdue accounts.

_____

50. If you have a need for help in the completion of your project, please make notification to Mr. Wills, my assistant.

_____

_____

51. When this metal undergoes expansion, it has a tendency to crack.

_____

52. Do not make an attempt toward the concealment of safety hazards.

---

53. I made the proposal that we effect the suspension of the issuance of coupons until next year.

---

54. He will have no knowledge of the answer until the completion of his project.

---

55. I am in amazement at the discovery that we have been making use of the wrong formula for the separation of these chemicals.

FOR CLASS DISCUSSION

Here are a few passages selected at random from the *Federal Register*. Discuss what you think each passage means; then try to improve its clarity by getting rid of as many abstract nouns as you can. Look especially for *-tion* and *-ment* nouns and convert them to verbs or verbals wherever possible. Put the class's consensus on the chalkboard.

Is the class's revision of each passage clearer than the original? Keep a copy of each revision for use in next chapter's Class Discussion.

A. The Department has 90 days to conduct an investigation and inform the recipient of its findings and an additional 90 days to resolve violations by obtaining a voluntary compliance agreement from the recipient. This is done through negotiations between the Department and the recipient, the goal of which is agreement on steps the recipient will take to achieve compliance.

B. Institutions are not required to upgrade teams to intercollegiate status or otherwise develop intercollegiate sports absent a reasonable expectation that intercollegiate competition in that sport will be available within the institution's normal competitive regions. Institutions may be required by the Title IX regulation to actively encourage the development of such competition, however, when overall athletic opportunities within that region have been historically limited for the members of one sex.

C. Compliance will be assessed in any one of the following ways:

(1) Whether intercollegiate level participation opportunities for male and female students are provided in numbers substantially proportionate to their respective enrollments; or

(2) Where the members of one sex have been and are underrepresented among intercollegiate athletes, whether the institution can show a history and continuing practice of program expansion which is demonstrably responsive to the developing interest and abilities of the members of that sex; or

(3) Where the members of one sex are underrepresented among intercollegiate athletes, and the institution cannot show a continuing practice of program expansion such as that cited above, whether it can be demonstrated that the interests and abilities of the members of that sex have been fully and effectively accommodated by the present program.

TEST YOURSELF

In items one through four, revise the sentence if it needs it. In items five through ten, list or revise as indicated. The answers are on page 44.

1. Mr. Kelly gave me his assurance that he would be here.

2. Ms. Porter gave an explanation of cost accounting to our entire staff.

3. Mr. Brown's delivery of his speech was slow and deliberate.

4. The safety officer will perform an investigation of the accident.

Here is the rough draft of part of a committee report:

> *(1) The deletion of unnecessary paragraphs was the intention of the review committee. (2) However, two members made objection to the omission of one paragraph which had relation to health-care benefits. (3) They were in agreement with the rest of the committee that all members had earlier made a decision about deletion of the paragraph, but they wanted a new discussion of the reasons for the deletion of it.*

5. List the nouns hiding action in sentence 1.

6. Revise sentence 1.

7. List the nouns hiding action in sentence 2.

8. Revise sentence 2.

9. List the nouns hiding action in sentence 3.

10. Revise sentence 3.

APPLY YOURSELF

Assume your colleague in the next office has been working on her rough draft of a letter responding to a customer's enquiry about a problem he has had with a soldering iron that he bought from your company. Suddenly your colleague gets sick and asks you to finish her letter for her so she can go home immediately. You have a few minutes free, so you agree. Here is your colleague's rough draft. Revise it into an acceptable final draft suitable for typing.

June 12, 19___

Mr. Robert Plaintree
3425 Grove Street
Milwaukee, WI 56948

Dear Mr. Plaintree:

We are in agreement that you should not have the necessity of replacement of the soldering tip on your Solder-Master after its utilization for only one week.

The owner's manual for your model makes the warning that your soldering iron can make use of only Solder-Master tips numbered 500 and above. We are of the belief that you are making use of the wrong tip for that model, and we make the recommendation that you immediately make a change in tips for the protection of your soldering iron's transformer.

You made mention of the fact that the original tip was broken when you first took reception of your Solder-Master in the mail. We are happy to make a replacement of that tip free of charge. It will make its arrival under separate cover.

We have the assurance that your Solder-Master will give you many years of dependable service.

Sincerely,

James B. Pearsen
Customer Service
Department

ANSWERS TO EXERCISES

1. After consulting the legal department, Ms. Winlock supervised the committee selecting personnel to administer the company's new retirement program.

gerund—*consulting*
verb—*supervised*
participle—*selecting*
infinitive—*to administer*

(As you perhaps noticed, you needed to rearrange the sentence a little in order to make it sound right after converting the *-tion* and *-ment* nouns into verbs or verbals.)

2. All the trainees wanted to complete the program.

3. Ms. Stokes wanted Mr. Bradley to study the guidelines.

4. The department manager cancelled the meeting.

5. Although budget cuts have curtailed our employee services, we will continue to provide free coffee for our customers.

6. B

7. A

8. A

9. A

10. B

11. B

12. A

13. A

14. B

15. (a) select (b) selecting (c) selected (d) selecting (e) to select

16. (a) decide (b) deciding (c) decided (d) deciding (e) to decide

17. (a) require (b) requiring (c) required (d) requiring (e) to require

18. (a) consider (b) considering (c) considered (d) considering (e) to consider

19. (a) explain (b) explaining (c) explained (d) explaining (e) to explain

20. (a) assure (b) assuring (c) assured (d) assuring (e) to assure

21. (a) develop (b) developing (c) developed (d) developing (e) to develop

22. revision

23. revise

24. revising

25. Revising the proposal took two weeks.

26. completion

27. complete

28. The crew completed the project by the deadline.

29. deferment

30. defer

31. to defer

32. The attorney wanted us to defer legal proceedings until the first of the year.

33. installation

34. install

35. installing

36. The mechanic cut his finger installing the safety shield.

37. authorization

38. authorize

39. authorized

40. The cost study authorized by Ms. Grandis is a good one.

41. authorization

42. authorize

43. Ms. Grandis authorized my cost study also.

44. All members agreed that a meeting was necessary.

45. No revision is necessary.

46. Rising costs increased our budget this year.

47. Ms. Jarvis approved my idea for reducing waste.

48. The committee members agreed to help Mr. Fain decide on priorities.

49. The managers discussed recovering overdue accounts.

50. If you need help completing your project, please notify Mr. Wills, my assistant.

51. When this metal expands, it tends to crack.

52. Do not attempt to conceal safety hazards.
OR
   Do not try to hide safety hazards.

53. I proposed we suspend issuing coupons until next year.

54. He will not know the answer until he completes the project.
OR
He will not know the answer until completing the project.

55. I am amazed to discover that we have been using the wrong formula for separating these chemicals.
OR
I am amazed to discover that we have been using the wrong formula to separate these chemicals.

ANSWERS TO TEST YOURSELF

1. Mr. Kelly assured me he would be here. (Did you slip up on this one? Remember, nouns that end in *-tion* and *-ment* are not the only ones that can hide action.)

2. Ms. Porter explained cost accounting to our entire staff.

3. Mr. Brown delivered his speech slowly and deliberately.

4. The safety officer will investigate the accident.

5. deletion, intention

6. The review committee intended to delete unnecessary paragraphs.

7. objection, omission, relation

8. However, two members objected to omitting one paragraph relating to health-care benefits.

9. agreement, decision, deletion, discussion, deletion

10. They agreed with the rest of the committee that all members had earlier decided to delete the paragraph, but they wanted to discuss the matter again.

3

Use Transitive Active Verbs

One of the quickest and surest ways to ruin a good letter or report, to drain it of all vitality and forcefulness, is to use a lot of passive-voice verbs in it. On the other hand, the best way to increase the liveliness, readability, and conciseness of your report or letter is to use as many active-voice verbs as you can.

Before we go any further, we had better clarify some key terms we will be using in this chapter; they are a bit unusual.

If you look up any verb in a good dictionary, you will find it listed as either *v.t.* (verb, transitive) or *v.i.* (verb, intransitive), and although we will be considering primarily transitive verbs, it might be useful to look at the whole picture.

All English verbs fall into one of the following categories:

I. Transitive Verbs (verbs that show action being received)
    A. Transitive active (action being received by a direct object)
        Example: The new machine *produces* very good copies.
    B. Transitive passive (action being received by the subject)
        Example: Very good copies *are produced* by the new machine.
II. Intransitive verbs (verbs that do not show action being received)
    A. Intransitive linking (subject being linked with a predicate noun, a predicate pronoun, or a predicate adjective)
        Example: The new machine *is* a welcome addition to our department.
        Example: The new machine *is* a good one.
        Example: The new machine *is* huge.
    B. Intransitive complete (subject not being linked with anything)
        Example: The new machine *vibrates*.

Now, the writer's job is to make the reader see very clearly what the message says, and we can take that word *see* almost literally. In the last chapter we learned that helping your reader get vivid mental pictures of the nouns you use is one way of making your letter or report interesting. An even more important way is by giving your reader vivid mental pictures of actions, and verbs are the proper carriers of the activity you are describing.

If you look at the several categories of verbs listed, you will notice that transitive verbs always show action, as do intransitive complete verbs— usually. Therefore, you might think that intransitive linking verbs are the one kind to avoid. After all, most linking verbs merely serve as an "equal sign" between the subject and a noun, pronoun, or adjective. You would be right—partly. It is true that the linking verb lacks power; it is not very forcible. But that is only part of the story.

Even more important than whether a verb shows action is whether it shows action *in the right direction.* Notice that transitive passive verbs show action being received by the *subject,* not by the *object* as transitive verbs do. It is very important that you keep your reader's mind working from left to right, from actor to action to recipient. But transitive passive verbs turn this backward. In reading a sentence with a transitive passive verb in it, the reader first imagines a subject that *receives* the action, then the *action* itself, and then, in a prepositional phrase that is optional, the *actor.* Here is a sentence with an active-voice verb:

The machinist measured the circumference of the spindle.

In this case the subject *machinist* is the actor, the verb *measured* is the action, and *the circumference* is the recipient of the measuring. But look what happens when we transform the sentence into the passive voice:

The circumference of the spindle was measured by the machinist.

Here the subject of the sentence, *the circumference,* is the receiver of the action; the verb *was measured* is the action; and the object of the preposition *by* names the doer of the action, *the machinist.* In this case we have the whole idea reversed: recipient, action, then doer. This makes the reader's mind run backward.

So the best way to help your reader *see* your meaning is to describe activity in the normal cause–effect sequence. It is much better, then, to say, "The research team reported its findings to the committee," than to say, "The findings were reported to the committee by the research team." It takes fewer words and it helps the reader *see* the meaning. First the reader imagines the research team, then the reporting, and finally the findings and the committee.

A further problem with the passive voice is that it will tempt you to leave out the actor. For instance, in the last example it would also be grammatical to say, "The findings were reported to the committee." Leaving out the prepositional phrase "by the research team" enables the writer to hide part of the message. This may be fine for the writer's convenience, but what about the reader's? Remember, KEEP YOUR READER IN MIND. Your reader needs to know *who did what to whom*, not just two thirds of that information.

"A fellow asked me how many people worked here, and I said not more than fifty percent."

Now, it is true that a single sentence in isolation seems almost as easy to read when its main verb is passive as when its main verb is active. But a whole report, or even a whole paragraph, filled with passive-voice verbs is deadly. Consider these two paragraphs, for instance:

Passive

It was assumed that the present automatic garage-door openers have been found to be adequate except in cold weather. Therefore, other brands that have been manufactured under the same specifications have been studied, but their ability to function in below-zero temperatures has primarily been considered. As is shown by the data that are contained in this report, two of these brands have been tested with positive results. The Yumite opener can be operated at temperatures down to ten below zero, and the Maline opener can be operated at temperatures down to twenty below zero. Our needs would be satisfied by either brand. It is recommended that the Yumite opener be purchased because it can be more easily operated.

Active

Because our present door openers function well except in cold weather, this report compares alternative brands differing from ours mainly in their capacity to function in the cold. Tests show that the Yumite operates at temperatures down to ten below zero, and the Maline operates at temperatures down to twenty below zero. Both satisfy our needs. This report recommends we buy the Yumite opener because it operates more easily.

It is easy for a writer to become addicted to the passive voice. If you use it in the first few sentences, you will find yourself likely to go on that way for the rest of the paragraph. You might call it a sort of domino effect; passive-voice verbs beget other passive-voice verbs, and active-voice verbs beget other active-voice verbs.

Now that you have seen how the passive voice can darken your sentences and tangle your reader's mental processes, you need to know how to recognize that annoying structure when you see it in your own rough draft. Every passive verb consists of some form of *be* followed by a past participle. Therefore, it's a good idea to learn and remember the following:

The various forms of <u>be</u>: <u>am</u>, <u>is</u>, <u>are</u>, <u>was</u>, <u>were</u>, <u>be</u>, <u>been</u>, <u>being</u>
The three "principal parts", or forms, or verbs:

Present tense: "Today I _____."
Past tense: "Yesterday I _____."
Past participle: "Often I have _____."

Whatever verb form fits into the last blank will be a past participle. For example, let's take the verb *drive* and find its past participle.

"Today I drive."
"Yesterday I drove."
"Often I have driven."

Driven is the past participle of *drive*. Actually, because we are interested only in the past participle here, you need remember only that last sentence, "Often I have _____."

Once you have learned these things, all you need to do to recognize a passive-voice verb is look for any form of *be* followed by a past participle, as in this sentence:

All the trucks have been driven by qualified drivers.

The form of *be* is *been*, and the past participle is *driven*. Try another:

All products that were inspected by the night crew will be spot checked by Ms. Appline.

Here we have two passive-voice verbs: *were inspected* and *will be spot checked*. Each contains a form of *be* and also a past participle.

Now let's get some practice recognizing passive-voice verbs. The answers are on page 63.

1. Go back to the passive paragraph about automatic garage-door openers and list all the passive-voice verbs you can find. Remember to look for a form of *be* and a past participle.

_____

_____

2. Next list all the passive-voice verbs in the paragraph alongside it.

_____

Now that you can easily recognize passive-voice verbs when you see them, you are ready to start weeding them out of your rough drafts, thereby tightening up your sentences, providing clearer mental pictures for your reader, and adding action and forcefulness to your letters and reports.
Right?
Not exactly.
If you are not somewhat skeptical of what you have read concerning active and passive verbs so far in this chapter, you soon will be when you see some of the effects of changing passive-voice verbs to active in your rough drafts. Sometimes the emphasis will shift away from where you want it. Sometimes you will have to put unimportant nouns in the position of subject. Sometimes you won't even know what to include as the doer of the action because the original sentence doesn't say what or who the doer

is. Furthermore, it will probably occur to you that, after all, the passive voice is not *un*grammatical and that someone once told you the passive voice insures a tone of objectivity—which the business writer ought not sneer at.

Let's examine this last argument first. It is true that the passive voice gives an air of objectivity. But such objectivity is more apparent than real. For instance, it is really no more "objective" to state:

It was decided that the committee would postpone discussion of salary increases until next month.

than to state:

The chairperson decided to postpone the committee's discussion of salary increases until next month.

Or

The committee decided to postpone discussion of salary increases until next month.

There is really less hiding of fact, and therefore more objectivity or impartiality, in the last two sentences than there is in the first one.

Of course, the writer of "It was decided that the committee. . . ." might argue that *who* did the deciding is immaterial, in fact, irrelevant to the meaning of the sentence. We have an answer for that one, too: Leave out the *deciding* business altogether and write

The committee postponed discussion of salary increases until next month.

Or, better yet, we could get rid of the nominalization (the *-tion* noun) and write

The committee will discuss salary increases next month.

In scientific writing the problem is more complex. Here you want to keep your reader's attention focused on physical objects, quantitative results, and the like—not on people. Yet, even in such writing it is better to say, for example, "the investigation showed that. . . ." than to say, "It was found that. . . ." Your reader will appreciate the subject-verb-object sequence because at least it points in the right direction.

Now let's consider those other objections. It is true that sometimes in changing passive voice to active in your rough draft you will shift emphasis away from where you want it. But there is a way to avoid that problem. For example, suppose a sentence in your rough draft reads like this:

These discount benefits will be received by part-time as well as full-time employees.

Merely changing passive voice to active would produce this:

> *Part-time as well as full-time employees will receive these discount benefits.*

Now, suppose you wish to keep your reader's attention focused on the discount benefits. That is, you want to keep those benefits in the subject position in your sentence. You can keep it there if you change the verb:

> *These discounts apply to part-time as well as full-time employees.*

Finally, let's consider the problem of revising a rough draft that has many passive-voice verbs, but no stated doers, or actors, for those verbs. How would you revise the following?

> *An estimate from Millar Products Company has been obtained on the cost of replacing the coffee machines that have been dented. This cost was found to be quite high.*

Here we do not know who obtained the estimate or who dented the coffee machines. Nor do we know who found the cost to be quite high. Luckily, our reader doesn't really need to know these things. The writer has actually implied doers where nobody cares who those doers are. This happens more often than you would think. Let's get rid of those implied doers like this:

> *The Millar Products Company's estimate on the cost of replacing the dented coffee machines is quite high.*

In summary, don't use the passive voice to try to sound "objective," "businesslike," or "official." You can be all these things *without* using the passive voice, and you will be much more clear and forceful besides. In short, *never* use the passive voice unless you absolutely have to. And I can't think of a situation where you will ever absolutely have to use it. But perhaps such situations do exist even though I can't think of one. In any case, remember that each time you use a passive-voice verb you should feel as if you have just lost a skirmish in the noble war against fuzzy, inflated, evasive, mealy-mouthed language.

Finally, it probably has occurred to you that sometimes the writer gains very little in brevity or forcefulness by using the active voice. Consider these two sentences:

> *All workers were given immunization shots.*
> *All workers received immunization shots.*

The second sentence uses an active-voice verb; the first one uses passive voice. Is the second very much better than the first? No. Both have the subject as the recipient of the action; both have the main sentence parts in the same sequence. In fact, the verb "received" seems to bounce the

51

action back to its subject even though grammatically the subject is the doer, the thing that *does* the receiving. Such is the English language! But actually the second sentence *is* better than the first. It doesn't imply an unnamed doer so obviously as the other sentence does. And the second sentence is shorter by one word. One must always choose conciseness that costs the writer nothing in clarity.

Therefore, choose the active voice even if it improves your effectiveness only a tiny bit. In writing, it's the tiny improvement consistently made that tips the scale of clarity and persuasiveness in your favor.

There is one other thing. It will probably occur to you that always trying to avoid the passive voice violates common sense because such efforts must sometimes fail. Most other textbooks insist that, although the passive voice is weak, it is quite appropriate when you want to be objective or when you want to imply the doer is unimportant or unknown. This may be good advice for the creative writer, but you as a business writer need to win your reader's confidence in your total grasp of the material, in your bold avoidance of innuendo, and in your dedication to clarity and readability. We are talking about a frame of mind here. If you accept the notion that passive voice is sometimes appropriate, you will soon convince yourself it is appropriate every time you feel like using it. And you will frequently feel like using it because it often requires less thought and certainty on the writer's part. In a short time your writing will be flabby.

Now let's return to the problem of how to avoid the passive voice and how to choose the most effective of the other three types of verbs. Here are a few rules that will help.

Never use a form of be followed by a past participle if you can possibly avoid it.

Use the active voice wherever you can.

Use intransitive complete verbs where you can't use active voice.

Use intransitive linking verbs only as a last resort.

If you consider these four rules, you will see that they really amount to a sort of "pecking order" among verbs. For the best effect on your reader you should choose your verbs in this descending order of preference: (1) transitive active, (2) intransitive complete, (3) intransitive linking, and (4) transitive passive.

I will try to demonstrate why this is so. The next four paragraphs all contain essentially the same information, but the main verbs in each are all of the same type. You be the judge. Rank the four paragraphs in terms of their clarity, vigor, conciseness, and overall effect on the reader.

A. *I was asked by you for a description of how our vacation-relief system is designed. It is assumed that because vacations are taken on an average of five weeks per employee each year, approximately 10 per cent of our workforce will be needed at any given time to fill in while vacations are being taken by some other employees. Therefore, 110 per cent of* the number that are needed so the plant can be operated have been hired. Each department in the plant is composed of approximately fifty employees, so on an average five vacations are being taken each week in each department. The departments have been authorized to be staffed for about five more employees than are needed so that vacations can be covered.

B.   You asked for a description of our vacation-relief system. Because vacations occur on an average of five weeks per employee each year, approximately 10 per cent of our workforce will be on vacation at any given time. Therefore, we usually operate with about 90 per cent of our total workforce. Because there are about fifty employees in each department, about forty-five are on the job and five are on vacation at any given time. In other words, about 10 per cent of each department's staff consists of vacation-relief personnel.

C.   The answer to your request about our vacation-relief system is the following: About 10 per cent of our workforce are vacationers at any given time during the year. The reason for this is that although our employees become eligible for additional weeks of vacation the longer they remain our employees, their average vacation time is five weeks a year. The average strength of each department is fifty employees, so in each department at any given time about forty-five will be workers and five will be vacationers. Thus, our total workforce needs to be about 10 per cent larger than it would be if vacations were nonexistent.

D.   I will try to answer your questions about our vacation-relief system. Our employees average about five weeks of vacation annually, or about 10 per cent of the year. We have hired 10 per cent more people than we absolutely need to maintain production, so that in each department about forty-five of them will be operating the plant and five will be taking their vacations.

I would rate these paragraphs like this:

Best: D
Second best: B
Third best: C
Worst: A

Did you rank them the same? If you didn't, I must have bungled my demonstration somewhere.

Answer the following questions. The answers are on page 63.

3.   What kind of verb appears in Paragraph A?

4. What kind of verb appears in Paragraph B?

_____

5. What kind of verb appears in Paragraph C?

_____

6. What kind of verb appears in Paragraph D?

_____

Now get some practice improving sentences.

7. List the passive-voice verbs in this sentence:
Your trip mileage is recorded and your receipt is given to you by the dispatcher.

_____

8. What are the subjects of these verbs?

_____

9. Who is performing the actions the verbs describe?

_____

10. Revise the sentence by making *the dispatcher* the subject and changing the verbs to active voice.

_____

_____

11. What is the verb in this sentence?
Your application has been considered by Mr. Thompson and me.

_____

12. Does this verb contain a form of *be* followed by a past participle?

_____

13. Revise the sentence by changing the verb to active voice.

_____

14. What is the verb in this sentence?
The relay must have been adjusted by the electrician during the night shift.

_____

15. Does this verb contain a form of *be* followed by a past participle?

_____

16. Revise the sentence by changing the verb to active voice.

_____

_____

17. List and classify the verbs in this sentence:
Gasoline consumption is being reduced by the smaller engines, and this reduces both costs and air pollution.

_____

18. Revise the sentence by changing the passive-voice verb to active voice.

_____

_____

19. List and classify the verbs in this sentence:
The treasurer's report will be audited by the finance committee as soon as it has been received.

_____

_____

20. Revise the sentence by changing the passive-voice verbs to active voice.

_____

_____

21. List and classify the verbs in the following sentence:
Employees are asked to bring their immunization records with them when they report to the health nurse.

_____

_____

22. Who is the doer of the passive-voice verb?

_____

23. Revise the sentence by getting rid of the passive voice.

_____

Check your answer to this one before going on. Does it surprise you that one of the alternative answers is "Employees should bring. . . ."? Some people object to using such words as *should, must,* or *ought* on the theory that modern business has no place for language that seems to command. But look at it from your reader's point of view. Would you rather read what you *should* do, or have some disembodied voice *ask* you to do something? In any event, again looking at the sentence from the reader's point of view, it would probably be better to cast the whole thing in second person rather than third person. After all, you are presumably writing to the employees themselves. Therefore, the best revision of all is probably the following:

> *You should bring your immunization records with you when you report to the health nurse.*

However, *any* of the revisions above are much better than the original with its fuzzy passive-voice verb.

While we're on this topic, let's try revising a few more of that type of sentence. The answers are on page 64.

24. List and classify the verbs in this sentence:
You are required to have your ticket validated before the plane can be entered.

_____

_____

25. Who is doing the requiring?

_____

26. Who is doing the entering?

_____

27. Revise the sentence by getting rid of the passive voice.

_____

_____

28. And now, since both clauses have the same subject, we can improve the sentence further by reducing the second clause to a phrase. Try it.

_____

_____

We will get into that kind of revision more fully in Part IV. For the time being, let's enjoy ourselves a little longer by playing with some more verbs.

29. List and classify the verbs in the following paragraph:

Your report is excellent. It properly includes all the latest Supreme Court decisions pertaining to our problem. However, local ordinances on the subject should have been included in Part II of the Discussion. Would you please check on these and submit your findings to me by Friday? They will be inserted by me before I send the report to Ms. Buss.

_____

_____

_____

_____

_____

30. Revise the paragraph by getting rid of the passive voice.

_____

_____

_____

_____

_____

_____

_____

FOR CLASS DISCUSSION

1. To the class's revisions of the *Federal Register* passages in last chapter's "Class Discussion," apply what you learned about verbs in this chapter. Are the passages clearer with most or all of the passive-voice verbs converted to active voice? Which chapter's revisions improved clarity more?

Again, keep a copy of the class's consensus. Future chapters should give you additional ideas for improving the passages.

2. Here is a paragraph from an army manual entitled *Office Management: Preparing Correspondence:*

> *This regulation has been made as complete as possible to avoid the need to issue additional instructions. Therefore, supplements to this regulation will be restricted to instructions which are unique to an agency or command. Copying examples from this regulation on local letterhead stationery for the purposes of illustration only is prohibited.*

Discuss the questions this paragraph raises in the reader's mind. Then offer suggestions for getting rid of the passive-voice verbs and put the revised paragraph on the chalkboard or on an overhead projector. Is the revision shorter? Is it more forceful? Is it clearer?

TEST YOURSELF

Revise the following sentences by converting as many verbs as possible to active voice. The answers are on page 65.

1. It is widely thought that all energy problems can be solved by modern technology.

2. The valves are opened by a camshaft, the camshaft is driven by a belt, and the belt is driven by the motor.

3. Ms. Sloan was replaced by Mr. Wilkins while Ms. Sloan was recuperating from the operation.

4. Our winter catalogue must be sent out by September 30.

5. The contract has been examined by our legal department.

6. Your application is being processed by the personnel committee.

7. When an enclosure is not attached to the correspondence but is sent separately, so state in the body of the correspondence.

8. A letterhead is used to identify the originator and to provide a mailing address.

9. I was told by the mechanic that two of our trucks must be overhauled.

10. It was agreed that the contract would be accepted by both labor and management.

APPLY YOURSELF

Select a page at random from three different printed sources (novel, newspaper, magazine, textbook) and classify the first ten verbs you find on each page. Do not include any quoted material or sentences the author inserted as examples (in case you choose a composition text). Determine what percentage of verbs are transitive active, what percentage are transitive passive, what percentage are intransitive linking, and what percentage are intransitive complete. Do you find any correlation between the readability of a passage and the type of verb predominant in it?

Write a paragraph explaining what you have learned, and try to use the same types of verbs you found in the selection you thought was clearest and most readable.

ANSWERS TO EXERCISES

1.   was assumed, have been found, have been manufactured, have been studied, has been considered, is shown, are contained, have been tested, can be operated, can be operated, would be satisfied, is recommended, be purchased, can be operated.

2.   There aren't any.

3.   transitive passive

4.   intransitive complete

5.   intransitive linking

6.   transitive active

7.   is recorded, is given

8.   mileage, receipt

9.   the dispatcher

10.   The dispatcher records your mileage and gives you your receipt.

11.   has been considered

12.   Yes.

13.   Mr. Thompson and I have considered your application.

14.   must have been adjusted

15.   Yes.

16.   The electrician must have adjusted the relay during the night shift.

17.   is being reduced—transitive passive
reduces—transitive active

18.   The smaller engines are reducing gasoline consumption, and this reduces both costs and air pollution.

19.   will be audited—transitive passive
has been received—transitive passive

20.   The finance committee will audit the treasurer's report as soon as they receive it.

21.   are asked—transitive passive
report—intransitive complete

22.   Nobody knows. It could be the person writing the sentence, or it could be the health nurse, or it could be almost anyone.

23.   We ask employees to bring their immunization records with them when they report to the health nurse.
OR

The health nurse asks employees to bring their immunization records with them when they report to him.

OR

Employees should bring their immunization records with them when they report to the health nurse.

24. are required—transitive passive
can be entered—transitive passive

25. Nobody knows.

26. You are, presumably.

27. You must have your ticket validated before you enter the plane.

28. You must have your ticket validated before entering the plane.

29. is—intransitive linking; includes—transitive active; should have been included—transitive passive; would check—intransitive complete; submit—transitive active; will be inserted—transitive passive; send—transitive active

30. Your report is excellent. It properly includes all the latest Supreme Court decisions pertaining to our problem. However, you should have included local ordinances on the subject in Part II of the Discussion. Would you please check on these and submit your findings by Friday? I will insert them before sending the report to Ms. Buss. (Again, in that last sentence we are able to tighten up the loose verbiage because both clauses now have the same subject.)

ANSWERS TO TEST YOURSELF

1. Many people think that modern technology can solve all energy problems.

2. The motor drives a belt, the belt drives a camshaft, and the camshaft opens the valves.

3. Mr. Wilkins replaced Ms. Sloan while she was recuperating from the operation.

4. We must send out our winter catalogue by September 30.

5. Our legal department has examined the contract.

6. The personnel committee is processing your application.

7. When you do not attach an enclosure to the correspondence but send it separately, state this in the body of the correspondence.

8. Use a letterhead to identify the originator and to provide a mailing address.
OR
    A letterhead identifies the originator and provides a mailing address.

9. The mechanic told me that two of our trucks need overhauling.
OR
    The mechanic told me that we must overhaul two of our trucks.

10. Both labor and management agreed to accept the contract.

4

Put Modifiers Where They Belong

Your writing style for business should not be flowery. It should rather be as clear and forceful as you can make it. That means your sentences ought to be sinewy, not sinuous; they ought to consist mostly of nouns and verbs, of subjects and predicates, that will keep your reader's mind attentive to your central meaning.

But you can't avoid using modifiers. Adjectives and adverbs are necessary to pinpoint your meaning, to specify your message exactly so that your reader cannot misunderstand you. The usual problem that business writers have with modifiers is not so much in choosing them, but rather in placing them. When you know what you want to say, the adjectives and adverbs will usually suggest themselves. But putting them in places where each can modify only one thing is no easy matter.

When we speak, our voice inflection lets us get away with an almost haphazard placement of some modifiers, especially of phrases and clauses. When we write, however, we must be much more careful of word order. The reader must depend on the modifier's position in order to decide what it's supposed to modify; there is no voice inflection to help.

No writer misplaces a modifier intentionally. Like sentence fragments, sentences with modifiers in the wrong place sound all right when we hear them in our minds before writing them. But that's because we mentally hear them with the same voice inflection we would use in speaking them. What is worse, they are invariably hard to correct when we revise our first drafts. As we read our own sentences, we "hear" them with the same voice tones we assumed when we wrote them.

For example, you might say the following sentence aloud so that it could have only one meaning:

All the typewriters do not need new ribbons.

If you stressed the word *all,* you would be telling your listener that some typewriters need new ribbons, but others don't. On the other hand, suppose the reader of that same sentence mentally stressed the word "not." Your reader would understand your sentence to mean that *none* of the typewriters need new ribbons. You might have prevented the misreading by revising your sentence to this:

Not all the typewriters need new ribbons.

But each time you read your draft you provide the same mental voice stress. You don't even realize your reader can read it a different way.

Therefore, the suggestions in this chapter are ones that even the best writers need to keep in mind, as we will see in the following example. It demonstrates what can happen when the writer isn't careful to place modifiers where they can modify only one thing. Suppose your boss sent you this memo:

Noticing several fire hazards in production areas that are inexcusable and need to be eliminated, a meeting will be held next Thursday at 2:30 P.M. to discuss safety policies still applied by some managers that are outdated and ineffective in conference room 401D. We will also consider employee awareness of fire hazards, which we need to increase.

Yesterday I discussed with the sanitation crew the need for more regular pickup of garbage and other combustibles in my office, and they agreed to explain what employees can do to help control the rubbish that necessarily accumulates at our Thursday meeting.

I am asking you to suggest some policy changes to prevent fires that you think our production departments need. Giving safety awards for the best suggestions, you may deposit your recommendations for preventing fires in Ms. Pendleton's mailbox, or simply leave them with the secretary stapled to this memo.

You would no doubt have mixed feelings about such a message. In the first place, you would feel sorry for that poor secretary stapled to your memo. Then, you would be delighted that somebody besides you recognized what accumulates at your Thursday meetings. Finally, you would certainly be happy to know that soon your boss's position will be vacant and perhaps you will get promoted to it. For surely your boss will not hold that job very long. Putting modifiers where they don't belong is a sure way to create confusion and to seem very incompetent.

What your boss probably meant to say is something like this:

I have noticed several inexcusable fire hazards that need to be eliminated in production areas. We will meet in conference room 401D next Thursday at 2:30 P.M. to discuss outdated and ineffective safety policies still applied by some managers. We will also consider the need to increase employee awareness of fire hazards.

Yesterday in my office I discussed with the sanitation crew the need

*for more regular pickup of garbage and other combustibles, and they
agreed to explain at our Thursday meeting what employees can do to
help control the rubbish that necessarily accumulates.*

*I am asking you to suggest some policy changes you think would
help our production departments prevent fires. We will give safety
awards for the best suggestions. You may put your recommendations
in Ms. Pendleton's mailbox, or you may simply staple them to this memo
and leave them with the secretary.*

It is true that you rarely find any letters or reports with so many ridicu-
lously misplaced modifiers in them as that first example has. And when
you do run into such gems, they are more entertaining than they are dangerous. When a misplaced modifier turns the sentence into a howler, at least
the reader knows that the writer didn't mean what the sentence seems
to say. But just a few modifiers out of place can ruin an otherwise good
piece of writing, especially if they give the reader a message that is wrong,
but plausible.

Let's change the situation a little. This time suppose you are an insurance
claims adjuster and one of your investigators sends you a report containing
this paragraph:

*The claimant is the wife of Gerald N. Pearsen, who was a passenger
in the car. Before the accident she said Gerald tried to avoid hitting
the truck, which swerved by making a sharp left turn into his lane.
He also slammed on the brakes. I have some doubts about her story,
however, witnesses' accounts seem to agree with it quite well.*

This is what the investigator really meant to say:

The claimant is Gerald N. Pearsen's wife, who was a passenger in the car. She says that before the accident, by making a sharp left turn and slamming on the brakes, Gerald had tried to avoid hitting the truck, which had swerved into his lane. I have some doubts about her story; however, witnesses' accounts seem to agree with it quite well.

The two paragraphs differ considerably. In reading the first one, you can't tell until you get to the second sentence that Gerald, not his wife, was driving the car; and you think the truck made a sharp left turn. In the last sentence, you don't know which clause *however* belongs in; it "squints," or seems to modify words before and after it, too.

In order to avoid the kind of absurdity we saw in that first example of the memo and the kind of unclear writing we saw in the insurance investigator's paragraph, we need to learn how to put modifiers where they belong; that is, arrange our sentences so that our readers *cannot* mentally connect modifiers to words we don't intend them to modify.

Let's take up that "squinting" modifier business first. First of all, you must put a semicolon either before or after such words as *however, consequently, nevertheless, moreover,* and *on the other hand* whenever you use them between two independent clauses. Otherwise your readers won't be able to tell which clause they belong to. Secondly, don't put adverbs like *frequently, eagerly, slowly, often,* and the like between two elements they could conceivably modify. For example, don't say, "He loses his tools often because he lets people borrow them." Say either "He often loses his tools because he lets people borrow them," or "He loses his tools because he often lets people borrow them."

Now let's review our grammar a little. There are two kinds of modifiers: adjectives and adverbs. Adjectives modify nouns or pronouns; and adverbs modify verbs, adjectives, or other adverbs. Both adjectives and adverbs can be single words, phrases, or whole clauses.

Here is a sentence containing a single-word adjective:

Cattle trucks arrived.

Here is one with two adjective phrases; the first is participial, and the second is prepositional:

Trucks carrying cattle must display a certificate of inspection.

And here is one with an adjective clause:

Trucks that carry cattle must pass inspection.

Here is a sentence with a single-word adverb:

Cattle trucks arrived slowly.

Here is one with an adverb phrase:

70

Two trucks arrived after dark.

And here is one with an adverb clause:

Two trucks arrived after the gates closed.

If you examine a few pages of English sentences, you will notice that single-word adjectives almost always come *before* the nouns they modify. Adjectives consisting of phrases usually come *after* the nouns they modify, but when they appear at the beginning of the sentence, they always modify the noun that immediately follows them. Adjective clauses always come *after* the nouns they modify.

Adverbs are not so predictable, but those modifying the main verb usually appear at the beginning or at the end of the sentence.

You would probably observe one other thing, if you examined enough sentences. Certain limiting modifiers—*only, nearly, quite, ever, scarcely, hardly, almost, just, merely*—can appear almost anywhere in the sentence and will usually modify the word or words that immediately follow them. For example, look how the meaning changes when we move the word *only* around in these sentences:

Only Brady could hope to win the hundred dollars.

Brady could only hope to win the hundred dollars.

Brady could hope to win only the hundred dollars.

Keeping these observations in mind, we can state a few simple rules that will help us to avoid almost all misplaced-modifier problems. We'll start with the last observation, the one about modifiers like *only, nearly,* and so on. Let's call them *limiters*. Since they usually appear immediately *before* the words they modify, that is where your reader expects to find them. Put them there. It is true that you can sometimes achieve a certain emphasis by putting them at the end. But then you are flirting with confusion. The word *nearly* in the following sentence can modify either *half* or *vacant,* depending on which word you stress:

Half of the rooms were vacant, nearly.

Therefore:

Put limiters immediately before the words you want them to modify.

This will prevent you from writing a confusing sentence like this: "Our deluxe models only have a lifetime guarantee," when you really mean this: "Only our deluxe models have a lifetime guarantee."

To get an even clearer idea of how these limiters attach themselves to the word that *follows* them, try inserting the word *only* or the word *just* at various places in the following sentence and notice how the meaning changes:

Mr. Elwood thinks he can find the problem.

You should also be careful where you put the word *not* in your sentences. We didn't list it as one of the limiters because it doesn't limit, it negates. But, like limiters, it should appear immediately before the word you want it to modify. Compare the meanings of these two sentences:

Not all the samples were acceptable.
All the samples were not acceptable.

Some careless writers will write the second kind of sentence when they mean the first. So many do, in fact, that when you read a sentence like "All the customers were not satisfied," you don't know whether the writer meant "Not all the customers were satisfied," or "All the customers were unsatisfied." Avoid this kind of confusion in *your* sentences; don't use *not* or *never* to modify the verb if you have the word *all* in the subject.

Let's practice placing limiters where they belong. Revise these sentences so that their meanings are clear. The answers are on page 86.

1. Eighty per cent of the bottles were empty, nearly. (Clue to meaning: Seventy-nine bottles out of a hundred had nothing in them.)

———————————————————————

2. Eighty per cent of the bottles were empty, nearly. (Clue to meaning: Eighty bottles out of a hundred contained two ounces instead of sixteen ounces of liquid.)

———————————————————————

3. All the fish in your last shipment were not frozen. (Clue to meaning: Some fish were frozen; some were not.)

———————————————————————

4. All the fish in your last shipment were not frozen. (Clue to meaning: Every fish had thawed out.)

———————————————————————

5. Only ship our canned goods in unrefrigerated boxcars. (Clue to meaning: All our products except canned goods need to be kept cold.)

———————————————————————

The second rule for keeping your modifiers clear is also a simple one:

Make sure every adjective phrase at the beginning of a sentence modifies the subject of the sentence.

Watch out especially for participial phrases that "dangle" at the beginning of a sentence. In Chapters 2 and 3 we discussed participles, forms of verbs used as adjectives. Here, briefly, is what we'll need to know about them in this chapter:

Present participles always end in *-ing,* and past participles are the verb forms that would fit in the blank of this sentence: "Often I have _____." Participial phrases consist of the participles and their objects and modifiers. Here are some examples of participial phrases; the first two begin with present participles, and the last two begin with past participles:

sitting by the workbench
tying the rope over the tarpaulin
eaten by a bulldog
expressed in simple terms

Earlier in this chapter we noticed that modifying phrases usually appear immediately *after* the words they modify. Therefore, a participial phrase at the beginning of a sentence momentarily leaves your reader's mind a little unsettled. Your reader needs to know what to *do* with those words; this means you must immediately give the noun the participial phrase modifies. Every reader expects it to appear right after the phrase, and if you don't put it there, your reader will surely misread your sentence. Sometimes this can produce ridiculous results, but the laughter will be at your expense. Here are some examples of this kind of misplaced, or "dangling," modifier. Correct them. The answers are on page 86.

6. Eating our lunches in the cafeteria, the boiler began to rumble and make other strange noises.

_____

_____

7. Anticipating a delay, the deadline was postponed by the committee.

_____

_____

8. Rusted out at the bottom and dented on both sides, Mr. Forbes was not interested in the car.

_____

_____

9. Making sputtering noises and emitting sparks, the electrician was prevented from completing the job on time by the faulty generator.

---

10. Barking loudly and jumping up and down, the insurance agent was startled by the dog behind the screen door.

Participial phrases are not the only kinds of phrases that can come at the beginning of a sentence and seem to modify what you don't want them to, of course. Infinitive phrases and prepositional phrases can be troublesome in that position, too. And they can be either adjective phrases or adverb phrases. The important thing to remember is that all of them must make sense when joined to the subject or verb of the sentence. In the following sentences they don't. Correct them. The answers are on page 86.

11. To open a checking account, certain information must be provided by you.

---

12. Before sending in the license fee, your car must have a safety inspection.

---

13. In order to keep a dog in these apartments, your dog must be on a leash at all times.

---

14. When writing for information, the model number of your stereo must be included in your letter.

---

15. To repair your camera, our estimate must be approved by you.

The third rule for placing modifiers is a little more complicated than the others. But if you learn it well, you will be able to clear up many misleading sentences. Here is the rule:

Make sure relative pronouns refer to the closest noun preceding them.

Let's suppose you are trying to eliminate sentence fragments from your rough draft. You know that one way to correct a certain kind of sentence fragment is simply to attach it to the previous sentence. When the fragment consists of only a relative clause, such as "which is just three feet wide," and the previous sentence is something like "On the side of the van is a sliding door," you can get rid of the fragment this way:

On the side of the van is a sliding door, which is just three feet wide.

But such a solution will work *only* if the relative pronoun (*who, which,* or *that*) of the fragment refers to the last noun in the preceding sentence. You have to find a different solution if it doesn't—if, for example, you have this instead:

The sliding door is on the side of the van. Which is just three feet wide.

Here you can't just tack the fragment onto the preceding sentence; if you did, you would be saying the *van* is just three feet wide. Your reader will always assume that any relative pronoun you use refers to the closest noun *before* it.

Remember that horrible example of misplaced modifiers at the beginning of this chapter? Let's examine the first paragraph for instances of relative pronouns seeming to refer to the wrong nouns.

Noticing several fire hazards in production areas that are inexcusable and need to be eliminated, a meeting will be held next Thursday at 2:30 P.M. to discuss safety policies still applied by some managers that are outdated and ineffective in conference room 401D. We will also consider employee awareness of fire hazards which we need to increase.

You can find several other instances in the other two paragraphs as well. Now examine the revision of that memo. Notice that the revision relocates those relative clauses so that they *do* logically relate to the immediately preceding nouns.

75

Let's practice doing some of that relocating ourselves. Place the relative clauses where they belong in the following sentences. The answers are on page 86.

16. Please take every letter directly to the post office that has an airmail stamp on it.

_____

_____

17. Ms. Baldwin designed new uniforms for our concert hall ushers that have padded shoulders and blue piping down the front.

_____

_____

Sometimes you can't simply move a misplaced relative clause to a different part of the sentence. For instance, moving the relative clause won't help much in these next few sentences. You will have to recast the sentences. Try it. The answers are on pages 86 and 87.

18. We have a rental-rate schedule which includes trailers that you can fold up and keep in your pocket.

_____

_____

19. I am returning this lamp which I ordered from your winter catalog that arrived in pieces.

_____

_____

20. Mr. Thomas revised the vacation schedules of hourly employees that contained inaccuracies.

_____

_____

The final rule for putting modifiers in the right place really doesn't have much to do with changing their location in the sentence. This rule simply recognizes that when you have two prepositional phrases modifying the same noun you can't put them both first. And whichever one you put second is not going to modify anything very clearly. The rule is simple, yet difficult to apply. And sometimes you may have to violate it in order to say what you mean. But apply it when you can; it will sometimes help untangle a confusing sentence. Here is the rule:

Don't modify the same noun with more than one prepositional phrase.

Notice that the rule applies only to prepositional phrases used as adjectives. Verbs frequently need several adverb phrases to make their meanings clear. Adverb phrases that designate frequency, time, manner, place, and purpose sometimes all appear in the same sentence modifying the same verb. Here is a sentence like that:

On Thursdays at 2:00 P.M. we will meet in small groups in the conference room for problem-solving discussions.

But adjective phrases are different. If you put one right after the other, the second will *seem* to modify the object of the preposition in the first one, especially if that first phrase is rather long, whether you intend it to do that or not. Consider what happens in a sentence like this:

The discussion of our many parliamentary procedure problems at the last meeting lasted half an hour.

The reader cannot guess whether "at the last meeting" modifies "discussion" or "problems." You can't remedy the situation by reversing the order of the prepositional phrases. "The discussion at the last meeting of our many parliamentary procedure problems" sounds silly. Did your problems hold a meeting? You can, however, resolve the ambiguity by changing one adjective phrase into an adverb phrase:

The discussion of our parliamentary procedure problems lasted half an hour at the last meeting.

Or, you could recast the sentence so it would have only the other meaning:

The parliamentary procedure problems at the last meeting took a half hour to discuss.

But notice that in each case, in order to make the sentence clear you had to get rid of one of the two prepositional phrases modifying the same noun.

Now let's get some practice. Assume the writer of the following sentence intended both prepositional phrases to modify the underlined noun. Revise the sentences by getting rid of the *first* of the two prepositional phrases. The answers are on page 87.

21. The <u>suggestions</u> of the committee on safety are very good ones.

_____

_____

22. The wiring <u>diagram</u> of the computer in the office is inaccurate.

_____

_____

23. The <u>summary</u> in the newspaper of the statement left out some very important facts.

_____

_____

24. Ms. Brome read an <u>article</u> on profit sharing by a corporate manager.

_____

_____

25. Mr. Clinton asked for our <u>inventory</u> of hammocks of last year.

_____

_____

Finally, let's put it all together and practice revising sentences that have various kinds of misplaced modifiers in them. The answers are on page 87.

26. Opening the valve slowly, the air pressure can be safely increased by an operator up to forty pounds.

_____

_____

27. Our fuel consumption is decreasing, however, the cost per gallon has increased, consequently, our expense listed for fuel in the budget has remained constant.

_____

_____

_____

28. Please list in your report all equipment in your department that needs repair.

_____

_____

29. All of the computer printouts are not available for the study of costs which you are preparing.

_____

_____

30. While typing Mr. Neal's report, two grammatical errors were found by the secretary on the first page.

_____

_____

FOR CLASS DISCUSSION

1.   In groups of four or five, tape record some informal conversation of your own. Then transcribe about ten sentences from the recording. How many sentences seem all right when spoken, but contain misplaced modifiers when written? Correct all the sentences so that they are clear in written form.

2.   Bring to class three or four confusing sentences you have found in your own reading. With suggestions from the rest of the class, revise each one on the chalkboard until it can mean only one thing.

3.   Discuss the following statements:
(a)   It is more important to avoid misplaced modifiers in a report to the head of your department than it is to avoid them in a business letter to someone outside the company.
(b)   Placing modifiers in exactly the right place makes me lose the conversational spontaneity I want to put into my business letters.
(c)   So what if my sentences have more than one meaning? My reader should be intelligent enough to decide which one is right.

TEST YOURSELF

Revise the following sentences. The answers are on page 88.

1. Medical science has found cures for many diseases that increase average life expectancy.

_____

_____

2. After verifying your bank statement, it should be kept on file for two years.

_____

_____

3. Expressed in simple language, the committee was easily moved to action by the report.

_____

_____

4. Mr. Doan suggested that we auction off our old machinery at the annual board meeting.

_____

_____

5. New textbooks have arrived for our first-aid training courses that contain achievement tests at the end of each chapter.

_____

_____

6. Reserve seats only have padded backrests, however, general admission seats are quite comfortable too.

_____

_____

7. We must take into account the costs of replacement parts that are rising.

_____

_____

8. Please send the prospect list to the sales department which you compiled last month.

_____

_____

9. The council decided to accept the proposal to build another warehouse in less than twenty minutes.

_____

_____

10. The decision to reduce noise by Mr. Lewis means that we have to put mufflers on all our vehicles that are very quiet.

_____

_____

_____

APPLY YOURSELF

1. Write a paragraph describing a fictitious incident in which a misplaced modifier was either costly or embarrassing to a business writer. Make sure you include both the faulty sentence that caused the trouble and the correct sentence that the writer should have written. Be careful to avoid misplacing any modifiers in your own sentences.

2. When your boss asked you how you manage to write such clear reports, you answered that you always check your first drafts for misplaced modifiers. Now your boss wants you to explain to the rest of the department how to do that. Write a paragraph or two that your boss can use in a memorandum for departmental distribution. Remember, it will be your boss's memorandum, not yours; so be careful how you use the pronoun "I."

ANSWERS TO EXERCISES

1. Nearly 80 per cent of the bottles were empty.

2. Eighty per cent of the bottles were nearly empty.

3. Not all the fish in your last shipment were frozen.

4. None of the fish in your last shipment were frozen.
OR
    All of the fish in your last shipment were unfrozen.

5. Ship only our canned goods in unrefrigerated boxcars.

6. Eating our lunches in the cafeteria, we heard the boiler begin to rumble and make other strange noises.
OR
    While we were eating our lunches in the cafeteria, the boiler began to rumble and make other strange noises.

7. Anticipating a delay, the committee postponed the deadline.

8. Rusted out at the bottom and dented on both sides, the car did not interest Mr. Forbes.

9. Making sputtering noises and emitting sparks, the faulty generator prevented the electrician from completing the job on time.

10. Barking loudly and jumping up and down, the dog behind the screen door startled the insurance agent.

11. To open a checking account, you must provide certain information.

12. Before sending in the license fee, you must have your car safety inspected (*or* inspected for safety).

13. In order to keep a dog in these apartments, you must have it on a leash at all times.

14. When writing for information, please include the model number of your stereo.

15. To repair your camera, we need your approval of our estimate (*or* we need you to approve our estimate).

16. Please take every letter that has an airmal stamp on it directly to the post office.

17. Ms. Baldwin designed new uniforms that have padded shoulders and blue piping down the front for our concert hall ushers.

18. We have designed this rental-rate schedule, which includes trailers, so that you can fold it up and keep it in your pocket.

19. I am returning this lamp, which I ordered from your winter catalog. It arrived in pieces.

20. Mr. Thomas revised the inaccurate vacation schedules of hourly employees.

21. The committee's suggestions on safety are very good ones.

22. The computer's wiring diagram in the office is inaccurate.

23. The newspaper's summary of the statement left out some very important facts.

24. Ms. Brome read a corporate manager's article on profit sharing.

25. Mr. Clinton asked for our hammock inventory for last year.

26. Opening the valve slowly, an operator can safely increase the air pressure up to forty pounds.

27. Our fuel consumption is decreasing; however, the cost per gallon has increased; consequently, our fuel expense listed in the budget (*or* our budget estimate for fuel) has remained constant.

28. Please list in your report all your department's equipment that needs repair.

29. Not all the computer printouts are available for the cost study you are preparing.
OR
    All the computer printouts are unavailable for the cost study you are preparing.

30. While typing Mr. Neal's report, the secretary found two grammatical errors on the first page.

ANSWERS TO TEST YOURSELF

1. Medical science has increased life expectancy by finding cures for many diseases.
OR
   Medical science has found many disease cures that increase average life expectancy.

2. After verifying your bank statement, you should keep it on file for two years.

3. Expressed in simple language, the report easily moved the committee to action.

4. At the annual board meeting, Mr. Doan suggested that we auction off our old machinery.
OR
   Mr. Doan suggested at our annual board meeting that we auction off our old machinery.

5. New textbooks that contain achievement tests at the end of each chapter have arrived for our first-aid training courses.

6. Only reserve seats have padded backrests; however, general admission seats are quite comfortable, too.

7. We must take into account the rising costs of replacement parts.

8. Please send the sales department the prospect list you compiled last month.

9. In less than twenty minutes the council decided to accept the proposal to build another warehouse.

10. Mr. Lewis's decision to reduce noise means that we have to put very quiet mufflers on all our vehicles.

5

Avoid Sexist Language

Perhaps you have noticed a difference between the language used in this book and the language used in similar books written just a few years ago. In older texts you often found sentences like the following:

> *The efficient manager gets input for his reports from the workmen in his section early, so that he can get his draft to his secretary in plenty of time for her to type it carefully.*
>
> *Each salesman must give a copy of his trip ticket to one of the office girls before leaving.*
>
> *Mrs. Binkman, the receptionist, said businessmen visiting the plant could use the men's or ladies' washrooms on the first floor.*

What's wrong with these sentences? Grammatically, absolutely nothing. But none of them would be acceptable in the business community today. Each contains sexist language.

Language is sexist when it implies that certain roles in society, certain job positions, or certain intellectual or emotional traits are more appropriate for one sex than for the other. Usually the writer does not intend such an implication, but that does not diminish its unfairness. In a way, unintended sexism is the most pernicious kind. It implies that sex discrimination in business is not very important. Otherwise, why wouldn't the writer take the time to recognize it and learn how to avoid it?

As a business writer, you *must* be sensitive to sexist implications in your letters and reports. Whether you consider sexist language from the point of view of justice and human dignity or from the point of view of good, cost-efficient business communication, you will come to the same conclusion: Avoid sexist language.

But you can't avoid it unless you can recognize it—even when it is very subtle, or rather *especially* when it is very subtle. There is no way to decide grammatically. Consider the underlined pronouns in this sentence:

Mr. Knox told his secretary that if a reporter calls this morning she should tell him to call back after 2:00 P.M.

The first two pronouns are fine, but the last constitutes sexist language. The pronoun *his* refers to a specific person, Mr. Knox, and therefore the masculine pronoun is appropriate. The pronoun *she* also refers to a specific person, Mr. Knox's secretary. It is true that secretaries may be either male or female, but the writer here refers to a specific one who happens to be female, so the feminine pronoun is appropriate. But the pronoun *him* implies that any reporter who calls will be a male. This subtly suggests that the job of a reporter is a man's job, not a woman's.

Now let's examine the three earlier sentences, the ones we said were typical of those ordinarily found in business writing and in textbooks a few years back. Here's the first one again, this time with the sexist language underlined:

The efficient manager gets input for his reports from the workmen in his section early, so that he can get his draft to his secretary in plenty of time for her to type it carefully.

All five masculine pronouns—*his, his, he, his,* and *his*—suggest very strongly that a manager, or at least an *efficient* manager, will of course be male. The feminine pronoun *her* suggests that the lower-status, lower-paid secretary will of course be female. The noun *workmen* clearly implies a group consisting of *men* who work.

Before we go any further, we must acknowledge that not everyone would agree with that last paragraph. Some would argue that the pronouns *he, his,* and *him*—as well as the noun *man* itself—can mean humankind generically. They would cite such examples as this:

Hope springs eternal in the human breast:
Man never Is, but always To be blest.
                    Alexander Pope, Essay on Man.

Certainly the writer meant "man" to refer to both men and women, and every reader interprets it that way. Or they might cite an example like this:

Each brother and sister did his part to hold the family together.

The reader can be sure that the pronoun *his* in that sentence refers to both males and females. Finally, they might argue that grammatical gender is *not* the same thing as sexual gender and therefore there is nothing inherently ungrammatical about using a masculine pronoun—or a feminine one, for that matter—to refer to a group made up of both males and females.

How could we refute such statements? We couldn't. All of them are absolutely true. But they are irrelevant. We are not concerned here with

"This ought to be good. The boss has been expecting a J. P. Blivins and his secretary."

whether a sentence is grammatical, but whether it implies, or even *can* imply, sex discrimination. Throughout this text we have stressed the importance of keeping your reader in mind. Nowhere is it more important than in avoiding sexist language. It matters very little what the *writer* intends a sentence to mean; it matters very much what the *reader* infers from the sentence. As the writer of the following sentence, I can tell you that I mean *his* in the generic sense; that is, as referring to either a man or a woman:

Each professor should correct his own examinations.

But my reader might take it to mean that it is somehow not appropriate for a woman to be a professor. It would be common sense, then, for me to choose another grammatical way to say the same thing without the possibility of such misinterpretation, like this:

All professors should correct their own examinations.

Could we do the same with that example from the beginning of the chapter? Well, the following keeps most of the essential meaning:

> *Efficient managers get input for their reports from the workers in their sections early, so that they can get their drafts to their secretaries in plenty of time for careful typing.*

Or, if we wanted to keep *manager* singular, we could write the sentence like this:

> *The efficient manager gets input for reports from the section workers early, in order to get the draft to the secretary in plenty of time for careful typing.*

Notice what we've done to eliminate the sexist language. In the first revision, we made *manager* plural; then we could use the plural pronouns *they* and *their*. In the second revision, we left *manager* singular, but simply dropped the personal pronouns entirely. These are the two most useful techniques for getting rid of sexist language.

Now you try it. In the following exercises, eliminate sexist language by changing some of the singular nouns and pronouns to plural. The answers are on page 106.

1. Every pilot must file his flight plan before taking off.

_____

2. The careful secretary proofreads her typing for spelling and punctuation.

_____

_____

3. Mr. Johnson gave every clerk a calendar for her desk.

_____

4. The well-organized teacher makes her lesson plans a week in advance.

_____

_____

5. We are sending a copy of the announcement to each department manager so he can post it on his department's bulletin board.

_____

_____

_____

The other technique we mentioned—dropping the personal pronoun alto-gether—sometimes requires restructuring the sentence. For instance, con-sider the following:

Faulty: The editor of the company newsletter must distribute his article coverage so that he includes something about every department in each issue.

We can simply delete the possessive pronoun *his*, but we need to do a little word shuffling to get rid of the *he:*

The editor of the company newsletter must distribute article coverage in order to include something about every department in each issue.

As a rule, possessive pronouns are often unnecessary, and you can merely delete them; however, getting rid of other sexist pronoun forms usually requires some revising. Practice on these. The answers are on page 106.

6. The beginning truck driver finds it difficult to estimate unloading time, so he should get help from experienced drivers in filling out his trip ticket.

_____

_____

_____

7. A good principal visits every teacher's class once a year so he can observe her teaching performance.

_____

_____

8. A receptionist should always keep her employer's appointment sched-ule up to date for him.

_____

_____

Sometimes you can't avoid using the cumbersome *he or she* or *she or he* expressions. But use them only as a last resort. Here are a few sentences that seem to demand them. The answers are on page 106.

9. A senator should try to find out the preferences of his constituents.

_____

_____

10. Each committee member announced the safety slogan chosen by his department.

_____

_____

There was another type of sexist language in that first example from the beginning of the chapter. We said the noun *workmen* implied a group of *men* who work. How can we get around this problem? When the noun itself specifies sex, and you don't want it to, you must choose some other noun. Usually, *person, persons,* or *people* can substitute for *man, men, woman,* or *women;* but sometimes such a substitution will produce an absurdly clumsy result. You wouldn't want to change *workman* to *workperson.* That would be about as silly as saying your handwriting is getting slovenly so you are going to practice your pen*person*ship! Fortunately, for many sexist nouns like *workman* there is a sensible alternate noun, like *worker.* Here are a few other sexist expressions and their acceptable equivalents that don't have the cumbersome term *person* in their makeup:

manpower—workforce
man-hours—work-hours
five-man committee—five-member committee
fireman—fire fighter
policeman—police officer
businessmen—business people
salesmen—salespeople
councilman—council member

However, there are some that require you to use *person* in order to avoid sexism. They are a bit clumsy sounding, but preferable to the sexist terms they replace. Here are some of them:

businessman—business person
spokesman—spokesperson
salesman—salesperson
chairman—chairperson

Sometimes you can avoid sexist language and the clumsy addition of *-person* by recasting the sentence, like this:

Faulty: Please send a furnace repairman as soon as possible.
Revised: Please send someone to repair our furnace as soon as possible.

Now let's get some practice. Try getting rid of the sexist terms in these sentences. The answers are on page 106.

11. The director appointed a four-man committee to study the problem.

_____

_____

12. Ms. Standish wants to give up her job as salesman in order to become a fireman.

_____

_____

13. We must increase our manpower during the harvest season.

_____

14. Edith Brownlee is chairman of the Planning Committee.

_____

15. We will elect three additional councilmen next spring.

_____

Now let's look at the second sentence from the beginning of the chapter. Here it is again, this time with the sexist language underlined:

> Each _salesman_ must give a copy of _his_ trip ticket to one of the office _girls_ before leaving.

What we haved learned so far in this chapter would enable us to get rid of some of the sexist language in this sentence, but not that term _girls_. The word _girls_ in this context is sexist because the term means female _children. Girl_ is the feminine counterpart of _boy,_ not of _man._ Also, _lady_ is the feminine counterpart of _gentleman,_ not of _man. Woman_ is the feminine counterpart of _man._ Never say _girl_ or _girls,_ or _lady_ or _ladies,_ when you mean _woman_ or _women._ In the sentence cited, however, there is no reason even to identify the office workers as women. They are office workers, so we should call them that.

Therefore, applying all this to the original sentence, we could revise it to read this way:

> Each _salesperson_ must give a copy of _the_ trip ticket to one of the office workers before leaving.

OR

> All salespersons must give copies of their trip tickets to one of the office workers before leaving.

Let's consider the third sentence. Here it is with the sexist language underlined:

> Mrs. Brinkman, the receptionist, said businessmen visiting the plant could use the men's or ladies' washrooms on the first floor.

We know how to handle *businessmen* and *ladies'*, but what about that term of address, *Mrs.?* It is perfectly acceptable to use *Mrs.* when referring to someone who refers to herself that way. The same is true of *Miss.* A good rule to follow when addressing a return letter, for example, is to use the same form the person used in the signature of the letter you are answering. But *Ms.* seems a more reasonable choice when you are in doubt. *Mr.* does not indicate whether the man is married or not; there is no reason why a woman should indicate her marital status either.

The best solution of all, and one that most of the larger corporations use as their standard policy, is to dispense with the *Mr., Mrs., Miss, Ms.* business altogether and use only the person's name, like this:

Thomas P. Wood
Judith Nelson
R. T. Moore
W. Sanders

When a person signs his or her name with only one or two initials and the last name, you have no way of knowing whether the person is a man or a woman, of course. Let's suppose someone writes to you and simply identifies herself or himself as *J. T. Rawlings.* How do you address that person in the salutation of your return letter? The only sensible solution is to omit the *Ms.* or *Mr.* entirely—and that's what you should do. In such a case, write "Dear J. T. Rawlings."

But in the sentence we are considering, we have only the person's last name. Therefore, we must use *some* term of address before it. In a case like this, use *Ms.* for women and *Mr.* for men.

Now we can revise the sentence to eliminate all the sexist language, like this:

> Ms. Brinkman, the receptionist, said business people visiting the plant could use the men's or women's washrooms on the first floor.

Let's try a few exercises. Eliminate sexist language in the following. The answers are on pages 106 and 107.

16. The chairman should announce his meeting agenda at least a week in advance.

17. The girls in the accounting department elected Miss Harriet Warner spokesman for their ladies' rights committee.

---

18. Department heads may take their wives to the convention, but not at company expense.

---

19. An executive should always tell his secretary how many copies he wants her to make.

---

20. The assistant clerk should sort her department's mail as soon as the mailman delivers it.

Finally, we need to be careful to avoid sexist language that seems to break down sexual stereotyping but strengthens the stereotype in the process. For example, this sentence seems to proclaim that a stereotype is breaking down:

Mr. Thompson wants to become a male nurse.

At first glance the sentence seems reasonable enough. Mr. Thompson certainly is a male, and he wants to become a nurse. This punctures some people's notion that nursing is a profession exclusively for women. What's wrong with that? Yet you wouldn't say

Ms. Snider wants to become a female nurse.

If you wrote that, your reader would probably assume Ms. Snider wants to become a nurse who nurses only females. Therefore, if Mr. Thompson wants to become a nurse, say so. Insofar as a person performs the job, it makes no difference whether that person is male or female. The same is true of other jobs or professions. The following therefore have sexist implications:

woman doctor
man schoolteacher
lady judge
woman lawyer
male stenographer
woman novelist

Such terms imply that "normal" or "real" doctors, lawyers, judges, and novelists are men and that "normal" or "real" schoolteachers and stenographers are women. Therefore, do not *add* gender to a genderless noun, even when stating an exception to sexual stereotyping.

It may occur to you that many of the writing habits we have been trying to acquire in this chapter tend to make our sentences less precise than they would otherwise be. It is certainly easier for the reader to get a clearer mental picture of a man or a woman than of persons or people. You might well ask, "If I avoid sexist language, won't my statements become less precise, less likely to give my reader clear mental pictures?"

I am afraid the answer would have to be "Yes." There is no denying that a sentence like "An executive should not have to remind his secretary to change her typewriter ribbon" is easier to visualize than "Executives should not have to remind their secretaries to change their typewriter ribbons." It is difficult to visualize a group of people, especially when the writer does not specify the sexes of those people. But it is precisely because the first sentence is specific that it has the power of locking in the stereotypes that prevent women from getting fair treatment in the business world. Therefore, although you should usually try to make your sentences as specific and concrete as possible, never specify male or female when you don't have to; take the lesser of two evils and be a little more general in those situations where being specific would do an injustice—and sexist language does considerable injustice.

Fortunately, avoiding sexist language does not *often* require you to be more general than you want to be. Remember that it's only when you are referring to managers, secretaries, and so on as groups or generic classes that you need to watch out for sexist language. Whenever you refer to a *specific* manager, secretary, executive, or whatever, you should use the appropriate masculine or feminine pronouns to refer to them. Most of the sentences in your letters and reports will be about specific people, so the problem of avoiding sexist language should not occur very often. But when it does occur, it is an important one.

Now let's practice getting rid of sexist language only when it's there. Some of these last five exercise items contain sexist language; some do not. If the sentence is all right, say so; if it contains sexist language, revise it. The answers are on page 107.

21. The personnel director who hired me is now a woman lawyer.

22. Sandra Jacobs asked her boss if she could postpone her vacation.

_____

_____

23. Management trainees heard F. P. Holloway's lecture on her concept of dynamic leadership.

_____

_____

24. We will conduct a special tour of the plant for elementary schoolteachers and their husbands next Saturday at 9:00 A.M.

_____

_____

25. A good department manager is careful to avoid sexist language; he often reminds all the girls in the secretarial pool to help him watch for it in his letters.

_____

_____

_____

FOR CLASS DISCUSSION

Discuss the following statement made earlier in this chapter: "Whether you consider sexist language from the point of view of justice and human dignity or from the point of view of good, cost-efficient business communication, you will come to the same conclusion: Avoid sexist language."

In what ways does sexist language violate justice and human dignity?

In what ways does sexist language cost the business writer? In money? In goodwill?

TEST YOURSELF

Some of the following sentences contain sexist language; some do not. Revise the sentences that do. The answers are on page 108.

1. Each of the men and women in our department wants his own individual locker.

_____

_____

2. The council decided that the city needs some new "Men Working" signs.

_____

_____

3. When a foreman authorizes his crewmen to work overtime, he should report the total overtime man-hours worked to this office during the next working day.

_____

_____

_____

4. Our lawyer has not yet given us his advice in the matter.

_____

5. A company lawyer should always give his advice in writing.

_____

6. Our new policy requires every secretary to eliminate sexist language in the letters she types.

_____

_____

7. The landscape consultant suggested we include a fountain of man-made stone.

_____

_____

8. A district manager may choose his own reporting dates.

---

9. A plant manager must submit his annual report each January.

---

10. Please check Diane Dillworth's absence record so that we can inform her of the number of days of sick leave she has remaining.

APPLY YOURSELF

You are assistant director of training in a large corporation. The director has asked you to construct a three-session course in avoiding sexist language. Three hundred and twenty executives, managers, department heads, secretaries, and production personnel will be taking the course, in groups of sixteen. About half of the students are women.

Decide whether you want to have the students grouped by job classification, by sex, or by random selection. Then construct three units of instruction that you think will cover what your students will need to know in order to avoid sexist language.

Hand in to your instructor four paragraphs of about 100 to 150 words each, the first explaining how you would divide the people into groups and the next three briefly describing what you would teach in each of the three sessions.

ANSWERS TO EXERCISES

1. All pilots must file their flight plans before taking off.

2. Careful secretaries proofread their typing for spelling and punctuation.

3. Mr. Johnson gave all the clerks calendars for their desks.

4. Well-organized teachers make their lesson plans a week in advance.

5. We are sending copies of the announcement to all department managers so they can post them on their departments' bulletin boards. (Did you put the apostrophe in the correct place?)

6. The beginning truck driver finds it difficult to estimate unloading time, so the beginner should get help from experienced drivers in filling out the trip schedule.

7. A good principal visits every teacher's class once a year to observe teaching performance.

8. A receptionist should always keep the employer's appointment schedule up to date.

9. A senator should try to find out the preferences of his or her constituents.

10. Each committee member announced the safety slogan chosen by his or her department.

11. The director appointed a four-member committee to study the problem.

12. Ms. Standish wants to give up her job as salesperson in order to become a fire fighter.

13. We must increase our workforce during the harvest season.

14. Edith Brownlee is chairperson of the Planning Committee.

15. We will elect three additional council members next spring.

16. The chairperson should announce the meeting agenda at least a week in advance.

17. The women in the accounting department elected Harriet Warner spokesperson for their women's rights committee.

18. Department heads may take their spouses to the convention, but not at company expense.

19. An executive should always tell the secretary how many copies to make.
OR
    Executives should always tell their secretaries how many copies to make.

20. The assistant clerk should sort the department's mail as soon as the mail carrier delivers it.
OR
    Assistant clerks should sort their departments' mail as soon as the mail carrier delivers it. (Did you put the apostrophe in the correct place?)

21. The personnel director who hired me is now a lawyer.

22. The sentence is all right.

23. The sentence is all right.

24. We will conduct a special tour of the plant for elementary schoolteachers and their spouses next Saturday at 9:00 A.M.

25. Good department managers are careful to avoid sexist language; they often remind all the secretaries in (*or* members of) the secretarial pool to help them watch for it in their letters.
OR
    A good department manager is careful to avoid sexist language, often reminding all the members of (*or* secretaries in) the secretarial pool to help watch for it in letters.

ANSWERS TO TEST YOURSELF

1. All of the men and women in our department want their own individual lockers.

2. The council decided that the city needs some new "People Working" (*or* "Work in Progress") signs.

3. When supervisors authorize their crews to work overtime, they should report the total overtime work-hours to this office during the next working day.
OR
    When a supervisor authorizes a crew to work overtime, this office should receive during the next working day a report of the total overtime work-hours.

4. The sentence is all right.

5. Company lawyers should always give their advice in writing.

6. Our new policy requires all secretaries to eliminate sexist language in the letters they type.

7. The landscape consultant suggested we include a fountain of artificial stone.

8. District managers may choose their own reporting dates.

9. A plant manager must submit the annual report each January.
OR
    Plant managers must submit their annual reports each January.

10. The sentence is all right.

Part III
Business Letters

6

Invite Goodwill with Tone and Form

In Part II we concentrated mostly on sentence structure, word choice, forcefulness, and clarity to help you develop the basic skills of writing for business. We necessarily lumped all business writing together as if there were no differences between letters and reports. Actually, there are some very important differences between them. Although both letters and reports depend for their success on clarity, visual imagery, and readability, the two differ fundamentally in tone. Tone, by the way, is the writer's *attitude* toward the subject and toward the reader.

The function of a report is to present accurate, factual information in as concise, clear, and readable form as possible to any readers that have a need or a desire to use that information. That means the report writer must focus attention on *things* and *actions,* on *causes* and *results,* on *ideas* and *solutions* to problems. For this, the report writer needs to take a no-nonsense, "let's-get-down-to-business" approach that tells the reader immediately that there will be no unnecessary, unusable parts in the report. Utility and efficiency are important aspects of report-writing tone.

The business-letter writer, on the other hand, must adopt a very different tone. Every business letter is, first and foremost, a goodwill letter. That is, whatever the purpose of the letter might be, it must either reinforce the reader's existing goodwill toward the writer's business firm, or establish that goodwill if for some reason it doesn't already exist. Furthermore, this book has always stressed the importance of keeping your reader in mind. If you think about that, you will see that letter writing and report writing are essentially different things. The report writer must write for many people with a variety of backgrounds and expertise. The letter writer almost always writes to just one person—a customer, a supplier, a specific official of another company. Even when addressed to more than one person, the letter must speak to each one individually, and it must do so on a personal level. It must be the written form of one human being talking to another human being. Therefore, when you write a letter, don't be too formal; don't make your reader think you are wearing cardboard underwear.

This does not mean your business letter should be chatty. On the contrary, chattiness, windiness, or too much informality can make your letter very annoying to your reader. But simply using such brief signals of courtesy as "please" and "thank you" can help you change a bare statement of fact into a warm, personal message. Every good business letter gives clear signals that show the writer sincerely considers the reader and is primarily concerned with how the message affects that reader.

Keeping this in mind, you can easily see why the supreme rule for effective letter writing is this:

Use the "You" approach.

It is true that *all* good writing requires the writer to keep the reader in mind, but the business writer, because clarity is so important in letters and reports, must be more careful than the creative writer in this regard. The business-letter writer must be even more careful than the report writer to construct sentences and organize paragraphs from the reader's point of view.

In the next few chapters we will discuss how you can arrange your ideas to suit your reader's needs and convenience by using the "You" approach. That can be a little complicated. For now, we will translate the rule this way: Use the words *you* and *your* as often as you possibly can in your letters.

Let's compare the tones of two letters to see what the "You" approach can do. The first one is an example of a nonmilitary letter included in *Army Regulation 340–15* (January 1979). It doesn't use the words *you* or *your* even once. The second is from an executive returning a report he has asked to see. He uses the words *you* or *your* seven times in nine sentences. Which letter would you rather receive? (I have, of course, substituted fictitious names in the second letter.)

Dear Mr. Brown:

Use nonmilitary letters for correspondence with civilians, civilian agencies, other Government agencies, and the Secretaries of the Army, Navy, and the Air Force.

Single space the body of a nonmilitary letter, with double spacing between paragraphs. If, however, a nonmilitary letter has only one paragraph, use double spacing within the paragraph (see figure 2–14).

Do not number or letter paragraphs of a nonmilitary letter. If possible, avoid subparagraphing. In instances when it is absolutely necessary, use letters of the alphabet (e.g., a, b, c, and d).

112

Identify inclosures by showing the total number and a brief description of each or use the phrase "As stated" if inclosures have been fully identified within the body of the letter.

Sincerely,

Dear Bill:

I'm returning your report as promised.

Congratulations on a nice, readable presentation. No doubt the recipients of your report will appreciate it throughout the year as a reference.

Your mention of the Atlanta "Dynamic Management" concept caught my attention. Is this something that might interest our ACCUWHIZ TODAY readers? Might a story help you promote the program at other locations?

I realize how busy you are at this point; so, in a week or two, I'll get back to you on this subject.

Thanks for letting me see your report. Again, congratulations on the creative cover and useful text.

Sincerely,

Clinton A. Bowers
Employee Publications Manager

Now let's get a little practice in using the "You" approach. Revise the following sentences so that they contain at least one *you* or *your*. The answers are on page 134.

1. I would like some advice on how to improve our training program.

2. As requested, we are returning the photographs.

3. Please indicate on the application form whether part-time or full-time employment is desired.

4. We appreciate the comments on the ACCUWHIZ Calculator recently purchased.

_____

_____

5. Be assured that our guarantee covers all the optional equipment ordered with the ACCUWHIZ.

_____

_____

Almost as important as frequently using *you* and *your* is using *I* and *we* whenever it seems natural to do so. Remember, your letter should read like normal talk from one human being to another. Keep the content of your message businesslike, of course; but make your reader aware that the words are coming from a warm, friendly, compassionate human being— you. There is nothing wrong with starting a sentence with *I* or *we*, or with expressing your own honest opinions and feelings *when they are positive, constructive ones.* But be careful not to focus attention on yourself; that violates the "You" approach. In other words, use fewer *I*'s and *we*'s than *you*'s.

Don't hide behind the plural *we*, either. Use *we*, *us*, and *our* only when you must speak officially for your company or for other people as well as yourself. Otherwise, help your reader to feel as if you personally are in his or her corner. Imagine yourself standing beside your reader while the both of you are looking at your company and the situation you are writing about. Then explain the content of your message as you would to a friend. If you do that, the *I*'s, *we*'s, *our*'s, *you*'s, and *your*'s will fall into place naturally.

Let's look at a few examples of self-centered statements and try to revise them so that they reflect the "You" approach.

> *First Draft: We are always happy to provide our customers with the latest tips on servicing our outboard motors. That is why we are enclosing this revised booklet on recommended lubrication for our S-200 model.*

> *Revision: I'm happy to send you this revised booklet on keeping your S-200 outboard motor properly lubricated. I'm sure you'll find, as I have, that the tips on page four are excellent time savers.*

Besides inserting the words *you* and *your* in the revision, the writer shows consideration for the reader by using *I* instead of *we*, thus personalizing the message. Any time a sentence implies a whole company is "happy" or "is of the opinion," the reader naturally begins to doubt the writer's sincerity. Use *I* instead of *we*, therefore, whenever you express emotion or opinion. When you make a mere statement of fact, though, *we* is sometimes appropriate. Consider the following:

114

First Draft: We no longer stock the model you asked for. We suggest you try one of our other distribution centers to see if they have any left.

Revision: We no longer stock the model you asked for. But I will try to locate one for you from one of our other distribution centers and let you know by next Thursday whether I've had any success.

Notice that this last revision not only replaces *we* with *I,* but also demonstrates a willingness to help the reader. If you received the first draft, you would probably say to yourself, "They can't be very eager to sell me anything." But the revision would probably get this reaction: "How thoughtful! The writer really cares about my needs and will do my searching for me." Notice, too, that the revision is more likely than the first draft to result in a sale.

Now you try some. Change *we, us, our,* or *ours* to *I, me, my,* or *mine* where appropriate in the following exercises. The answers are on page 134.

6. We are happy to inform you that your company's bid on remodeling our reception area was lowest. We are enclosing a contract for you to sign. Please return the yellow copy to us by Friday, March 23.

_____

_____

_____

_____

7. If we can be of any further help, please call us at our west side office (499–3476) or write directly to our home office in Sunnydale.

_____

_____

_____

8. Here is our latest brochure on how to select the best savings plan for you. We think you will find it helpful in selecting one of the plans we recommended in our phone conversation last Thursday.

_____

_____

_____

_____

9.   We are delighted you agree with our suggestion to shorten Chapter 4. Your idea of expanding Chapter 3 is more practical than ours, though; and we think you should consider giving Chapter 5 the same treatment. If you run into any problems on Chapter 6, please let us know; we would like to help you as much as we can to meet the November 15 deadline.

_____

_____

_____

_____

_____

10.   If you wish, we can have our colleague, Mr. John Perkins, meet you in Grosse Pointe to assist you in your research.

_____

_____

There is one other very important matter of tone you must remember when you compose your business letters:

Be positive!

Merely by assuming your reader will take an affirmative attitude toward your message you can do much to encourage that attitude. The power of suggestion is a strong power indeed.

Your job as a writer is to call up vivid pictures in your reader's mind. Your job as a business-letter writer is to make sure those mental pictures are pleasant ones. Examine your own thoughts as you open a letter someone has sent you. Your first questions, as you open the envelope, are always ones like these: "Why is this person writing to *me?* How will this letter affect *me* or *my* job? What's in it for *me?* What kind of person does this writer think *I* am?" When you write to someone, then, you know that your reader will have those same questions in mind when opening *your* letter. If your letter is to invite goodwill, as every business letter must, you need to make sure that it provides answers your reader will feel good about. This involves courtesy, tact, dignity, sincerity, and many other qualities a respectable business person should have. But it also requires one other thing that all these qualities depend on: You must keep negative thoughts *out* of your reader's mind.

How can you do this, especially when your message is not very pleasant? First, you need to realize that the content of your message and the tone of your message are two entirely separate things. It's possible to give *good*

116

news so tactlessly that your reader will feel insulted; it's also possible to give *bad* news so considerately that your reader will feel goodwill toward you and your company despite the disappointing news. No matter what the message is, your reader will get a better self-image and therefore be more willing to cooperate with you and your company if you keep the ideas running in a positive direction. For example, suppose you included this sentence in one of your letters to bank customers:

Our bank is not open before 9:00 A.M. nor after 5:00 P.M.

Your readers would begin thinking about the times it would be more convenient to stop at the bank before 9:00 A.M. or after 5:00 P.M. But if you gave that same sentence a positive twist and expressed the idea this way:

You may do your banking anytime between 9:00 A.M. and 5:00 P.M.

your readers would begin to think of the best times for them to get to your bank after you open or before you close.

Similarly, suppose you are writing to a potential customer and you explain your guarantee this way:

We do not guarantee our barn paint against cracking, blistering, peeling, or fading for more than thirty-six months from the date of application.

Your reader will immediately think about a barn with the paint falling off in about thirty-seven months. But if you phrase it this way:

We guarantee our barn paint will remain bright, smooth, and weatherproof for thirty-six months.

your reader will imagine an attractively painted barn that stays that way a long time.

Now, if we apply the "You" approach to that positive statement, we get an even more effective message:

You can be sure that thirty-six months from now the paint on your barn will still be bright, smooth, and weatherproof. We guarantee it.

Let's get some practice. Change the following statements into positive, reader-oriented sentences. The answers are on pages 134 and 135.

11. We cannot accept reservations after 4:00 P.M. this Friday.

_____

_____

12. Anyone not showing the usher an invitation will not be permitted to enter.

---

13. If you don't pay by the end of the month, your excellent credit rating will be ruined.

---

14. If you do not want to sign up for this added insurance coverage, you will be saving only three dollars on your monthly insurance premiums.

---

15. If you are not satisfied with this explanation, do not hesitate to ask me about the parts you do not understand.

You should also be careful to answer your reader's unspoken question, "What's in it for me?" You must do this without implying that your reader is somehow being selfish for even asking it. Always assume your reader is a bit selfish, but never let that assumption show. This may sound like cynicism, but it is not; it is merely good psychology. For instance, which of the following messages do you think would be more likely to get the desired response from the reader?

    A.   *In order to update our records we need you to answer the following questions for us:*
          How many of your children have drivers' licenses?
          How many of those children are on the honor roll at school?
          Do you smoke?
    B.   *So that we can determine whether you are eligible for a reduction in your insurance rates, please send us the following information:*
          How many of your children have drivers' licenses?
          How many of those children are on the honor roll?
          Do you smoke?

Experience shows that less than 5 per cent of the readers would answer the first request; more than 90 per cent would respond to the second. Can you see why?

Revise the following sentences so that they stress the positive and answer the reader's question "What's in it for me?" The answers are on page 135.

16. I hope you will not refuse to send some samples of XYZ Corporation's letters that I need for the textbook I am writing.

_____

_____

_____

17. I need the enclosed questionnaire completed and returned to me by the end of June; otherwise, I cannot use the information on it.

_____

_____

_____

18. We must receive all Christmas orders for toboggans before November 15.

_____

_____

19. If you apply for membership, don't leave any lines blank on the form or you won't receive our newsletter promptly.

_____

_____

20. If you order from us again, use these new order forms. The old ones will probably cause your order to be delayed.

_____

_____

It all really boils down to this: Be as _helpful,_ as _thoughtful,_ and as _considerate_ as you can be in your letters. This is not only good manners; it is good business. When someone sends you a reasonable request for information that you don't have, don't merely reply "I don't know." Find out; and if you can't find out, then at least suggest some other way your reader might get that information. Don't limit your reply to just the questions asked, either. Perhaps the person didn't know enough about the subject

119

to ask all the right questions. Use common sense and put yourself in your reader's place. Include whatever you think your reader will need to know. This kind of thoughtfulness wins goodwill, and goodwill is the foundation of good business.

Now let's try a different kind of exercise. For these next five items you do not have to revise any sentences. Instead, you are to select the best word to fill the blank. The answers are on page 135.

21. No matter what purpose a business letter might have, it must always

be a _____ letter.
(a) request (b) sales (c) goodwill (d) one-page

22. A good business letter will use the word _____ as often as possible.
(a) we (b) you (c) I (d) they

23. The writer should always assume the reader will ask,

_____ .
(a) "How can I help this writer?" (b) "Is this a form letter?"
(c) "Do I need to reply?" (d) "What's in it for me?"

24. A good business letter contains as few _____ statements as possible.
(a) negative (b) positive (c) factual (d) reader-oriented

25. The letter writer can invite goodwill by adopting a pleasant tone and by using an acceptable letter _____ .
(a) jargon (b) form (c) vagueness (d) sarcasm

If you answered that last one correctly, you already know that an acceptable form—a form that does not outlandishly call attention to itself—is important in establishing the reader's goodwill. A simple, efficient form clearly implies that the writer respects the reader and is meticulous, orderly, and friendly—in short, businesslike.

It would be nice if you would be able to put together a decent business letter from scratch by the time you finish this chapter. Until now, I've been loading you up with what to say and what not to say in your letters, so that you have an armload of ideas and principles, but no container to put them in. Let's look for one.

Actually, there are a lot of containers, or forms, for business letters. The trouble is, some of them are so unusual or extravagant that the recipient spends more time in marveling at the curious package than in examining the contents. So you'll just have to stand there a while longer with your arms full until we can select an appropriate form.

The best guide in choosing a form or forms is common sense, which demands that we always keep our reader in mind. Therefore, unless your company, or your secretary, has a strong preference for some other style,

"I'd like a boutonniere that won't clash with my outfit."

you would do well to choose either the block or the semiblock because they are the most common and, consequently, the least distracting to your reader.

But before we look at these forms, perhaps we ought to consider some questions you are probably asking yourself right now, questions like "Why should I learn to type a letter? Won't some secretary be doing that for me?"

Whether you dictate a letter or write it out in longhand before giving it to the typist, you should know something about what happens at the typewriter. Such knowledge can help you construct letters that your secretary can easily make into neat, attractive typewritten messages. Besides, you will sometimes find it convenient, or even necessary, to generate your letter, revise it, and type it up yourself. When this happens—and it will— you should remember these few basics:

1 Use letterhead stationery for the first page, plain paper for subsequent pages.

2 Single space within paragraphs; double space between paragraphs and also between other letter parts.

3 Leave equal margins at least an inch wide at right and left; leave at least a one-inch margin at the bottom (and also at the top, when you are not using letterhead stationery).

4 Leave four blank lines (double space twice) between "Sincerely," and your typed name in the signature block.

Following these four rules will enable you to produce a presentable letter that doesn't distract your reader's attention from your message. Of course, it is always nice to have a secretary who can "dress up" your correspondence into eye-appealing documents suitable for framing; but even if you have such a secretary, the knowledge that you could sit down at the typewriter and eventually make an effective business letter all by yourself does wonders for your self-confidence.

ESSENTIAL PARTS

There are just a few other things you should know before we practice with block and semiblock formats. One of them is that all business letters have only five *essential* parts: heading, inside address, salutation, body, and signature block.

Here is a brief description of each of those parts:

Heading

The heading is indispensable because it tells your reader how to address a letter he or she might wish to send to you. It also shows when you wrote the letter, and that can sometimes be very important. The heading consists of the printed letterhead and the typed date. Always use letterhead stationery when writing in your business capacity, even if you own the business and are the only person in it. Do *not* use letterhead stationery when writing as a private individual, or any other time you are not writing in your capacity as a business person. In such cases, the heading consists of your complete address (but not your name) and the date.

Inside Address

The inside address is necessary to prevent any confusion as to who is supposed to be reading the letter. This is especially important in large companies that have rather complex routing systems. It consists of the complete name and address of the person you are writing to. It must be identical to the name and address on the envelope you use to mail the letter. This makes it possible for the recipient to discard the envelope and still have all the useful information it contained. The only abbreviations permissible here are titles like *Mr., Mrs., Ms., Dr., Ph.D.,* and the two capital letters identifying the state. Do not abbreviate *Street, Boulevard, Road, Lane, Court,* or other words in the address. Be sure to include the zip.

Salutation

The salutation is important because it establishes the tone of the letter; therefore, it must always be courteous and invite goodwill. It consists of the word *Dear,* followed by the reader's name, followed by a colon.

The necessity of avoiding sexist language sometimes makes writing a courteous salutation difficult. The modern business writer must no longer assume that if I. L. Brown is a woman, she should overlook being addressed as "Mr. Brown." Therefore, the most sensible approach seems to be the following:

1. Use *Mr.* or *Ms.* only when you are sure such a title is accurate. *(Of course, use Mrs. or Miss if you know the person prefers it.)*
2. Omit the *Mr.* or *Ms.* if you don't know whether the person is a man or a woman, but then you must include the person's first name or initials.
   For example: Dear Pat Jones:
   Dear I. L. Brown:
3. Use the all-purpose title *Director* or other reasonable alternative when you don't know the person's name.
   For example: Dear Personnel Director:
   Dear Billing Director:
   Dear Accounting Director:
   Dear Editor:
4. Use *Dear* and just the person's first name only if the two of you are intimate friends.
   For example: Dear Jim:
   Dear Marilyn:
5. Some people find the following forms objectionable; don't use any of them:
   Dear Accounting Department:
   Dear Sir:
   Dear Sirs:
   Gentlemen: *(even if they are all men)*
   Ladies: *(even if they are all women)*

Body

The body is essential because it is the message itself. Whenever possible, keep the paragraphs short and the total contents brief enough so that the entire letter will fit on one page.

Signature Block

The signature block is important because it establishes the authenticity of the message. It consists of the complimentary close (use the all-purpose

123

closing "Sincerely,"), your typed name (put your signature immediately above it), and your office or title. If you are writing as an official representative of the company you work for, you can indicate that by typing the company's name in capital letters two spaces below "Sincerely," and leaving four blank lines for your signature between the company's name and your typed name. Including the company's name this way alters the legal responsibility for the letter. Check with your boss first.

Now let's look at some examples. For our present purposes, we are interested in only two things: the eye appeal of the letter page and the ease of typing. Figure 6–1 shows the block form; Figure 6–2 shows the semiblock:

ST. NORBERT COLLEGE
DE PERE, WISCONSIN 54115

```
The date goes here.

The inside address
goes on these four
or five lines, depending
on the length of the
address.

The salutation goes here.

This is the body of the letter.  You should try to keep
your message to three or four paragraphs, ideally. But
don't use the form as a Procrustean bed to lop off or
stretch your message for the sake of a balanced page.

Notice that I double-spaced between paragraphs.  That
makes indenting unnecessary because your reader can easily
see how your message breaks down into its component parts;
the paragraphs stand out as units with white space all
around them.  Of course, if your message consists of only
one paragraph, you should double-space within it instead
of single-spacing as I am doing.

You should also notice that if you leave too wide a margin
on the right when using this form, your letter will have
a decided lopsided tilt to the left.  All the black letters
towards the left and all the white space on the right will
make the page look as if it is listing to portside.

Sincerely,

Block Form

Your typed name goes here,
four lines below the complimentary
close.  So does your job title.
```

Figure 6–1. Block Form.

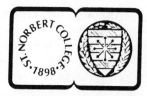

ST. NORBERT COLLEGE
DE PERE, WISCONSIN 54115

The date goes here.

The inside address
goes on these four
or five lines, depending
on the length of the
address.

The salutation goes here.

　　　This is the body of the letter. As with the block
form, the semiblock has most eye appeal if you keep your
message to three or four paragraphs.

　　　This form has a better balanced, "picture frame" look
than the block form has; but it requires a little more ingenuity at the typewriter. Besides the left-margin tab of
14 for pica and 16 for elite (This is the same for both
block and semiblock), you need to set the paragraph-indent
tab 19 for pica and 21 for elite. Furthermore, you need
to set the tab for the date, the complimentary close, and
the signature block at 44 for pica and 51 for elite.

　　　However, once you have made these three tab settings,
it will take you no longer to type the semiblock than it
does to type the block--except for having to push the tab
button seven or eight additional times. Many people think
that's a small price to pay for producing a letter that
looks so nicely balanced. It certainly is prettier than
the block form.

　　　Don't ask me why you have to double-space between paragraphs when you also mark them off by indenting. The only
reason I can give is that it looks nicer that way.

　　　　　　　　　Sincerely,

　　　　　　　　　Semiblock Form

　　　　　　　　　Your typed name goes here;
　　　　　　　　　so does your job title. Line
　　　　　　　　　them up with the date.

Figure 6–2. Semiblock Form.

　　　No doubt you are tired of standing around with your armload of do's
and don't's, your "You" approach, and your positive attitude, and I'm sure
you are eager to dump what you've learned into a block or semiblock form
and get down to writing some letters. But there are a few odds and ends
that we need to take care of first. So be patient.

125

Although it is true that you need to use only the five essential parts in order to make a good business letter, you should know what the optional parts are, too. It's nice to know what they mean when they show up on letters you receive. Sometimes they serve a very important purpose; but when they don't, you shouldn't clutter up your letter with them.

Anyway, here they are:

1. Attention line—This enables the writer to address the letter to a company, but direct it to a specific person. Its value is doubtful, except when you don't know the first name of the addressee, *e.g.,* *Attention Mr. Jamison.* But in that case you'll have trouble with the salutation, anyway; the salutation should refer to the first line of the inside address, not to the person named in the attention line.

2. Subject line—This may aid a little in filing the letter, but if you construct a decent first sentence of the body, your reader won't need the subject line. It usually appears alongside the salutation or below it and centered on the page.

3. Reference or file number—This is strictly to aid in filing. Some companies require it, but you shouldn't use it unless you have to. When it appears, it's usually somewhere slightly above the body of the letter.

4. Reference initials—These are the initials of the author followed by those of the typist, like this: RJL:ms. They appear at the left margin, below the signature block.

5. Enclosure notation—This can be of help to envelope stuffers or mail openers, but serves hardly any other useful purpose if you tell your reader in the body of the letter what you are enclosing. It usually appears under the reference initials.

6. Copy notation—This can be important if you want other people to get copies of your letter and want a record of who got them. It usually appears under the enclosure notation.

7. Postscript—some writers of sales letters use this to gain attention. It usually seems sophomoric. Don't use it without good reason. It appears below everything else in the letter.

Finally, you need to know how to begin a second page in case you can't get the whole letter on one page. One inch from the top and at the left margin of a blank sheet of paper, you should type the addressee's name. On the next line, also at the left margin, type "Page 2." On the next line, also at the left margin, type the date. Double space, and finish your letter.

All right, you've stood there eagerly panting long enough. Now you get a chance to write a letter. Your last five exercises for this chapter consist of this: Take a sheet of 8½" x 11" typing paper and draw a line across it 2" from the top. That's the bottom line of the letterhead. Next, using the semiblock form, type a response to the following letter:

839 Pine Street
Denver CO 80272
March 21, 19XX

Ms. Sylvia Christensen
Planning Director
Accuwhiz Widget Company
413 Cherry Street
Green Bay, WI 54304

Dear Ms. Christensen:

Your article in the February Accuwhiz Today *was delightful, but it left me with some questions about your meaning in a few places.*

What did you mean when you said, "Accuwhiz Widget is planning to centralize its accounting system?" Does that mean my sister who works in the accounting department of your Denver branch is going to lose her job? If she loses her job, I'm going to stop buying your widgets and tell all my friends to stop buying them too. It's always "centralize this" and "centralize that" until people in your branch offices don't have jobs. What kind of rotten game are you playing, anyway?

Also, what did you mean by "modernizing our boilers"? Haven't you people wasted enough money on "modernizing"? Pretty soon we stockholders won't get any dividends at all; there won't be anything left.

Otherwise, I liked your article. You are a good writer. But I wish you would have explained some parts of it better.

Sincerely,

Victor A. Johnquist

Here are the facts: (1) The accounting departments in your branch offices will tie in with the computer in your home office in Green Bay starting next month. Nobody will lose his or her job because of this. Besides, this improvement in accounting is sure to reduce waste and therefore increase profits and dividends. (2) The EPA has required modification of your boilers so that they meet antipollution standards. The cost of this to Accuwhiz Widget Company is minimal because of government tax incentives.

Now write your letter to Mr. Johnquist, employing what you learned in this chapter.

After you have finished, answer these questions about your letter. The answers are on page 135.

26. Did you omit all reference to Mr. Johnquist's offensive sentence about the "rotten game" he thinks you are playing?

_____

27. Did you concentrate on what you *did* mean in your article, rather than on what you *did not* mean?

_____

28. Did you express appreciation for Mr. Johnquist's interest in your article and for his taking the time to write to you about it?

_____

29. Did you succeed in telling Mr. Johnquist that his dividends will increase *without making him feel embarrassed for thinking they would decrease?*

_____

30. About how many inches from the right edge of the paper did you *start* the signature block?

_____

FOR CLASS DISCUSSION

Bring to class the letter you wrote to Mr. Johnquist for exercises 26–30 and exchange it with one of your classmates.

Assume you are Mr. Johnquist. Would you agree with your classmate's answers to questions 26–30? Does your classmate agree with your answers to those exercise questions?

After you have discussed your differences of opinion with your neighbor (no fist-fights, please), the instructor will solicit the entire class's sentence-by-sentence suggestions for the body of the letter and write them on the chalkboard. In your notebook, copy down the class's solution from the chalkboard and compare it with your own letter. Which one is better? Does the definition of a camel as a horse put together by a committee apply to what you discovered in this class exercise?

TEST YOURSELF

Revise the following sentences so that they reflect the "You" approach and show a positive attitude. The answers are on page 136.

   1. Don't buy our X-47 tires for a taxi fleet; we didn't design them specifically for that kind of use, the way we did our X-50 tires.

_____

_____

_____

   2. With every order we receive we send a booklet on how to plan an inexpensive vacation.

_____

_____

   3. When anyone opens an account with us, we offer a choice of gifts—either a stadium blanket or a coffee maker.

_____

_____

   4. Don't lose the sales slip; we won't exchange the drapes for a different size without it because the other sizes are not on sale.

_____

_____

_____

   5. If anything else goes wrong, please don't hesitate to call.

_____

_____

   6. We are always glad to hear from a customer who is not the least bit unhappy with our service.

_____

_____

7. If you don't call by Friday, I'll know our offer is not acceptable.

_____

_____

8. If you order twelve or more, we give a 10 per cent discount.

_____

_____

9. I think working for your company can help me achieve my career goal of becoming a personnel manager.

_____

_____

10. I cannot meet with you anytime except on Wednesday afternoons from 2:00 P.M. to 4:00 P.M.

_____

_____

APPLY YOURSELF

Suppose you are captain of your softball team. This is the team's first year in the league, so you decide to write to Accuwhiz Widget Company and ask them to sponsor you. Here are the facts, some of which you will need and some of which you won't:

1. It costs five hundred dollars for shirts, caps, and monograming.

2. About 150 spectators attend each game.

3. You play thirty games each summer.

4. You cannot join the league without a sponsor.

5. A competitor of Accuwhiz sponsors another team in the league.

6. The league charges a sponsor's fee of twenty-five dollars.

7. Deadline for registering your sponsor is thirty days from now.

8. Accuwhiz sells its widgets only through their mail-order catalog.

9. Your shortstop's uncle is a shipping clerk at Accuwhiz.

10. Your team hasn't decided on a name for itself yet.

11. You don't expect to win many games your first year in the league.

12. The local newspaper covers only the league championship games.

13. Accuwhiz's address:
    Accuwhiz Widget Company
    2145 Pine Street
    Peoria, IL 63491

14. Ms. Delores Barnes is public relations director at Accuwhiz.

Use the semiblock form and be careful to use the "You" approach. Be sure you stress the positive.

ANSWERS TO EXERCISES

1. I would like your advice on how to improve our training program.
OR
   Would you please give me your advice on how to improve our training program?

2. As you requested, we are returning your photographs.

3. Please indicate on your application form whether you desire part-time or full-time employment.

4. Thank you for your comments on the Accuwhiz Calculator you recently purchased.
OR
   Thank you for your comments on your new Accuwhiz Calculator.

5. We assure you that your guarantee covers all the optional equipment you ordered with your Accuwhiz. (The guarantee now belongs to the customer, so this enables you to call it "your guarantee" rather than "our guarantee.")

6. I am happy to inform you that your company's bid on remodeling our reception area was lowest. I am enclosing a contract for you to sign. Please return the yellow copy to me by Friday, March 23.

7. If I can be of any further help, please call me at my west side office (499–3476) or write directly to our home office in Sunnydale.

8. Here is our latest brochure on how to select the best savings plan for you. I think you will find it helpful in selecting one of the plans I recommended in our phone conversation last Tuesday.

9. I am delighted you agree with my suggestion to shorten Chapter 4. Your idea of expanding Chapter 3 is more practical than mine, though; and I think you should consider giving Chapter 5 the same treatment. If you run into any problems on Chapter 6, please let me know; I would like to help you as much as I can to meet the November 15 deadline.

10. If you wish, I can have my colleague, Mr. John Perkins, meet you in Grosse Pointe to assist you in your research.

11. Please make your reservations before 4:00 P.M. this Friday.

12. Please show your invitation to the usher at the door.

13. To protect your excellent credit rating, please send us the amount due by the end of the month.

14. For only three dollars more a month, you can have this extended insurance coverage.

15. I will be happy to answer any further questions you might have. (However, this revision seems to invite further questions. It would be better, if

possible, to eliminate the sentence entirely and thank the reader for taking an interest in whatever it was you needed to explain.)

16. The letter samples you send will surely help improve the writing skills of the next generation of XYZ executives.

17. I will be happy to send you a copy of the tabulated results of all question-naires received if you will complete yours and return it to me by the end of June.

18. You can have your toboggan by Christmas if we receive your order before November 15.

19. To make sure you receive your newsletter promptly, please fill in your complete address on the membership application.

20. When you order again, please use these new forms to insure prompt delivery.

21. c

22. b

23. d

24. a

25. b

26. Yes.

27. Yes.

28. Yes.

29. Yes.

30. 4½

ANSWERS TO TEST YOURSELF

1. I suggest you put our X-50 tires on your taxi fleet; we designed them specifically for that kind of use.

2. As soon as I receive your order, I will be happy to send you our booklet that tells you how to plan an inexpensive vacation.

3. You can choose either a stadium blanket or a coffee maker as a gift when you open an account with us.

4. Please save your sales slip until you are sure the drapes will fit.

5. Please call me if you need any further help.
OR
    If I can help you again, please call.

6. Thank you for telling us you liked our service.
OR
    I am happy you are pleased with our service.

7. Please call me by Friday if you decide to accept our offer.

8. When you order twelve or more, you receive a 10 per cent discount.

9. I believe I can be an asset to your personnel department.

10. I will be happy to meet with you any Wednesday afternoon between 2:00 P.M. and 4:00 P.M.

7

Make First and Last Paragraphs Count

Every piece of communication, whether oral or written, has a beginning, a middle, and an end. "Big deal!" you say? "Who doesn't know that?" Apparently, many business writers either forget that simple three-part division of their messages or else fail to realize what it implies. When business letters are unclear, it's usually because the writer did not take enough care to introduce the message and to conclude it *from the reader's point of view.*

The first part and the last part of almost every language unit—from the simple phrase right on up to the lengthy speech, the formal report, and even the novel—are places of natural emphasis. Readers and listeners pay most attention to the beginnings and endings of phrases, sentences, paragraphs, letters, reports, books, and every other message they read or listen to. That is one reason why sponsors put commercials at the beginning and at the end of television programs. It is also why football fans seldom yawn during the opening kickoff or during a "two-minute offense" at the end of a game.

You can capitalize on this psychological phenomenon by making sure your opening and closing paragraphs satisfy your reader's expectations at those points. First, we'll see how you can do this in your opening paragraphs.

When you first open a letter someone has sent you, your eyes naturally skip down to the first paragraph, and your first question is either "Why is this person writing to me?" or "What's in it for me?" Your reader will invariably do the same. Therefore, the first rule of beginning your opening paragraph is this:

Make sure your first sentence concisely tells your reader what your letter is all about.

Construct that first sentence carefully. Try to be concise, yet complete. Make it as specific as you can. Include the date of the letter you are answer-

137

ing, for example. If you do it right, the entire opening paragraph should have to be no more than three or four lines long. The important thing is that by reading your first sentence your reader will know what the letter is about. And by reading your first paragraph your reader will understand why you are writing. This will provide a context for understanding your middle paragraphs.

Let's try some exercises that involve evaluating opening sentences. Suppose you are writing to the manufacturer of your power drill because you want to order a fish-scaling attachment for it. The answers are on page 157.

1. From your reader's point of view, what is your letter about?

_____

2. Here is a possible first sentence for your letter:
I like my power drill very much.
This sentence (a) includes the subject of the letter.
          (b) uses the "You" approach.
          (c) is concise.
          (d) is complete.
          (e) is none of the above.

3. Here is another possible first sentence:
My power drill did not come with an attachment for scaling fish, even though some of the newer models now have them as standard equipment.
This sentence (a) includes the subject of the letter.
          (b) uses the "You" approach.
          (c) is concise.
          (d) is complete.
          (e) is none of the above.

4. Here is another possible first sentence:
Please send me one of your fish-scaling attachments for my model 4200 power drill.
This sentence (a) includes the subject of the letter.
          (b) uses the "You" approach.
          (c) is concise.
          (d) is complete.
          (e) is none of the above.

5. Here is another possible first sentence:
I've really been catching a lot of fish up here in northern Minnesota all summer.
This sentence (a) includes the subject of the letter.
          (b) uses the "You" approach.
          (c) is concise.
          (d) is complete.
          (e) is none of the above.

Notice that from *your* point of view the sentence in example 5 probably contains the most important subject of all: your success in fishing. But from your *reader's* point of view the prospect of selling you a fish-scaling attachment would undoubtedly seem more important.

From these exercises you should have learned at least two things:

1.   It's very hard to decide whether a first sentence is complete, or even concise, when it doesn't express the main purpose of the letter. Your reader would have the same kind of trouble understanding what you are driving at.
2.   The most direct but courteous way to begin the first sentence of a letter asking for something your reader will <u>want</u> to send is to write simply, "Please send me. . . ."

But what about the opening sentence of a letter asking for a favor, persuading, or giving bad news? It's bad psychology to hit your reader immediately with a statement that is sure to cause some degree of resistance. But the general rule still applies: Tell your reader what the letter is *about* in that first sentence. For instance, suppose someone has suggested a change in your company's family-insurance plan. Your job is to tell her that the company has rejected her suggestion. You can still inform her of the *subject* of your letter in the first sentence without springing the bad news on her immediately, if you write something like this:

Our personnel committee has carefully considered your suggestion for changing our family-insurance plan.

It is true that an experienced reader of that opening sentence will know you didn't adopt her suggestion; she will understand that if you *had* adopted it you would have told her so right away. Yet, she will probably maintain her goodwill toward you and the company, simply because you were considerate enough *not* to tell her the bad news as if you couldn't wait to disappoint her. Yet, you have let her know at the very beginning of the letter that your main purpose is to announce your decision to her.

It really makes no difference, then, what kind of letter you are writing; sales letters, persuasive letters, good news letters, bad news letters—*all* should begin with a sentence that lets your reader know what the letter is about.

Some writers find it difficult to get right down to business in that first sentence, for fear of sounding abrupt. If you worry about that, you may find the following suggestions helpful.

When you write a letter, you will frequently find yourself doing one of three things:

1.   asking for something
2.   answering something
3.   acknowledging something

These are very general categories, but they can be useful in deciding how best to phrase an opening sentence. When you are asking for something, you can usually start with the word "please":

Please send me your spring catalog.
Please return the manuscript of my short story "Igloo," which I sent you April 4.
Please accept my apology for losing your manuscript.

When you are answering something, you can often begin your first sentence with the word *here:*

Here is the market analysis you asked for in your letter of December 19.
Here are the extra copies of the new tax-rate schedules you called me about last Wednesday.
Here is the accident report you requested in your June 30 memorandum.

When you are acknowledging something, you should try to begin your first sentence with the words *thank you:*

Thank you for returning the contract so promptly.
Thank you for your helpful suggestions on improving our training course.
Thank you for letting us know how you like your new Accuwhiz computer.

All of these examples get right down to business, yet they avoid curtness and a stiff formality because they include either the courteous words *please* and *thank you,* or they exemplify the "You" approach, or they do both.

Now let's practice writing a few opening sentences. The answers are on page 157.

6. Your colleague who is a chemical engineer for Accuwhiz Widgets in Toledo has written to you suggesting you apply for a job that has opened up in his engineering department. It would mean a higher salary for you, but you don't want to leave Omaha. You decide not to apply. What would be your opening sentence in the letter you send your colleague explaining your decision?

---

7. You have asked for, and received, a report on traffic congestion in Milwaukee. But page four of the report is missing. What would be the first sentence of your letter to the Milwaukee transportation director?

---

8. A social worker in San Francisco has written to you, asking for a copy of a speech you gave at a convention of criminologists last December. What would be the first sentence of the letter you send with the copy of the speech?

---

9. In a letter dated June 10, your insurance agent has asked you for a list of items damaged in a fire in your warehouse. What would be the first sentence of the letter you send accompanying the list?

---

10. On June 14 you sent the letter described in item 9. But on June 16 you discover four more items damaged in the fire. What would be the first sentence of your letter asking your insurance agent to add the four items to the list you sent?

This rule of telling your reader what the letter is all about in the first sentence is a good one, and you should follow it *in most cases*. But common sense will sometimes suggest that you bend it a little. The degree of familiarity between you and your reader will determine how closely you should observe the rule: the more intimate you and your reader are, the more you can relax the rule.

For example, this salutation and opening sentence from the first letter I received from my editor reflect the appropriate formality and decorum the writer must use when writing to someone for the first time:

Dear Professor Londo:

My colleague Mr. Phil Wagner reports that you contemplate developing a text in business report writing.

That first sentence told me exactly what the letter was about. Compare that with the following, which I received from the same editor ten months later, after we had written to each other many times:

Dear Dick:

The first four months of this year have passed so rapidly that I have, for the first time in my career, barely met the schedule imposed on all wage earners by the IRS. The sudden and nearly catastrophic appearance of this deadline has reminded me that there are others out there in the misty future and that I should take some steps now to avoid running into them at careless full steam like the Titanic.

This is the first paragraph of the editor's letter asking me to verify the scheduled due date for the manuscript of this textbook and requesting that I inform him if I foresaw any difficulty in meeting that date. The first sen-

141

tence gives no hint of what the letter is about, except for that one word *schedule*. Is this therefore a bad opening? Certainly not. (You didn't think I would criticize my editor and then submit this chapter for him to edit, did you?) The salutation is the tipoff. When you address someone by his or her first name, you are saying, "Let's be a little more chatty and informal than strict business etiquette will allow." In fact, after having corresponded with this editor for so long, I would have felt a little chill if he had done it this way:

> *Dear Professor Londo:*
>
> *Please let me know if you expect any difficulty in meeting the deadline for your manuscript of Common Sense in Business Writing.*

And I would have felt nearly insulted if he had begun the letter this way:

> *Dear Professor Londo:*
>
> *Please inform me whether your understanding of the deadline for your manuscript agrees with mine.*

Notice, too, that the whole first paragraph of his actual letter is a bit longer than what would be usual in a more formal one. That's another hint of good-natured friendliness, quite appropriate in this situation.

But be sure you state your business in the first sentence whenever you write to someone for the first time. And keep doing it that way in subsequent letters until you feel a first-name-only salutation would not seem impertinent. Then you can postpone the real business of your letter as far as your second paragraph if you want to.

Some people, no matter how often you correspond with them, will prefer to maintain some degree of formality. In such cases, follow the rule; state your business in the first sentence—but always be friendly and courteous, even in the most formal of letters.

Now, how about the rest of the opening paragraph? First of all, keep it short. Secondly, after telling *what* the letter is about in the first sentence, tell your reader *why* you are writing in the rest of the paragraph. Often you can cover both *what* and *why* in the first sentence. In that case, you have a one-sentence opening paragraph. Here are a few examples of one-, two-, and three-sentence first paragraphs:

> *Please send me a list of all foot injuries at our plant for the month of February. We need to include this information in our monthly safety report to our central office.* (Your next paragraphs would explain exactly what kind of information you need and tell your reader how to report it.)
>
> *Here is the summary of insurance options you asked for in your letter of June 9.* (Your next paragraphs would consist of the summary.)
>
> *Would you please let me know whether our employees are eligible for your 10 per cent discount on safety shoes? One of our workers told*

142

me she received the discount. Two others, who ordered through your catalog, said they did not receive it. (Your next paragraphs would describe whatever details your reader might need to know in order to explain why one got the discount and others did not.)

Now you try some. For the next five exercises, write both an appropriate salutation and a one-, two-, or three-sentence opening paragraph. Don't forget that you must never give bad news in the first paragraph. The answers are on pages 157 and 158.

11. You are an instructor at a technical school. You learn about a new textbook that may be suitable for your course Introduction to Electronics. The title of the text is *The Transistor Revolution,* published by Columbine Press and written by James L. Jamison. You would like an examination copy before June so that if you like it you could adopt it for the fall semester. Begin your letter to Ms. Anita Donnely, manager of the college sales division of Columbine Press.

_____

_____

_____

_____

_____

12. You are manager of customer services at Lamblock's Mail-Order Store. A customer, Mr. Jerry Quinn, has written to you asking for the owner's manuals for his five-year-old snowblower, his two-year-old stereo, and his seven-year-old chainsaw. By mistake, when cleaning out his garage, he threw out the copies that came with the equipment. He says he is willing to pay for the replacement manuals. You have no more copies of the owner's manual for the chainsaw, but have found copies of the other two manuals and will send him those free of charge. Begin your letter to him.

_____

_____

_____

_____

_____

13. You are personnel manager of a two-hundred-employee manufacturing plant. Five local photographers have responded to your newspaper ad calling for bids on the job of photographing each of your employees for your personnel records. Photographer Philip Green won the job, and you are sending him a contract. Start your letter to Mr. Green.

_____

_____

_____

_____

_____

14.   Given the same situation as in exercise 13, start a letter to Mr. James Yalbert, one of the four photographers who did not get the job.

_____

_____

_____

_____

_____

15.   You are dean of Hollingsworth College of Nursing. In preparing a proposal to your faculty that you change from your current grading system to one of pass/fail, you discover an article in a nursing journal that says Mercycare Nursing School has recently decided to return to traditional grading after two years of experimenting with the pass/fail system. The dean of Mercycare is Dr. Lois Van Eck. Begin a letter to Dean Van Eck in which you ask for the details of why Mercycare decided to abandon the pass/fail system.

_____

_____

_____

_____

_____

CLOSING PARAGRAPHS

The other place of emphasis in the body of your letter is, of course, the last paragraph.

When you get near the end of a letter someone has sent you, especially if the letter is lengthy, you begin to ask yourself, "How does all this affect *me*?" or "What does the writer expect *me* to do about this?" Your reader will want answers to those questions, too.

If your letter is a request for something, the last paragraph is an excellent place to be very specific about what precisely you are asking for. Include such things as the date you need it by, your telephone number, or anything else you can think of that will make it *easy* for your reader to do what you are asking.

If your letter is a response to a request, your last paragraph is a good place to offer additional assistance, if needed. You might include here some information which your reader didn't specifically ask for, but which you know will probably be useful. The last paragraph is also an excellent place to summarize, to "tie it all together" for your reader if your message is rather complex.

If your letter is simply an acknowledgment, the last paragraph is the place to do some plugging for your company. For instance, if you are acknowledging receipt of a final payment on an account, you should do a little selling in that last paragraph. Try to get your reader interested in

"Send a letter to the Weyauwega Widget Works and tell them 'Phooey!' Put a nice opening and closing on it."

continuing to do business with you, in making a new purchase, or in at least thinking well of you and your company.

Remember, every business letter is a goodwill letter. The natural emphasis of your final paragraph makes it ideal for reinforcing that goodwill. Your reader should finish reading your letter feeling good about your business relationship.

There is one sure way to ruin that goodwill at the end of a letter, and that is to trot out some old cliché that both you and your reader have seen a hundred times in the last paragraphs of other letters. Such sentences as "Please don't hesitate to call if I can be of any further assistance," "Thank you in advance for your help in this matter," and "I assure you that this will never happen again" are bad endings for several reasons. First of all, like all other clichés, they give your reader the impression that you have simply pulled a sentence off the shelf and tacked it onto the end of your letter without really thinking about what the words mean. Secondly, "Please don't hesitate to call. . . ." is extremely negative. The mental pictures it calls up are of someone hesitating, and then deciding *not* to hesitate. Be positive. Tell your reader what to do, not what to avoid doing. "Thank you in advance. . . ." is presumptuous. If your reader thinks about your meaning at all, he or she will feel indignant that, having already received your thanks, there is no way to avoid giving you what you want. Don't try to subtly coerce your reader this way; it is likely to meet with resistance. Finally, it is foolhardy to promise that something will *never* happen again. Accidents do happen, and they sometimes happen more than once no matter how hard you try to prevent them. Consider how embarrassed you will feel, if your luck is like mine, when it *does* happen again.

On the basis of these observations, we can make two general rules about ending paragraphs. The first is

Depending on the nature of the letter, your final paragraph should do as much of the following as possible:
1. *make it easy for your reader to comply with your request*
2. *offer additional help to your reader*
3. *summarize the content of your letter*
4. *reinforce your reader's goodwill*

The other general rule will help you avoid cliché conclusions:

Whenever possible, refer to your reader by name in your last paragraph.

Of course, it's hard to do this in a form letter, but whenever you take the time to generate a letter to a specific individual you should try to capitalize on that by reminding your reader that you think of him or her as a unique person. A final paragraph like the following does that:

If you need any further help constructing your questionnaire, Ms. Richards, please call me any weekday afternoon at 337–3118.

This personalized "You" approach is particularly effective in final paragraphs. It always reinforces the reader's goodwill.

Here are a few exercises to give you practice in recognizing a good final paragraph when you see one. If you know what an effective one looks like, you are well on your way to writing effective ones yourself. For these last five exercises, select all the answers that apply. The answers are on page 158.

16. *Contact me if I can be of any further help.*
This conclusion (a) uses the "You" approach.
                (b) is specific.
                (c) summarizes the rest of the letter.
                (d) does none of the above.

17. *If you are interested, please fill out the enclosed application form, Mr. Birdwell, and return it in the self-addressed envelope by August 17. We will then be able to let you know our decision before September 1.*
This concluding paragraph (a) uses the "You" approach.
                        (b) is specific.
                        (c) makes reader response easy.
                        (d) reinforces reader's goodwill.

18. *Wishing you the best of fortune in all your future endeavors, I remain*
                                          Sincerely,
This ending (a) uses inflated language.
            (b) is a cliché.
            (c) sounds insincere.
            (d) is none of the above.

19. *Please call by phone if we can be of any further service.*

This ending (a) makes reader response easy.
           (b) uses the "You" approach.
           (c) contains a redundancy.
           (d) reinforces reader's goodwill.

20. *For these reasons, Mrs. Hartwig, we need your written permission to transfer the funds. Please sign, date, and return this permission form in the enclosed postpaid enevelope.*
This ending paragraph (a) reinforces reader's goodwill.
                  (b) makes reader response easy.
                  (c) summarizes the rest of the letter.
                  (d) does none of the above.

FOR CLASS DISCUSSION

Comment on the opening and closing paragraphs of the following letters. All three are genuine, except that I have changed all proper nouns to insure anonymity.

Letter A

ACCUWHIZ WIDGET CORPORATION
212 Oneida road
Elmira, Colorado 80314
(303) 867–1010

Executive Offices

February 5, 19__

Mr. Neal Volsces
285 Elmira Street
Esperanto, NJ 08937

Dear Neal:

Thank you for consenting to handle some photography for ACCUWHIZ TODAY.

As for the specifications for the story on Ed Larabee and Herb White and their participation in the Happy Worker program, those listed below should provide you with enough direction.

Black and white film, with available light, will be fine.

Shoot Larrabee and White in counsel with a local business person at his/her place of business. A candid environment is best.

For purposes of example, if the local person is a baker, you might shoot the threesome in the kitchen area with the baker still with his hands white from cooking flour. If he is a local service station operator, you might shoot the men with the open hood of an auto as a back drop. In short, use your imagination. I want to convey the environment as well as the men.

After you make arrangements with Herb and Ed, but before you do the shooting, please call me at (303) 867–1018. I'll need a price estimate from you before I give you the go ahead. I'm certain that will be no problem, however.

When the job is over, please forward the processed film as well as a set of contact sheets. To save time, we'll have prints made here from your negatives.

I'll be in contact with you again in the near future concerning another job at the ACCUWHIZ plant.

Thanks again.

Sincerely,

Cliff Barnard

Cliff Barnard
Manager, Employee Publications

Letter B

ACCUWHIZ WIDGET CORPORATION
212 Oneida Road
Elmira, Colorado 80314

Executive Offices

November 4, 19__

Mr. Dave Danielson, Director
ACCUWHIZ SOUTHERN NEWSLETTER
Lambeth, GA 57123

Dear Dave:

Thanks once again for your phone call relative to ACCUWHIZ TODAY. Your comments are well taken and we will continue to be sensitive to publicizing issues that are contrary to your local efforts.

After our chat, I went to my "Intercom" library and found that I am not receiving a copy of your newsletter. Can you send me a copy of the most recent issue and put me on your distribution list for the future?

Thanks again for rattling my cage just a bit. We in Elmira can use that from time to time.

Regards,

Cliff

Cliff Barnard
Manager, Employee Publications

Letter C

UNITED COMMUNITY FUND, INC.
4132 Estroit Place
Nota Bene, CO
93132

February 11, 19__

Mr. Robert Evans, Editor
ACCUWHIZ TODAY
Accuwhiz Widget Corporation
212 Oneida Road
Elmira, CO 80314

Dear Mr. Evans:

The United Community Fund Publications Contest has been judged, with Widgetmaster Corporation being judged the most outstanding entry in competition. The judging was very difficult as there were many excellent entries from which to choose.

All entries were judged on editorial and writing content, creativity in makeup and layout, and value to the United Fund campaign.

On behalf of the United Community Fund, I would like to honor your efforts with this Gold Award for outstanding service to your community. If it were possible, you would all be judged winners.

Thank you for your participation and for your fine efforts in telling the story of services offered by United Community Fund agencies. I hope to see you participating again next year.

Sincerely,

Louisa M Allworthy

Louisa M. Allworthy
Associate Director, Communications

TEST YOURSELF

The answers are on page 159.

A. Rewrite the following opening paragraphs:

1. I received your letter of June 29. In it you asked for a list of charges made to your account since February 1. Here is that list.

_____

_____

_____

_____

2. I noticed your advertisement announcing the improved garbage compactor. I think I saw it in *Good Homekeeping* on Page 132. It was the July issue, I believe. I would like more information about it. My old garbage compactor keeps acting up on me. I need to know the name of the nearest dealer who handles them. Your ad said you would send that information to anyone who asked for it.

_____

_____

_____

_____

3. As you may recall, I asked you for your reasons for converting from the pass/fail system back to traditional grading. I also asked for a copy of the questionnaire you used in making that decision. Both arrived in this morning's mail. They will be very helpful to us. Thanks.

_____

_____

_____

_____

4. It sure is hot here in Alabama this week, and the weatherman tells us there will be many more hot, humid weeks ahead. Every year as this kind of weather rolls around it reminds me that soon it will be time for our annual sales convention in Mobile. But this year we're changing all that. We'll see you in Dallas instead. Sorry about those previous announcements about having it in Mobile, but we only recently found out that remodeling of our convention hall in Mobile won't be finished by convention time.

_____

_____

_____

_____

5. I am refusing your request for travel funds for the welders' convention in Cincinnati. I met with the personnel committee last week and we thought of the following reasons for rejecting your request.

_____

_____

_____

_____

B. Rewrite the following closing paragraphs:

1. I need this information by July 10. Therefore, hoping to hear from you soon, I remain

Sincerely,

_____

_____

_____

2. If I can be of further assistance, please don't hesitate to call.

_____

_____

3.   I would like an interview. Call me if you are interested in further examining my qualifications as a chemical engineer. I can get to Accuwhiz for the interview any time because I'm out of work.

_____

_____

_____

4.   NOTE: This is the last paragraph of a letter to Mr. Paul A. Genter:

I hope this explanation is sufficient. If it is not, call me and I'll try to explain more fully the parts you don't understand.

_____

_____

_____

_____

5.   The cost list you send can help me compile my report only if I get it by October 12. Thank you in advance for responding to my urgent need.

_____

_____

_____

_____

APPLY YOURSELF

Supply an opening paragraph and a closing paragraph for the following letter:

1240 Griggs Avenue
Grand City, WI 55010
August 18, 19__

Director, Pansy Airlines
Blockminster Airfield
Jet Plains, WI 54687

Dear Director:

_____

_____

_____

_____

If it were physically impossible for anyone in the passenger compartment of an airplane in flight to communicate with, or have access to, the cockpit—and if the public knew that—a would-be hijacker would know that any attempt to commandeer an airplane would be doomed to failure.

Any hijacking attempts then would require communication of threats to the cockpit by control towers' ground-to-air radio. The complexity and difficulty of doing this might well discourage most would-be hijackers from making the attempt; it certainly would eliminate all one-person, spur-of-the-moment attempts made while in flight.

Sealing off the cockpit from the rest of the plane would require toilet facilities, and the like up front, I suppose; but it wouldn't rule out one-way communication from the cockpit to the passenger area.

_____

_____

_____

_____

Sincerely,

Harvey L. Halley

Harvey L. Halley

ANSWERS TO EXERCISES

1. Selling you a fish-scaling attachment

2. c

3. e

4. a,b,c,d

5. e

6. Thank you for telling me about the engineering job.

7. Please send me page four of the report on traffic congestion in Milwaukee.

8. Here is the copy of my speech you asked me to send you.

9. Here is the damage list you asked for in your letter of June 10.

10. Please add the following items to the list I sent you on June 14.

11. Dear Ms. Donnely:

   Please send me an examination copy of *The Transister Revolution* by James L. Jamison for possible adoption in my course Introduction to Electronics. I will need it before June in order to consider it for use in the fall semester.

   (In the subsequent paragraphs you could explain such details as the number of sections you teach, the usual class size, etc.)

12. Dear Mr. Quinn:

   Here are the snowblower and stereo manuals you asked for. I am happy to send them to you without charge.

   (In the subsequent paragraphs you would explain that the owner's manual for the chainsaw is not available.)

13. Dear Mr. Green:

   I am happy to send you the enclosed contract for photographing our employees.

   (In the subsequent paragraphs you could give Mr. Green such details as how soon you must have the contract returned, when he should report to your plant to take the pictures, and so on.)

14. Dear Mr. Yalbert:

   Thank you for answering our call for bids on the job of taking our employees' pictures for our personnel records.

   (In subsequent paragraphs you would state–or, better yet, *imply* clearly— that you have selected another photographer for the job.)

157

15. Dear Dean Van Eck:

Would you please tell me your reasons for deciding to return to traditional grading after your two-year experiment with the pass/fail system? We at Hollingsworth have recently been thinking about changing from a traditional to a pass/fail system. Certainly, we would be grateful for whatever information you could give us to help us decide wisely.

(Subsequent paragraphs would include such things as specific questions you would like answered, how soon you need the information, assurance that you would be glad to return a similar favor in the future, and the like.)

16. d

17. a,b,c,d

18. a,b,c

19. c

20. a,b,c

ANSWERS TO TEST YOURSELF

A.

1.   Here is the list of charges made to your account since February 1, as you requested in your letter of June 29.

2.   Please send me the name of the nearest dealer who handles the improved garbage compactor you advertised on page 132 of the July issue of *Good Homekeeping*.

3.   Thank you for the list of reasons for changing back to traditional grading and for the sample questionnaire I asked you for. Both will be very helpful to us.

4.   This year we will hold our annual sales convention in Dallas because remodeling our Mobile convention hall is taking longer than we expected.

5.   The personnel committee and I have thoroughly considered your request for travel funds for the welders' convention in Cincinnati.

B.

1.   May I please hear from you by July 10?

2.   Please call me at (give your phone number) if I can be of any further assistance.

3.   May I please have an interview with you, at your convenience, so that we can further discuss what I could do for Accuwhiz as one of its chemical engineers?

4.   If you have any questions, Mr. Genter, please call me at (give your phone number). I want to help all I can.

5.   Would you please send me the cost list by October 12?

8

Organize Good-News Letters Deductively

You must organize your business letter so that each idea enters your reader's mind at precisely the right psychological moment. This means that you must give careful thought to both the arrangement of paragraphs within the body of the letter and the arrangement of sentences within each of those paragraphs. In this chapter and the next, we will discuss mostly the body paragraphs that come between the opening one and the closing one, but it may be a good idea to review openings and closings briefly before we begin.

Your opening sentence should tell your reader what your letter is about, and your opening paragraph should explain why you are writing. If you have good news for your reader, give it in the first sentence.

Your closing paragraph should summarize, conclude, or state exactly what you are asking your reader to do. It must always be a very *positive* paragraph, avoiding all negative terms and stressing the most optimistic aspect you can find in your message. Offer help here, and be specific.

Now, all business letters fall into one of two very general categories. Either they include information that your reader will resist in some way, or they do not. Any time the main purpose of your letter is to *sell* your reader something, to *ask* your reader for a favor, or to announce a decision that will *disappoint* your reader, you know that your message will encounter some degree of resistance. Whenever you are trying to persuade your reader to give you time or money, or whenever you have to say "No" to your reader, you are writing what we will call a Bad-News letter. It is true that some letters in this group do not necessarily contain bad news for your reader; a sales letter, for instance, *could* meet immediate acceptance—if you're lucky. But we need a very general category here, and Bad-News letter seems as good a name for it as any.

A Good-News letter is any letter that is not a Bad-News letter, as we have defined it. In a Good-News letter you do not expect your reader to resist your message in any way, so you use deductive, rather than inductive, organization.

Perhaps we should say something about these two basic organizational patterns, deductive and inductive. (Some texts call the deductive the "direct approach" and the inductive the "indirect" or the "psychological approach," but our terms will do as well.)

When you work *inductively,* you begin with many specific facts, and you end with a general conclusion derived from those facts.

When you work *deductively,* you begin with a general statement, and you go on to list specific facts and details that support or explain that statement.

When writing Good-News letters, you should always arrange the parts of your message deductively. Put the good news at the beginning. Let's see what happens when the writer doesn't do that. Suppose, in response to an employment ad in a professional journal, you have written to Accuwhiz Widgets, Inc., applying for the position of assistant production manager. You feel confident that your résumé and application letter are impressive. Today you receive a letter from Accuwhiz. Here is the body of that letter:

> *Thank you for responding to our ad announcing a vacancy in our production department.*
>
> *You are one of seventy-eight applicants for the job, most of them with outstanding qualifications. We were so surprised by this large number that it took us a week longer than expected to decide on the three we would like to interview. That is why I am writing to you almost a week later than our ad said we would.*
>
> *But we wanted to make sure we would be interviewing only the best persons available. Therefore, we certainly did not want to rush our decision.*
>
> *And we're sure our careful deliberations paid off. We think you are one of the three best qualified applicants for the position. Congratulations. Please call me for an appointment.*

How would you feel receiving such a letter? I suppose you might answer that any time someone invites you to interview for a job you are going to be happy. But do you really want to work for a company that is so self-centered it sends you a letter focusing on its own problems in selecting three applicants for interviews? How do you feel about a company that ignores you and your interests until the last paragraph, and then announces you got the interview almost as an afterthought?

Wouldn't you feel better about going to that interview if Accuwhiz had written you a letter like the following?

> *I would like to interview you for the assistant production manager position you applied for. Your letter and résumé suggest you may be the person we want for the job.*
>
> *Could you meet with me next Thursday afternoon, June 27, at 2:00 P.M. in my office so that I can explain the position further and discuss with you your qualifications for it?*

162

Please call me at 618–3240 to confirm the appointment. I am looking forward to meeting you, Ms. Jones.

Let's look at this situation more closely. The writer has some information to communicate to you, the reader, and that information gives rise to some necessary action on your part. The message *announces* the good news that you succeeded in getting a job interview. But that news creates some questions in your mind: "What's the next step I should take? What do I do now?" The writer of that first letter wasn't really thinking about you, but rather about what's been going on at Accuwhiz during the selection process. That's probably important to the writer, but it doesn't answer *your* natural question about what you are supposed to do to get what *you* want—that job. At the very end of the letter, the writer finally gets around to you and tells you to call for an appointment, as if there is no urgency in the matter.

The writer of the second letter, on the other hand, wisely looked at the situation from *your* point of view. This writer knew that once you learned the good news you would want details telling you what to do next. And those details—time, place, and purpose of the interview—appear just when you are asking yourself, "What do I do now?" After giving these details, the writer also knew that you would probably want to do something right away, to "nail down" the interview, to show your interest and willingness to cooperate, so right then the writer conveniently provides the phone number so you can do that. Notice, too, the *positive* attitude shown in that last paragraph. In assuming you will call to *confirm* the appointment, the writer also assumes you will find the time and date acceptable. That way, changing the appointment won't even occur to you unless you *have* to do it.

Now let's look at the *internal* structure of the second letter's paragraphs.

The opening paragraph is deductive. It begins with a sentence telling what the letter is about: the good news. Then follows a sentence that explains the *reason* for that good news.

The second paragraph is deductive, too. It contains only one sentence, but the sentence itself begins with the main idea—"Can you meet . . ."— and ends with the details and the *reasons* for the meeting or interview.

The final paragraph is also deductive. Its first sentence states what the reader should do, and the last sentence graciously gives an additional *reason* for complying.

This is the way it should be. You should arrange your sentences, your paragraphs, and the body of your entire letter deductively when you write a Good-News letter. You set up a rhythm when you do that; every element first blurts out the news, then follows it with reasons and details. It's an exciting rhythm; and if your letter has it, your reader will feel you are sharing his or her excitement over the good news. That's how you generate good will.

It's time now for you to get some practice. Revise the following sentences so that they are deductive: The answers are on page 184.

1.   I am always glad to have an opportunity to help the Boy Scout program; therefore, I enthusiastically accept your invitation to serve as director of your fund drive.

_____

_____

_____

2.   Because you were so prompt in returning our questionnaire, we are sending you a copy of the preliminary results of our survey.

_____

_____

_____

3.   Our records show your account is paid in full, so we are returning your check for $25.62.

_____

_____

4.   Although we are not yet sure how many pages we want our brochure to be, we have decided to award you the contract for printing it.

_____

_____

_____

5.   Because your proposal for our fall advertising campaign is so thorough, we accept it; our sales should increase considerably.

_____

_____

_____

You should realize, of course, that if you write all sentences with a *reason* clause or phrase at the end, your letter will become monotonous. Vary your sentence length; use simple sentences, too. But always keep the key idea near the beginning of each Good-News sentence. Grammarians call such structures *loose sentences;* these are easier to read and understand than *periodic sentences,* which keep the reader guessing about what the main idea is until near the end of the sentence.

So much for Good-News sentences. How about a little practice rearranging paragraphs? For the next five exercises, list the proper sequence of sentences to make the paragraph suitable for a Good-News letter. The answers are on page 184.

6. (a) Our costs last month were down 7 per cent from the previous month.
   (b) I think we were too close to the problem to see what was wrong.
   (c) Your suggestion for reducing costs worked very well.

---

7. (a) The camera you returned does have a defective shutter spring.
   (b) As you pointed out, our guarantee covers defective materials as well as faulty workmanship.
   (c) We are sending you a new camera.

---

8. (a) Ordering in this quantity will save us $532 a year.
   (b) We wish to increase our order from fourteen dozen filters to two gross.
   (c) We have storage space available and can take advantage of your new lower rates for gross lots.

---

9. (a) We ordinarily permit only college graduates to attend our seminars.
   (b) Here is your permit to register in our computer science seminar.
   (c) However, the screening committee agreed that your experience qualifies you to enroll in this course.

---

10. (a) Your new "Metal-Flo-Roof" process could be the answer to our problem.
    (b) We would like you to give us an estimate on weatherproofing the roofs on four of our warehouses.
    (c) Mr. James Colbert, our superintendent of buildings, can show you what needs to be done.
    (d) Two have already begun to leak slightly.

That was fun, but a little too easy—for you, at least. I had to think up all the sentences, and all you had to do was rearrange them and jot down three or four letters of the alphabet. Now I'm going to sit back and let you construct some paragraphs of your own. For each of the next five exercises, write a three-sentence paragraph that would appropriately follow the given opening paragraph of a Good-News letter. When checking your answers on page 184, consider only whether you have the information in the correct *order*.

11. Opening paragraph:

We conditionally accept your short story "Dangerous Trek" for publication in Good Homekeeping. It could be just the kind of story we are looking for to lead our adventure series next winter, if you would shorten it a little.

(Your paragraph must include the following information:
(a) The story needs to be about five hundred words shorter.
(b) When submitting the manuscript, the author offered to revise the story to suit your needs.
(c) You are sure the author could easily delete several paragraphs at the beginning of the story without diminishing its effect.
(d) You think the story, if revised according to your wishes, could perhaps win your "New Authors" award.)

_____

_____

_____

_____

_____

12. Opening paragraph:

Here is our wine-making supplies catalog you requested. We are sure you will find it useful in your new hobby of making your own wine.

(Your paragraph must include the following information:
(a) Catalog prices do not include 4 per cent state sales tax.
(b) Tear-out order forms appear after page 39.
(c) To those who order from you for the first time, you send a free booklet of twenty wine recipes.
(d) When you receive an order, you send the customer a coupon good for a 5 per cent discount on the next order.)

_____

_____

_____

_____

_____

_____

13. Opening paragraph:

I will be happy to present Acme Music Company's new products at your Friends of Music Festival on October 17. Thank you for inviting me again this year.

(Your paragraph must include the following information:

(a) You will need an electrical outlet for your filmstrip projector.
(b) Acme's new "History of the Flute" filmstrip will be ready for you to use at the festival.
(c) You will need a projection screen.
(d) You will bring your own filmstrip projector.)

_____

_____

_____

_____

_____

_____

14. Opening paragraph:

I am happy to answer your questions about Gerald L. Lureen, who has applied for a position in your accounting department. Gerald worked for me for three years, so I feel I know him very well.

(Your paragraph must include the following information:

(a) Gerald sometimes worked late to get a job finished.
(b) Gerald often skipped lunch rather than disrupt something he was working on.
(c) Gerald is a hard, conscientious worker.
(d) Gerald takes pride in doing a thorough job and in finishing it on time.)

_____

_____

_____

_____

_____

_____

15. Opening paragraph:

I think your idea for adding calorie information to our food labels has merit. I have forwarded your suggestion to our package design department.

(Your paragraph must include the following information:

(a) You are grateful for customers' suggestions on how to improve the usefulness of your product.

(b) You are sending your reader a complimentary variety package of your food products.

(c) The package you are sending contains a new product—canned fortune cookies.

(d) You would be glad to hear what your reader thinks of your new product.)

_____

_____

_____

_____

_____

_____

Just because you got most of those right, I suppose you feel pretty smart right now. Well, then, let's see how you do on these next exercises. You will write an entire Good-News letter this time. Yes, right in this book. I will give you a list of jumbled-up information, some of which you will want to put into the letter and some of which you will want to leave out. Organize the useful information and compose your letter. Here are the steps you should take:

1. Underline the information you will use in the letter.

2. On another sheet of paper, sort this usable information into groups corresponding to the five essential parts of a letter.

3. Under the group headed "Body," make several subgroups arranged deductively, one for each paragraph of the body.

4. Within each subgroup of the body, arrange the information deductively.

168

"The manufacturer wrote, and you'll be thrilled to know a free brake job awaits you."

5. Employing the "You" approach, stressing the positive, and using what you learned about sentences in Part II of this book, write your letter.

6. After you have polished the language in your draft, copy your final version in the text and then compare it with the solution on pages 176 and 177.

(Incidentally, the general pattern of this procedure is good to follow whenever you write, at least until you develop a "feel" for organizing your letters.)

Here is the information you will need to know. Remember, some of it does not belong in the actual letter.

1. You are Jordan B. White, customer relations manager at Accuwhiz Swimming Pool Company, 2371 Oak Drive, Akron, Ohio, Zip Code 37842.

2. Use the current date.

3. Ms. Olive Drabb has written to you demanding reimbursement for her flattened chaise longue, which your workers backed over with their truck when they delivered the swimming pool she had bought from you.

4. She says the chaise longue was only two months old and costs $38.95 to replace.

5. She insists that you fire the truck driver.

6. You have spoken to the driver, and she has promised to be more careful in the future.

7. Use the all-purpose complimentary close.

8. The driver said Ms Drabb distracted her by constantly talking to her while she was backing the truck.

9. You know where Ms. Drabb could get a good chaise longue for $29.95.

10. Your company makes a profit of $102.00 on the kind of swimming pool Ms. Drabb bought.

11. You decide to reimburse Ms. Drabb, even though she was partly at fault.

12. You wish to apologize to Ms. Drabb for the damage your driver caused.

13. Ms. Drabb said in her letter that your apology meant more to her than the $38.95 she was demanding.

14. Your truck driver has worked for you for seven years, and this is the first time she has damaged anything.

15. Your truck driver agreed she should have been more careful and promised such a thing would never happen again.

16. The filter pump on the type of pool Ms. Drabb bought has a tendency to burn out.

17. Part of your job is to keep customers happy with their swimming pools by providing prompt repair service when needed.

18. Your phone number is 689–3737.

19. Your driver reported the accident to you yesterday, the day after it happened.

20. Ms. Drabb's address is 372 Park Vista Lane, Akron, Ohio 37843.

21. You will not fire the truck driver.

Write Your Letter on the Next Page.

Accuwhiz Swimming Pool Company
2371 Oak Drive
Akron, Ohio 37842
(Today's Date)

_____

_____

_____

Dear _____

_____

_____

_____

_____

_____

_____

_____

_____

_____

_____

_____ ,

_____

_____

Now answer the following questions. The answers are on page 185.

16. Why did you use item 13 in your first paragraph?

_____

_____

17. Why did you use item 6 ahead of item 14 in your second paragraph?

_____

_____

18. Why did you leave out the part about "repair service" when you included item 17?

_____

_____

19. Why did you use item 18 in your last paragraph?

_____

_____

20. Why did you decide *not* to mention item 21 in your letter?

_____

_____

Let's try one more like that. Remember earlier we said a Good-News letter is any that is not likely to meet reader resistance. This means that letters intended simply to announce or inform—letters that give information your reader will not regard as either good news or bad news—should follow the deductive pattern, too. Such neutral messages make up the bulk of routine business communication, but you should be on the alert to convert as many of these routine letters into genuine good-news messages as you can. Try to find something your reader will like in your message, and then lead off with that. Don't be too obvious about it, of course; exaggerated good news is easy to detect and will quickly make your reader doubt your sincerity. But you should always capitalize on whatever positive elements there are in your message.

When you can't find any, and yet your message isn't really bad news either, organize it deductively—just as if it did contain good news.

This next exercise will give you some practice in doing that.

Suppose you are program director for a management conference your company will host five weeks from now, on Thursday, October 21, and

Friday, October 22. Last month you invited a well-known management consultant, Mr. George V. Lindell, to give a speech the first day of the convention and perhaps to participate in a panel discussion on the second day.

A few weeks ago Mr. Lindell wrote to you and agreed to your request, but he needs to know some details that were not available when you first wrote, such things as the exact topic you want him to speak on and whether or not you will need him to participate in the panel discussion. You and your planning committee have now worked out the whole convention program, and your job is to write to Mr. Lindell and let him know those details.

Follow the same steps you did for the last exercise. The solution is on page 177.

Here is the information you will need to know. Remember, some of it does not belong in the actual letter.

1. You have scheduled Mr. Lindell's speech for Thursday, October 21, at 11:00 A.M. in Conference Room C.

2. Mr. Lindell is president of Acme Consulting Service, 230 West Avenue, Los Angeles, CA 91340.

3. Use the all-purpose complimentary close.

4. You have never met Mr. Lindell.

5. Today's date is September 16 of the current year.

6. The topic of the second day's panel discussion will be "Avoiding Discrimination in Management Recruiting," which will tie in with Mr. Lindell's Thursday morning speech topic.

7. Mr. Lindell's Thursday morning presentation should be about forty-five minutes long.

8. The panel discussion Friday afternoon will be from 2:00 P.M. to 3:00 P.M. in Conference Room B.

9. You yourself will speak to the conference's entire membership at 1:00 P.M. Friday on Affirmative Action core groups.

10. In his letter accepting your invitation, Mr. Lindell said he was prepared to speak on "The History of Management" or on "Changing Trends in Management Recruiting."

11. You would like Mr. Lindell to use the last fifteen minutes of his speaking time Thursday morning to answer questions from the audience.

12. Nobody on your planning committee was interested in Mr. Lindell's history-of-management topic.

13. In his letter accepting your invitation, Mr. Lindell said he would be willing to talk to media reporters.

14. Your planning committee thought Mr. Lindell's speech on "Changing Trends in Management Recruiting" would fit the theme of the conference very well.

15. The planning committee suggested that you take advantage of Mr. Lindell's offer to give a television interview immediately following the panel discussion, and you have made the arrangements with the local television station.

16. You will meet Mr. Lindell at the airport Thursday morning.

17. You are Jennifer A. White, director of personnel services at Accuwhiz Widget Company.

18. You have settled the matter of Mr. Lindell's fee in your previous correspondence with him.

19. You have read several articles by Mr. Lindell in trade journals, and you liked all of them but the last one, which you thought was asinine.

20. Last week your boss hinted that there may be a promotion in store for you if this conference runs smoothly.

21. When you called the local television station to arrange for the interview, the news director said he would tape the interview, but would put it on the air only if there was a shortage of news that day.

22. If the interview gets on the air, it would be a big public relations boost for your conference.

23. You are sending Mr. Lindell a copy of the conference schedule.

24. Your main purpose in writing to Mr. Lindell is to give him the conference details you promised him earlier.

Write Your Letter Here.

Accuwhiz Widget Company
1627 Beaumont Street
Sandusky, Ohio 37913
September 16, ____

_____

_____

_____

_____

Dear _____ :

_____

_____

_____

_____

_____

_____

_____

_____

_____

_____

_____

_____

_____

_____

_____

_____ ,

_____

_____

Now answer the following questions: The answers are on page 185.

21. In the second paragraph, why did you use item 14 before items 7 and 11?

_____

_____

22. Which sentence of the third paragraph contains the key idea of the paragraph?

_____

_____

23. Which sentence of the fourth paragraph contains the key idea of the paragraph?

_____

_____

24. Why did you decide to omit item 20?

_____

_____

25. Why did you decide to omit items 12 and 21?

_____

_____

Accuwhiz Swimming Pool Company
2371 Oak Drive
Akron, Ohio 37842
(Today's Date)

Ms. Olive Drabb
372 Park Vista Lane
Akron, OH 37843

Dear Ms. Drabb:

Please accept our apologies and this check for $38.95 to replace the chaise longue our delivery truck damaged.

The driver has promised to be more careful in the future. Her excellent record for the past seven years convinces me that she is sincere. This was her first accident.

We are sure you will be happy with your Accuwhiz swimming pool and with our prompt service. If you have any questions or problems, please call me at 689–3737. I will be glad to help in any way I can.

Sincerely,

Jordan B. White
Customer Relations Manager

Accuwhiz Widget Comapny
1627 Beaumont Street
Sandusky, Ohio 37913
September 16, _____

Mr. George V. Lindell, President
Acme Consulting Service
230 West Avenue
Los Angeles, CA 91340

Dear Mr. Lindell:

Here are the conference details I promised you. The enclosed schedule will give you an overview of our program.

Our planning committee decided your topic "Changing Trends in Management Recruiting" would fit the theme of our conference very well. About a thirty-minute speech followed by fifteen minutes for audience questions would be fine.

Please notice that we have also scheduled you to participate in Friday's panel discussion at 2:00 P.M. The topic will be "Avoiding Discrimination in Management Recruiting." This will give you an opportunity to elaborate on parts of your Thursday morning speech.

I have arranged for you to give a brief television interview immediately after the panel discussion. You said you would be willing to do that, and we would be grateful for the public relations boost it would give to our conference.

I am looking forward to meeting you on October 21, Mr. Lindell. I will meet you at the airport when you arrive that Thursday morning.

Sincerely,

Jennifer A. White
Director of Personnel Services

FOR CLASS DISCUSSION

A. Discuss the organization of the following paragraphs. On the chalkboard, revise the ones that use inductive organization into deductive paragraphs suitable for a Good-News letter. You may wish to omit some of the content.

1. The photos you sent on our Northwoods project are excellent. Each one illustrates an important phase and focuses on the people responsible for its success. The outdoor shots are especially good; they certainly create a woodsy atmosphere for Jim's article on the project.

2. The service manuals you asked for have been out of print for some time now. But I thought I remembered seeing some of them on a workbench in the welding shop a few months ago. After asking around a bit, I managed to collect all but one, and that one I found, without a cover, behind my own filing cabinet. So now I have them all, and I will send them as soon as I get approval to do so. You should have them in a few days.

3. You sent your complaint to the wrong department. It went to Public Relations instead of Customer Relations, and that's why you had to wait so long for an answer. Your claim is certainly justified, so we are enclosing a check for the $17.50 we overcharged you on the drapes. In the future, please address all claims to our Customer Relations department.

4. We have increased your line of credit to $15,000 as you requested. The higher value of your collateral and your excellent record of payments enable us to do this. We are glad to be of help in your plans to expand your business and wish you every success in this new venture.

5. Four companies besides yours submitted bids on our landscaping project. One of those companies submitted a bid lower than yours, but when we examined it we found it did not meet our specifications for quality of lawn seed. Therefore, yours was the lowest acceptable bid, and so we are awarding you the contract.

B. Bring to class some Good-News letters you have received. After explaining to the class your own reaction to the letters when you first received them, ask for suggestions for improving them. Are they deductive in organization? Would reorganizing them help?

TEST YOURSELF

Each test question contains information for inclusion in one paragraph of a Good-News letter. Select the information you would use to *begin* the paragraph. The answers are on page 186.

1. (a) You are always happy to hear from your customers.
   (b) The customer asked for a refund.
   (c) You are sending the refund.

   _____

2. (a) Mr. Nellow is very dependable.
   (b) Mr. Nellow is never late for work.
   (c) Mr. Nellow always attends staff meetings.

   _____

3. (a) You are sending the cost figures your reader requested.
   (b) You have checked the accuracy of the cost figures.
   (c) The cost figures do not include costs shared by other departments.

   _____

4. (a) You directed the Charity Fund Drive two years ago.
   (b) You agree to direct the Charity Fund Drive this year.
   (c) The Charity Fund is a very worthy cause.

   _____

5. (a) You have checked your records.
   (b) Your reader's claim is correct.
   (c) Your reader claims you charged him for the same item twice.

   _____

6. (a) Your reader has asked you whether her insurance policy has lapsed, since her premium payment was a week late.
   (b) Your policyholders have a fifteen-day grace period for making their payments after the due date.
   (c) Your reader's insurance policy has not lapsed.

   _____

7. (a) You wish to welcome your reader as a new member of your historical society.
   (b) You have received your reader's membership application and first year's dues for your historical society.
   (c) All members of your historical society receive a monthly newsletter.

   _____

8. (a) Your reader's score on the manual dexterity test was twenty points higher than that needed to pass.
   (b) Your reader's score on the theory portion of the test was eleven points higher than that needed to pass.
   (c) Your reader passed both portions of the qualifying examination.

---

9. (a) You received your reader's credit application last week.
   (b) You have checked the reader's references.
   (c) You have decided to allow your reader the credit line of five thousand dollars she asked for.

---

10. (a) You wish to thank your reader for entering your company's local photo contest.
    (b) Your reader's entry won the fifty-dollar prize for second place.
    (c) This year's entries were generally much better than those of any previous year.

APPLY YOURSELF

You are Dr. Canister B. Quandary, dean of admissions at Bellaston College, Sleepy Hills, Illinois, Zip Code 61304.

Of the 875 applications for freshman enrollment, you have accepted the best 450. Write a form letter informing those 450 applicants that your college is accepting them for the fall semester. Because this is a form letter, it will not have an inside address.

Here is background information, some of which you will include in your letter and some of which you will not:

1. Freshman orientation will begin on August 27 at 9:00 A.M.
2. The Financial Aid Office has given you two forms and business-reply envelopes to include in your mailing. All new students applying for financial aid must fill out these forms.
3. Sixty per cent of this year's freshman class were in the top 20 per cent of their high school graduating class.
4. All students who have not had a physical examination in the last year will need to have one by August 27.
5. Today's date is June 24.
6. Your college is planning a reception for new students and their parents, but the date and details are still incomplete. You think it will be the evening of August 27, however.
7. This year's freshman class scored higher on the Scholastic Aptitude Test than any previous Bellaston freshman class has scored.
8. You will send each new student information on housing, meal plans, and the like in about two weeks.
9. The first installment on tuition payments is due on September 30.
10. Last year two freshmen ended up in the hospital after a touch football game sponsored by the college during registration week.
11. All students must take English 101, freshman composition.
12. You are enclosing a copy of the student handbook, which explains all college regulations.
13. The student handbook tells them that they may not drive motor vehicles or own pets on campus.
14. All new students must attend an orientation lecture at 9:00 A.M. August 27 in the student union building.
15. Of this year's freshman class, 54 per cent are female.
16. You would like as many parents of the new students as possible to attend the first two days of orientation.
17. Bellaston is trying to enhance its reputation as an academic institution and to diminish its reputation as a "party-goers'" college.
18. You encourage new students and their parents to visit your campus during the summer months.
19. Your staff conducts summer tours of the campus.
20. Your phone number is (424) 338–9264.
21. Plans for the reception for new students and their parents will be complete in about a week from now.
22. Tuition at Bellaston increased $175 a semester this year.

Select the information you will include and write the form letter.

ANSWERS TO EXERCISES

1. I enthusiastically accept your invitation to serve as director of your fund drive; I am always glad to have an opportunity to help the Boy Scout program.

2. We are sending you a copy of the preliminary results of our survey because you were so prompt in returning our questionnaire.

3. We are returning your check for $25.62 because our records show your account is paid in full.

4. We have decided to award you the contract for printing our brochure even though we are not yet sure how many pages we want it to be.

5. We accept your proposal for our fall advertising campaign; it is very thorough and should increase our sales considerably.

6. c,a,b

7. c,b,a

8. b,c,a

9. b,a,c

10. b,d,a,c

11. We like your story so much, in fact, that we would also consider it for our "New Authors" award if you would revise it to suit our needs, as you offered to do. We think you could easily delete a few paragraphs at the beginning without diminishing the story's effect. This would reduce the story by about five hundred words, making it the right length for our use.

12. You will receive our free booklet containing twenty wine recipes with your first order. We also include with each order a coupon entitling you to a 5 per cent discount on your next order. Please use the convenient tear-out order forms following page 39, and remember to add the 4 per cent state sales tax to the total.

13. I am sure those attending your festival will enjoy Acme's new "History of the Flute" filmstrip, which I intend to show as part of my presentation. I will provide my own filmstrip projector, but will need a screen. Of course, I will also need an electrical outlet for the projector.

14. Gerald is a hard, conscientious worker. He takes pride in doing a thorough job and in finishing it on time. When he worked for me, he often skipped lunch and even worked late in order to do that.

15. I am sending you a complimentary variety package of our food products to show our gratitude for your suggestion. The package includes one of our new products, canned fortune cookies. Please let us know how you like them.

184

16. This item tells you how to *begin* your first sentence. It is what Ms. Drabb says she is most interested in.

17. Item 6 comes closest to what Ms. Drabb wants you to do about the truck driver; item 14 explains why you were not so severe as Ms. Drabb wanted you to be and therefore will meet more resistance than item 6.

18. "Repair service" is a negative term to someone who has just bought the product. Don't imply her new pool is likely to need repair soon.

19. This permits you to be specific in offering your help.

20. You can clearly *imply* it; *mentioning* it would antagonize Ms. Drabb.

21. Items 7 and 11 give the details of item 14.

22. The first sentence contains the key idea.

23. The first sentence contains the key idea.

24. Item 20 is irrelevant to your purpose.

25. These items would deflate Mr. Lindell's self-esteem, and you don't want to do that. Every letter is a goodwill letter!

ANSWERS TO TEST YOURSELF

1. c
2. a
3. a
4. b
5. b
6. c
7. a
8. c
9. c
10. b

9

Organize Bad-News Letters Inductively

Nobody likes to get a Bad-News letter. Nobody likes to write one, either. In ancient times the bearer of good news received a reward, and the bearer of bad news received scornful looks, if not a beating. The sentry in Sophocles's *Antigone* says to the king:

> . . . *you had to be told the news*
> *And one of us had to do it! We threw the dice,*
> *And the bad luck fell to me. So here I am,*
> *No happier to be here than you are to have me:*
> *Nobody likes the man who brings bad news.*

And the sentry was right. The king did not talk to him very gently after hearing the bad news that someone had violated a royal decree.

Human nature has not changed over the centuries since then. As unfair as it may seem, the frustration and disappointment of receiving bad news will ordinarily lead the reader into feeling resentment and ill-will toward the writer who communicates that bad news—unless the writer has very carefully observed the principles we are about to discuss.

Before we look at those principles, we should review what we learned about Bad-News letters in the previous chapter, where we briefly defined the term in order to better understand what a Good-News letter is. We said a Bad-News letter is one in which the writer tries to *sell* the reader something, *asks* the reader for a favor involving time or money, or announces something that will *disappoint* the reader. In short, whenever you expect your letter to encounter reader *resistance* in any way, you are writing a Bad-News letter. It may seem unreasonable to include sales letters in this group, but any time you are trying to separate your reader from his or her money, you know your letter must overcome some reader resistance. In fact, the whole point of a sales letter is to persuade your reader that

187

the good of gaining whatever it is you are selling outweighs the bad of parting with the price of it. An effective sales letter, then, is one that you have managed to transform from Bad-News to Good-News, at least from your reader's point of view.

Now let's return to those general principles for writing Bad-News letters. In the last chapter we learned that *deductive* organization consists of putting the key idea, the general statement, first, and then following it with examples, reasons, details, and other specifics. *Inductive* organization is just the reverse. When you organize inductively, you *begin* with reasons, background, explanations, and other details, and then you *follow* them with the main idea. For example, this paragraph is *deductive;* the topic sentence comes first:

> *Congratulations to you and your staff on the splendid "Industrial Issues" program you put together for the Alameda conference. The topics you chose for the afternoon session were especially good; both speakers suggested helpful ideas for improving systems design. Since the conference, we have tried a few of those ideas, and the results are encouraging. The "competitive teams" concept alone saved us $2,000.*

This paragraph is *inductive;* the topic sentence comes last:

> *Since attending your Alameda conference on "Industrial Issues" last year, two of our managers have used the "competitive teams" concept of systems design you and the other speakers recommended. We tried it first in our shipping department, but found it required two additional clerks to keep track of vouchers. Another manager tried the concept on one of our production lines, and our average cases per day dropped 2 per cent. It is unlikely both managers misapplied the concept; they worked independently of each other. Therefore, we have to think there is something wrong with the "competitive teams" concept itself.*

Although I tried to keep these two paragraph examples about equal in length, the second one turned out a bit longer. This is typical of Bad-News paragraphs. It usually takes more words to *explain*, to *prepare* your reader, than it takes to blurt out good news. Good-News letters generally tend to be short and sweet; Bad-News letters must always be long enough to persuade the reader that the writer's message—as distasteful as it might be— is really the only reasonable one possible.

Therefore, brevity is not necessarily a good quality in a Bad-News letter. If your letter is too brief, your reader will regard you as an adversary who refuses to be bothered with the simple courtesy of providing an explanation for the bad news. Even if your reader does not see the validity of your explanation, he or she will subconsciously thank you for trying to give one and will regard you as an ally rather than as an adversary. A Bad-News letter that is a little too long is much better than one that is a little too short.

You must not, of course, just fill up a Bad-News letter with wordiness in order to avoid curtness or undue brevity. Use the first part of each paragraph, whenever you can, to convince your reader that you *are* on his or her side. Show that you would really prefer to be telling your reader good news; the bad news you communicate must come out as something you regret, never as something you or your company *could* change but have whimsically decided not to. That means it is never acceptable to give merely "our company's policy" as your reason for the bad news. From your reader's point of view, a company policy that results in bad news is unreasonable—unless you can *show* that it *is* both reasonable and necessary.

It says, "The people who saw me hit your car assume that I'm leaving my name and address. But they're wrong."

When we discussed the Good-News letter in the last chapter, we learned that everything in it, from the sentences right on up through the body of the letter itself, should follow the deductive pattern. Everything in the Bad-News letter, from the sentences right on up through the body of the letter itself, should follow the inductive pattern. Let's practice on a few sentences.

Change the following sentences from deductive order (loose sentence) to inductive order (periodic sentence). The answers are on page 210.

1. Your suggestion would cost more than we can afford right now; however, it does show considerable ingenuity, attention to detail, and a sincere concern for our passengers.

_____

_____

_____

2. We cannot replace your oil heater free of charge because the warranty expired two years ago.

_____

_____

3. The committee decided not to approve your request for a transfer after thoroughly discussing all the considerations I have listed above. (*Besides making this sentence inductive, try to get rid of the negative term* not.)

_____

_____

_____

4. We think you will need to replace the entire boiler because corrosion has weakened at least 40 per cent of the plate surface.

_____

_____

_____

5. Your short story does not fit our needs right now, but we like it very much.

_____

_____

Now let's try arranging a few paragraphs inductively. Look again at the Bad News paragraph about the "competitive teams" concept on page 188. Actually, the paragraph is rather weak in that the evidence given does not entirely justify the concluding sentence. There are several other possible reasons for the failure of the "competitive teams" concept besides the ones given in the paragraph. Perhaps neither manager adequately explained the concept to the workers, for instance. Yet, the overall organization of the paragraph is right. The evidence, shaky as it is, comes first; and the conclusion drawn from that evidence, even if not entirely justified, comes last. The paragraph may have some faults, but organization is not one of them.

Try your hand at organizing this way. In each of the next five exercises, one of the sentences is really a result or consequence of the other two. Rearrange the sentences so that they are in proper sequence for a Bad-News paragraph and write the paragraph. Be sure to provide appropriate transitions like *therefore, as a result, consequently, but,* and the like. You may combine some sentences, if you wish. The answers are on page 210.

6. (a) Please send us your check for $5.95, so we can send you the jacket you ordered.
   (b) The $25.00 you sent was the price of the sport jacket in last year's catalog.
   (c) This year's catalog, which went into effect last June 1, lists the jacket at $30.95.

----

7. (a) The $512 balance on your account is now six months overdue.
   (b) We have no choice but to take legal action.
   (c) You have not responded to any of our requests for payment, and the last one we sent by registered mail four weeks ago.

----

8. (a) I will be unable to speak at your Parent–Teacher Association meeting.
   (b) I will be in Washington, D.C., the week of September 8.

(c) Thank you for inviting me to speak at your Parent–Teacher Association meeting on September 11.

---

9. (a) I will need your report a month earlier, by the end of June.
   (b) I realize I wrote you last week that the deadline for your report was the end of July.
   (c) The government has notified me that my summary must be in by July 15.

---

10. (a) Plant safety statistics will not be available until June 28.
    (b) I need the plant safety statistics for the second half of my report.
    (c) I cannot possibly get my report to you before July 6.

Up to now we've been practicing inductive organization in the sentence and in the paragraph. Soon we will try arranging a whole Bad-News letter inductively. But before we do, we need to take care of a few odds and ends that pertain to the overall tone of such a letter. We need to keep the following rules in mind all the while we write a Bad-News letter so that we maintain a persuasive attitude toward the person we are writing to:

1. Be firm.

When the bad news is final, you need to make that fact clear. Do not let the courtesy of your language suggest that your reader could persuade you to change a decision that you know must stand. Don't give false hope.

2. Don't Lie.

Don't "manufacture" explanations or excuses. Make sure the reasons you give are *real* ones, even if they are not the *only* ones.

3. Imply rather than state, whenever possible.

Sometimes to protect yourself legally you must state the bad news directly. But when you can, you should try to state your reasons so clearly that there will be no need to state the bad news those reasons add up to. For instance, we would probably improve the paragraph we wrote for exercise 8, above, if we simply dropped sentence *a* and substituted a more positive sentence, like this:

> *Thank you for inviting me to speak to your Parent–Teacher Association meeting on September 11. Unfortunately, I will be in Washington, D.C., that week, but perhaps I will be able to accept such an invitation sometime in the future.*

4. Always give your reader the benefit of the doubt.

If you are asking for an overdue payment, assume your reader *forgot* to send it; if your reader is at fault for something, assume it was an *honest* mistake. Do not answer a sarcastic letter with a sarcastic letter of your own, or you will only make matters worse. Be sincerely courteous, respectful, and friendly; remember *every* letter is a goodwill letter.

5. Be especially careful in your opening and closing paragraphs.

In Chapter 7 we learned that opening and closing paragraphs are always very important. But they pose unusually difficult problems for the writer of a Bad-News letter. For instance, we learned that the first sentence of an opening paragraph should tell the reader what the letter is about, but in the present chapter we discover that the bad news must never come early in the letter. You can solve that problem by letting your reader know only the *general topic* of your letter in that first sentence, and withholding the bad news itself until after you have given enough explanation to prepare your reader for it.

"... 'and if you do not immediately remit the money owed us, be assured
we will prosecute you to the full extent of the law.' New paragraph:
'By the way, Mom. . . .'"

Final paragraphs, too, require special care. No matter how negative the
news is, you must end your letter on a *positive* note. Let's take an extremely
difficult situation—the one we saw in exercise 7. A positive last paragraph
for that letter could be something like this:

*We plan to turn the matter over to our lawyers in ten days. May
we please hear from you before then?*

That's about as much as you can do to end such a negative letter positively
and constructively.

Now let's turn to the arrangement of paragraphs, the overall strategy
of a Bad-News letter. You should use inductive order for the body, just as
you did when writing the sentences and the paragraphs that make up that
body; *ease* your reader gradually into accepting the bad-news part of your
message.

Earlier we said that there were at least three kinds of Bad-News letters:
the sales letter, the request for a favor, and the announcement of a decision
that will disappoint your reader. Although all three require inductive organization, each differs from the other two enough to warrant separate consideration. We'll take sales letters first.

SALES LETTERS

The easiest way to write a successful sales letter is to follow the AIDA formula:

A—*Attention.   Get your reader's attention by appealing to his or her curiosity or self-interest. Every reader, upon first opening a letter, asks, "What's in for me?" Answer that question.*

I—*Interest.   Once you have your reader's attention, you must get him or her interested in the product or service you are selling. Appealing to your reader's curiosity is a good way of doing this.*

D—*Desire.   This is the crucial part. The best way to get your reader to want what you are selling is to provide clear mental pictures of your reader using your product, enjoying its advantages, or somehow benefiting from owning it. You must draw vivid word pictures here, and that means you must use specific language. Always include your reader in the word pictures you draw.*

A—*Action.   This is the Bad-News part, from your reader's point of view; it tells what action your reader must take in order to get what you are selling. Two things are important here: (1) You must describe the cost in as attractive a form as you can (eleven cents a day sounds less expensive than $40.15 a year), and (2) you must make it as easy as possible for your reader to act (include a business-reply envelope, for example).*

If you can manage to *blend* Attention, Interest, and Desire, so much the better. But always put the Action step last, of course.

A real danger in applying this formula is getting carried away with your own enthusiasm for your product. The "super-amazing-colossal-stupendous" type of appeal may catch your reader's attention, but it raises doubts about your credibility. You don't want your reader to toss your letter aside as just so much sales "propaganda" or "rhetoric." And don't just appeal to your reader's emotions, either. A sales letter addressed to the head as well as to the heart is most likely to succeed. Be sensible; show your reader that you are a realist and that desiring what you have to offer makes good economic sense, too. Consider the following appeal made by a well-known research hospital. Although it asks for charitable contributions, it is in every other respect a sales letter.

Dear Friend:

It must seem strange to many that we are giving away money in a Sweepstakes—while we are begging for the contributions we must have to exist!

The answer: we receive much more than we give away. But, we do give lots of money—more than two hundred cash prizes, with a twenty thousand dollar first prize, maybe YOURS.

195

Everyone likes a chance to win big money; that's why our Sweepstakes works. And, there's another reason: Unselfish, warm-hearted, people enjoy helping a dying child to go on living!

With no charge, and regardless of race or creed, we treat four thousand little patients here. Each child's life depends upon us, just as we must depend upon you.

Amazingly rapid medical research here now saves half of our patients—children who would certainly have died only fifteen years ago. But, half still die. We just can't accept that. Our doctors now feel we are on the threshold of being able to save many of the "hopeless" cases.

At this crucial point, we need your prayers and your contribution. Your gift is not obligatory to enter our Sweepstakes, but suffering children really do need your help.

Merciful Americans who don't refuse to aid a dying child are our only support. Please, send a check today, along with your Sweepstakes tickets.

Sincerely and gratefully,

(Signature of founder)

Let's examine the letter paragraph by paragraph and trace the probable thoughts of most readers as they read each one.

First Paragraph: "Yes, I am curious about that, now that you mention it. If you're so much in need of support, why give away all that prize money?"

Second Paragraph: "Oh, of course. That makes sense. Some people will contribute only in hopes of winning twenty-thousand dollars. Don't think I'm one of those. But you say 'maybe YOURS,' and I have to admit it is a pleasant thought."

Third paragraph: I agree. Some people will contribute just for a chance to win the money. But your second sentence is the one that appeals to warm-hearted people like me."

Fourth Paragraph: "Now that's real charity! They must really need a lot of contributions in order to keep going."

Fifth Paragraph: "Nor can I accept the deaths of 2,000 children. I'm beginning to understand the urgency of your request."

Sixth Paragraph: "I'm glad you said a contribution wasn't necessary for me to enter the Sweepstakes. I want to make my donation strictly out of compassion for those kids, not as a means of winning something for myself. I certainly wouldn't enter the Sweepstakes without contributing something. How would I feel if I won $20,000 from those kids if I hadn't donated?"

Seventh Paragraph: "I am one of those 'merciful Americans' and will certainly send a check along with my Sweepstakes tickets. Who knows? Maybe I'll win. If I do, I won't feel guilty because <u>somebody</u> is going to win; the prize money will go whether I enter or not. And if I don't win, at least I will have contributed to a good cause."

The letter begins by getting the reader's Attention and Interest through curiosity, proceeds to stimulate Desire by appealing to the reader's self-interest, then *transforms* that Desire into an altruistic concern for the dying children, and finally calls for Action as a result of that double-based Desire. And the letter employs no trickery, either. It clearly states that the reader may try for a prize without contributing. It candidly explains the reason for the Sweepstakes. The writer counted on two psychological probabilities: (1) Most readers would want a chance to win the sweepstakes, and (2) most readers would feel guilty about entering the Sweepstakes without contributing something.

Now answer these questions about the letter: the answers are on page 210.

11. Which paragraph includes the transition between appealing to the head and appealing to the heart?

_____

12. Which two paragraphs include *specific* information about the good the reader's contribution will do?

_____

13. Judging from the way the writer organized the letter, is self-interest or altruism more likely to capture the reader's attention and stimulate interest?

_____

14. On the return envelope, in place of a stamp these words appear: "Your stamp gives more to the children." Does this appeal to the head or to the heart?

_____

15. The stub, which the reader is to fill out and retain, says, "Please retain this stub for your tax records." Does this appeal to the head or to the heart?

_____

Now let's look at another kind of Bad-News letter. When you write to ask someone for a favor, like speaking to your organization or sending you some information, you need to consider reader benefits, too. Remember that every reader first asks, "What's in it for me?" In this kind of letter the reader's benefits usually are in the form of enhanced reputation, favorable publicity, good public relations, and the like. Yet, nobody wants to admit to doing a favor for selfish reasons. Therefore, you must not *mention* such reader benefits; just make sure your reader will understand that they are *there.* You must be much more subtle in asking for a favor than in trying to sell a product. In a sales letter you can, and usually should, blatantly announce what's "in it" for your reader; in a letter asking for a favor, you must never do that.

How do you persuade your reader to do what you ask, then? You will seldom succeed if you begin by stressing how desperately you need the favor, though with some readers that will work. Your best bet is to concentrate on your reader's excellent reputation, superior expertise, or helpfulness in the past. Or, if your reader has promised to help you, you might remind him or her of that. But whatever you concentrate on, DON'T LET IT SOUND LIKE FLATTERY! Put yourself in your reader's place. Would *you* like people to think they can get you to do anything they want just by flattering you?

Use the same kind of psychology concerning reader benefits. In general, you should start with these two assumptions: (1) Your reader will not grant your favor unless there's "something in it" for him or her, and (2) Your reader will not grant your favor if you state what that "something" is.

Starting with these assumptions, we can devise a general plan that will be a slight modification of the AIDA strategy we discussed earlier. You still need to get your reader's attention and interest at the outset; but because the only reader benefit you can offer is prestige, your gratitude, or heightened goodwill, you should focus on *why* you are asking for the favor. However, don't concentrate on yourself and your problems; get your reader into the picture. For instance, suppose you wish to invite a local management specialist to talk to a group of your managers, but you have no budget for outside speakers. Your letter might look like this:

Dear Mr. Reynolds:

Your speech at this year's Progressive Management convention very accurately described some of the morale problems we have recently had at Accuwhiz. We are especially concerned with our growing absentee rate.

Absences have increased 12 per cent over the last six months. And improvements we made to the working environment two months ago seem to have had no effect on the problem. In your convention speech you mentioned some experiments you have conducted on several incentive programs. Would you please be our guest at one of our group managers' meetings and tell us more about what your studies have shown? We are especially interested in the "competitive teams" program you said showed considerable promise. Perhaps you could explain how we might adapt it to our needs. I am certain you can give us some new insights and suggestions on how to attack the problem.

I would be happy to pick you up at your office any day next week at 11:00 A.M. and drive you to our plant, where you can be my guest for lunch. Afterward, you can meet with our group managers for about a half hour. I promise to get you back to your office by 1:00 P.M.

Please call me at 489-7474 to let me know which day you prefer. We are all eager to hear your suggestions and would be most grateful for your help.

Sincerely,

This letter's opening sentence both lets Mr. Reynolds know what your letter is about and subtly pays him a sincere compliment: you not only heard his speech, but found it accurate. The next sentence stimulates reader interest by introducing a problem that needs solving.

The next few paragraphs describe your problem more completely and convince Mr. Reynolds that his specific suggestions would greatly help you improve employee morale. There's another hidden compliment in that. Next comes the actual invitation to speak, followed by a detailed explanation of all the ways you are prepared to make his acceptance convenient—such as providing him your personal transportation, having him as your guest for lunch, and so on.

Finally, the Action paragraph makes it as easy as possible for him to accept. It explains how he can reach you and says he can set the date at his own convenience. It assures him you would be grateful for the favor, but it does *not* thank him in advance!

The letter does use AIDA strategy. But to stimulate *Desire*, it uses a challenge to the reader's pride, rather than a description of a product being sold.

Now answer these questions about the letter. The answers are on pages 210 and 211.

16. Which reader benefits does the letter *state?*
(a) enhanced reputation as an expert
(b) a free lunch
(c) the letter writer's friendship and goodwill
(d) free transportation

---

17. Which reader benefits does the letter *imply?*
(a) enhanced reputation as an expert
(b) self-satisfaction as a problem solver
(c) media publicity
(d) the reader's chance to gather additional experience in the field

---

18. Which paragraph gives details that will help the reader decide how to prepare for the meeting?
(a) First paragraph
(b) Second paragraph
(c) Third paragraph
(d) Fourth paragraph

---

19. The first sentence of the fourth paragraph demonstrates which of the following principles?
(a) Provide for easy action.
(b) Use the active voice.
(c) Take a positive approach.
(d) Use the "You" approach.

---

20. The organization of the letter is not entirely inductive because its main point—that is, the actual request for the favor—appears near the
(a) beginning.
(b) middle.
(c) end.

Finally, a "Bad-News" letter that announces a decision your reader will not like, or that informs your reader of some other disappointing fact, is a little easier to organize, but much more difficult to write. Organization is simple: Explain fully first, and then state or imply the bad news, following it with a short paragraph that stresses whatever positives there are. Every sentence and paragraph in the letter should be inductive; that is, the main idea should come last. However, since you know your reader will strongly resist your message, you need to be very careful in preparing the trail of logic that leads inevitably to the disappointing conclusion. You simply cannot do that very well if you think only about *your* side of the situation. Look at the reader's side and ask yourself what questions you would ask if *you* received the letter. Be sure you plug up all the holes in your explanation by answering those questions.

For instance, suppose as a vegetable farmer you own several flatbed trailers. A member of a college fraternity has asked to use one of them for a homecoming float. But you need all of your trailers that week for harvesting. You might write the following first draft of a paragraph:

> *Although we were happy to lend your fraternity one of our flatbed trailers for your homecoming float last year, we will be unable to let you use one this year.*

If you read that sentence from *your* point of view, it will probably seem entirely adequate. It begins with something positive and proceeds to the

200

bad news at the end. But if you don't mention the reason, your reader is likely to think you are upset with something the fraternity did to your trailer last year or that somehow you have recently become just plain selfish. You won't see this deficiency in your sentence, though, unless you read it from your *reader's* point of view.

Here's how you might revise it so that it includes everything your reader needs to know:

> *We were happy to lend you one of our flatbed trailers for your homecoming float last year. And we would like to let you use one again, but the unusually late harvest this year means we cannot spare any of them during that week.*

This paragraph lets your reader know that you cannot help making the refusal. Showing you don't *want* to give bad news keeps your reader's good-will. Always show that you would *like* to accommodate your reader *if you could*.

Also, if you look at the situation from your reader's point of view, you will see that once your reader gets the disappointing news, he or she is sure to ask, "What do I do now?" Try to give some constructive suggestion, some other solution to your reader's problem. For instance, if you must refuse a request for a loan, make sure you explain what your reader can do to qualify for it in the future, or suggest another place to try for it now. Or, if you don't have what your reader asked for, suggest some other place to write for it. Try to be as helpful as you can.

Now you try one. Here's the situation: A customer who bought a watch from your mail-order catalog has sent the watch back to you with this explanation:

> *I bought this watch three weeks ago, and now it doesn't work.*
>
> *My year's guarantee says it is water resistant, but I wore it swimming only once and it stopped running.*
>
> *I like the watch and want you to either fix it free or give me a new one exactly like it.*
>
> *Sincerely,*
>
>
> *Thelma Thomas*

Examining the watch, you notice deep scratches on the back, as if someone had tried to remove the back cover. Therefore, you cannot possibly take the watch back and give her a new one. Furthermore, the watch she bought is not waterproof, only water resistant. The instructions and the guarantee clearly tell the owner that immersing the watch in water or removing the back cover invalidates the guarantee.

You are willing to repair the watch, charging Ms. Thomas for labor and the parts needed to replace the water-damaged ones. This will total $7.50. You must get Ms. Thomas's agreement to pay before you begin the repairs.

Before starting the letter, answer these questions. The answers are on page 211.

21. How can you let Ms. Thomas know that you will not give her a new watch without stating it?

_____

22. Should you accuse Ms. Thomas of trying to pry off the back of the watch?

_____

23. Are there any good-news items you can begin with?

_____

24. What part of your message requires Ms. Thomas to act, and where should you put that part?

_____

25. Now write the letter.

_____

Dear Ms. Thomas:

_____

_____

_____

_____

_____

_____

_____

_____

_____

_____

_____

_____

_____

Sincerely,

_____

FOR CLASS DISCUSSION

A. Discuss the following statements:

1. If a customer makes a foolish complaint, I feel I have a right to give a foolish answer. Many times all the customer had to do was read the label on the product to find out there is no justification for the complaint.

2. When I mean "No," I say "No." My reader ought to realize I wouldn't refuse without good reason.

3. In explaining where my readers are wrong, I try to make them squirm a little. When people feel embarrassed, they are not so quick to complain the next time.

4. Why should I answer people courteously who write to say they will never buy our product again? There's no chance of gaining their goodwill or their future business anyway.

5. I try to make my readers feel like simple-minded children. That way they never ask for further explanations.

B. If we were to generalize on the basis of the letter samples given in this chaper, we would conclude the following: In a sales letter the sentence containing the worst news for the reader occurs in the final paragraph, in a request for a favor it occurs near the middle of the letter, and in a letter containing unfavorable news it occurs just before the final paragraph. Discuss whether there are any psychological reasons supporting such placement of the "bad news."

TEST YOURSELF

The answers are on page 212.

I. Some of the following sentences are inductive; some are deductive. Change the deductive ones to inductive.

1. I can give you only a partial report because two of the committees will not meet to discuss the issue until next Thursday.

_____

_____

_____

2. Your roof sustained additional damage during the winter; therefore, my new estimate is fifty dollars higher than last year's.

_____

_____

_____

3. Because your bid arrived after the deadline had passed, we are returning it unopened.

_____

_____

_____

4. We cannot extend the loan period on the film you borrowed because we have already promised another group they could have it on the 29th.

_____

_____

_____

5. We must add the ten-dollar late payment charge to your account because even though you wrote the check on June 4, we did not receive it until June 19, Mr. Adams.

_____

_____

_____

II. Here are five sentences, jumbled out of sequence, from an inductive ("Bad-News") paragraph:

1. Clause VII of your policy specifically exempts the insurance company from liability in such a case.

2. Our investigator interviewed a representative of the Fire Department to establish the cause of the fire.

3. We have no choice but to disallow your claim and cancel your insurance, effective this date.

4. The investigation of your claim for twenty thousand dollars in fire damage to your warehouse on December 3, 19— is now complete.

5. The Fire Department representative said two firefighters reported finding a piece of metal in place of one of the fuses in the main fusebox.

List the proper sequence of the sentences.

APPLY YOURSELF

Assume you are customer-relations manager of a large department store. Today you receive the following letter from an irate customer:

Dear Whatever Your Name Is:

I have always bought my clothes at your store. But NO MORE!

This week I bought a swimsuit you had on sale. "Thirty-five dollar swimsuits reduced to $22.50," your ad said.

Is there something wrong with the lights in your store? When I bought the suit it looked blue, but when I got it home it was <u>green</u>! Everybody knows how horrible I look in green. And when I got it wet, it turned the most atrocious shade of green you ever saw. It even made <u>me</u> look green.

It doesn't fit me, either. It's too big. But that's not surprising; your clerk wouldn't even let me try it on first.

When I tried to return it, your clerk wouldn't take it back. She said it was against the law. What kind of law is <u>that</u> if now I have to be stuck with a baggy green swimsuit I <u>wouldn't</u> be seen dead in?

Can't you make an exception and exchange it for one I can wear? If you don't, you won't see me in your store again.

Sincerely,

Bertha Rogers

You cannot, of course, make an exception for Ms. Rogers. As a protection to consumers, state law clearly forbids allowing customers to try on swimwear or to exchange any of it. Furthermore, your store's policy is that all purchases of sale merchandise are final.

There is a large sign in your swimwear department that quotes the state law. There is also a smaller sign explaining that the swimwear on sale is from a manufacturer whose sizes run slightly large.

There is nothing wrong with the lights in your store. When you asked your clerk whether she remembered Ms. Rogers, she said, "Oh, that must have been that pretty girl with the big blue sunglasses." The sunglasses are probably what made the swimsuit look blue to Ms. Rogers.

Bertha Rogers has indeed been a good customer of yours, and you would like her to remain so.

Now write your letter to Ms. Rogers.

ANSWERS TO EXERCISES

1. Your suggestion shows considerable ingenuity, attention to detail, and a sincere concern for our passengers; however, it would cost more than we can afford right now.

2. The warranty on your oil heater expired two years ago, so we cannot replace it free of charge.

3. After thoroughly discussing all these considerations, the committee decided you are more valuable to the company in your present location.

4. Because corrosion has weakened at least 40 per cent of the plate surface, we think you will need to replace the entire boiler.

5. Although we like your short story very much, it does not fit our needs right now.

6. The twenty-five dollars you sent was the price of the sport jacket in last year's catalog. But this year's catalog, which went into effect June 1, lists the jacket at $30.95. Therefore, please send us your check for $5.95, so we can send you the jacket you ordered.

7. The $512 balance on your account is now six months overdue. Yet, you have not responded to any of our requests for payment, and the last one we sent by registered mail four weeks ago. Therefore, we have no choice but to take legal action.

8. Thank you for inviting me to speak to your Parent–Teacher Association meeting on September 11. Unfortunately, I will be in Washington, D.C., the week of September 8 and therefore will be unable to speak at your meeting.

9. I realize I wrote you last week that the deadline for your report was the end of July. But the government has notified me that my summary must be in by July 15. Therefore, I will need your report a month earlier, by the end of June.

10. I need the plant safety statistics for the second half of my report. But these statistics will not be available until June 28. Consequently, I cannot possibly get my report to you before July 6.

11. 3

12. 4 & 5

13. self-interest

14. to the heart

15. to the head

16. b, d

17. a, b, d

18. b

19. a, b, c, d

20. b

21. By stating what you *are* willing to do, you can clearly imply what you are *not* willing to do.

22. No. Whether she tried to remove it or not will not affect your decision to charge her for the repairs; she admits to immersing the watch in water, and that invalidates the guarantee. But you should remind her not to tamper with the back cover in the future.

23. Yes. You can repair the watch, and Ms. Thomas is correct in saying her watch is water resistant.

24. She must sign an agreement to pay for the repairs. You should put that immediately before the last paragraph.

25. Dear Ms. Thomas:

I am glad to tell you that we can repair your watch for you.

You are right in saying that your guarantee states your watch is water resistant. Very high humidity or even rain will not damage it.

However, it is not waterproof. The owner's instructions and the guarantee specify that immersing the watch in water or removing its back cover invalidates the guarantee.

Before we can work on your watch, we need you to sign and return the enclosed agreement to pay the $7.50 repair charge.

You should receive your watch as good as new within ten days after we receive your authorization.

Sincerely,

_____

ANSWERS TO TEST YOURSELF

I. 1. Because two of the committees will not meet to discuss the issue until next Thursday, I can give you only a partial report.

2. The sentence is already inductive.

3. The sentence is already inductive.

4. We have already promised another group they could have the film on the 29th, so we cannot extend the loan period on the film you borrowed.

5. Even though you wrote the check on June 4, we did not receive it until June 19, so we must add the ten-dollar late payment charge to your account, Mr. Adams.

II. The proper sequence of the sentences: 4,2,5,1,3

10

Application Letters and Résumés

Applying for a job and constructing a résumé of your qualities and accomplishments are not things you do every day. Ideally, you should have to do these things only once in your lifetime—when you apply for, and get, the *perfect* job—one that suits your talents exactly, has unlimited opportunities for advancement, and enables you to pursue your career objectives happily ever after. Unfortunately, it seldom happens that way in the real world. But even if it should, you would still have to write that one letter and résumé to get it.

You should, of course, apply to many prospective employers. However, don't spread your efforts too thin. Select only the ones you would really like to work for, and tailor an application letter for each one specifically. The more you know about the particular kind of job you want, the easier it is to construct an effective résumé, too. But we will discuss résumés later.

The one fatal mistake you must avoid in your application letter is to ignore your reader's point of view. Remember we said earlier that every reader first asks, "What's in it for me?" The prospective employer who opens your application letter will certainly ask that question, too. If you can't answer it, you aren't ready to write the letter.

Put yourself in your reader's place. If an applicant wrote to you for a job, you would want to know two things about that person: (1) Is the applicant sincerely interested in *helping your company* achieve its corporate objectives? and (2) Is the applicant *sufficiently qualified* to do that? As an applicant, then, you must provide affirmative answers to these questions, and that's where planning your letter should begin.

Before you even start the draft of your letter, examine your own talents and abilities carefully. Be completely honest with yourself. Are you good at collaborating with colleagues, or do you work better alone and independent of others? Are you better at math skills or verbal skills? Do you write well? Is there some type of work you definitely dislike? Assess your qualifica-

213

tions and desires thoroughly. Maybe you really are *not* interested in the job you are applying for or are *not* really qualified for it. In that case, choose another prospective employer.

Once you have decided you *do* have the qualifications and *are* truly eager to work at the kind of job you are applying for, you are ready for the next step: **Find out all you can about the company.** Send for their brochures; check *Standard Statistics, Reference Book of Manufacturers, Business Periodicals Index,* and any other pertinent reference books in the library; call the company's switchboard for the proper name, title, and address of the person you should send your application to if you don't know them. Find out what the company's accomplishments have been and what its goals are. You not only want to avoid making erroneous assumptions about the company in your letter—you also want to convince your reader that you would fit right into their system easily.

But the most important thing this research does is show your prospective employer that you actually took the time and expended the effort to become familiar with the company! That's the most convincing evidence there is that you really want to become part of their team.

Now you are almost ready to begin a draft of the first paragraph of your application letter. But not quite. Remember that the first sentence of your business letters should tell your reader what your letter is about, and the first paragraph should explain why you are writing. The job application letter is no exception. But the way you do that will depend on whether you are answering an employment ad, writing for a job a friend has told you about, or applying entirely on your own. When answering an ad, follow the ad's directions exactly and tell your reader what publication you saw it in. When someone tells you about the job opening, by all means mention the person's name if you think the name will mean something to your reader. If you don't have any such lead-ins, at least let your reader know in your first sentence that you are applying for a specific job—and name the job.

The following would be good opening paragraphs for an application letter, then:

I wish to apply for the position of public relations coordinator, described in your ad that appeared in the July issue of Cowkeeper's Journal. Your new Consumer Publications Department seems especially interesting to me because I have conducted some research on the subject in a seminar here at the university.

Professor Jonas T. Flood has told me of an opening in your computer services department. He said you asked him if he knew someone who could revise operating manuals clearly. My two years as editor of the college newspaper have taught me how to express complex ideas in plain language.

I would like to work for Accuwhiz as a systems analyst trainee. Your emphasis on computerization at your East Shore plant convinces me that my major in mathematics would help me do a good job for you.

214

"I'd feel better about this prospective proofreader if he hadn't addressed his letter to 'Pennyprinter Packing.'"

In each of these openings the writer tells what the letter is all about in the first sentence, states or clearly implies the reason for writing, shows some specific knowledge about the company, and suggests how the writer's competencies fit the company's needs. Eagerness to work for the company shows through the entire paragraph.

Now check your understanding of what makes a good first paragraph for an application letter by answering these questions. Choose ALL answers that apply. The answers are on page 229.

1. Which two of the following would make good opening sentences?
(a) My name is Quentin Deerfield and I am a student here at Midwest State, expecting to graduate next June.
(b) I wish to apply for the position of copy editor of your new magazine.

(c) Do you have a job in your accounting office I could apply for?

(d) Don't read any further if you don't want a bright, energetic young engineer on your staff.

(e) Your ad in the July 17 issue of *The Wall Street Journal* says you are looking for an assistant director of student housing.

---

2. Which two of the following would make good opening sentences?

(a) I know I'm just the person you're looking for.

(b) Wanted: A good-paying employer who desires to hire a sharp, aggressive personnel director.

(c) Ms. Selma Quinstet has informed me of a vacancy in Accuwhiz's customer relations department.

(d) I am dissatisfied with my present job here at Accuwhiz.

(e) I wish to apply for the chemical engineer position you advertised for in the September issue of *The Industrial Chemist.*

---

3. What are the two questions your reader is sure to ask when beginning to read your application letter?

(a) Is the applicant sincerely interested in helping the company achieve its corporate objectives?

(b) How much salary does the applicant expect?

(c) What are the applicant's career objectives?

(d) Is the applicant qualified?

(e) What are the applicant's hobbies?

---

4. Finding out as much as you can about a prospective employer accomplishes which of the following?

(a) It helps you avoid making erroneous assumptions and blunders in your application letter.

(b) It tells you which of your qualifications and credentials to stress.

(c) It helps you decide whether or not you really want to apply for the job.

(d) It helps you address the letter correctly.

(e) It convinces the prospective employer that you are interested in the company.

---

5. Which of the following is most important when writing a letter of application?

(a) Use the active voice.

(b) Look at the situation from your reader's point of view.

(c) Provide adequate transitions.

(d)   Show confidence in yourself without being arrogant.

(e)   Avoid negative terms.

Now let's turn to the middle paragraphs of your application letter. Again, look at the situation from your reader's point of view. Immediately after reading your first paragraph, in which you show your interest in helping the company, your reader will want to know what makes you think you can do the job. Your résumé will list your qualifications in detail, but you don't want your reader to start browsing through that—yet. You need to provide a context for interpreting your résumé in terms of the company's needs. That's what you give your reader in these middle paragraphs. You select, explain, and highlight the parts of your educational or work experience *that pertain to the specific job you are applying for.*

For example, let's take one of those sample first paragraphs from earlier in the chapter and see what kind of middle paragraphs might be effective after it.

> *Professor Jonas T. Flood has told me of an opening in your computer services department. He said you asked him if he knew someone who could revise operating manuals clearly. My two years as editor of the college newspaper have taught me how to express complex ideas in plain language.*
>
> *Because our college paper has almost as large a circulation among our alumni as among our students, we need to make sure our news, features, and editorials avoid the kind of campus-jargon that would be puzzling to our alumni. As editor, I worked hard at this and succeeded in getting excellent alumni response as well as four state awards in the annual journalism competition, including a first place for one of my editorials.*
>
> *I have also worked part time for the past six months as copy writer for the local radio station. This has taught me to work quickly as well as accurately.*
>
> *I would like the opportunity to write or edit your operating manuals. The work sounds like a real challenge, but I think I could learn to do it well.*

The applicant's résumé, of course, will support these claims of achievement as well as provide many other facts about his or her background. But the application letter points to only those parts of the résumé that are related to this specific job, and it elaborates on those parts.

When you apply, you should try to match your strengths to the company's needs. The middle paragraphs of your application letter are the proper places to call your reader's attention to that matchup.

Assume each of the following is another fact about the writer's background. Which ones might have been appropriate to include in the middle paragraphs? The answers are on page 229.

6. The writer's hobby is fishing.
(a) appropriate
(b) inappropriate

---

7. The writer took elective courses in computer science.
(a) appropriate
(b) inappropriate

---

8. The writer served two years in the army infantry.
(a) appropriate
(b) inappropriate

---

9. The writer has had two short stories published.
(a) appropriate
(b) inappropriate

---

10. The writer would like to know whether the company pays the moving expenses of new employees.
(a) appropriate
(b) inappropriate

The last paragraph of your application letter, like the last paragraph of any other letter, must show a positive attitude. Be optimistic; assume your reader will want to interview you, and make it as convenient as possible for your reader to do that. You should not include your phone number or mailing address here, because they will appear on your résumé. But if you will be in the reader's city on a visit or a business trip, or if you will be attending a convention which the reader or some other company representative will also be attending, by all means mention that. Try to be as accommodating as you can. If your reader sees that interviewing you will cost the company little or no money, you may well get an interview you might otherwise not have. And try to phrase your interview request as a question. Merely stating when you are available makes it seem as if you are *allowing* the interview to happen. But when you ask a question, you make your reader feel it would be somewhat discourteous *not* to answer.

Here, then, would be a good closing paragraph for the application letter we have been constructing:

> *I will be visiting relatives in San Francisco the week of October 17. Would it be possible to meet with you sometime that week to discuss my qualifications further?*

Now you try some. Revise these five sentences so that they would be appropriate for the closing paragraph of an application letter. The answers are on page 229.

11. If you want to interview me, it will have to be some Wednesday afternoon.

_____

_____

12. Since I'll be in your city on September 11, anyway, I might as well stop by your office for an interview.

_____

_____

13. If there's anything in my résumé you don't understand, I'd like a chance to explain it in an interview, at which time I could also find out more about Accuwhiz.

_____

_____

_____

14. Write and tell me when you are free for an interview, and I'll let you know if I can make it or not.

_____

_____

15. If I don't hear from you in ten days, I'll know you are not interested in getting the names of my references.

_____

_____

_____

One of three possible things will happen within two weeks of mailing an application letter and résumé: (1) You will get a response inviting you to an interview, (2) you will get a response telling you that you didn't get the job, or (3) you will get no response at all.

If you do not get a response, send another copy of your original application and résumé with a brief, courteous letter like the following:

Dear Ms. Appline:

Because I have received no reply to my June 10 letter applying for a position at Accuwhiz, I assume it has become lost in the mail.

Therefore, I am enclosing another copy of the letter and résumé.

May I please hear from you soon?

Sincerely,

If you receive a response telling you that someone else got the job, you should immediately write back, thanking the person for considering you and asking that the company keep your application on file in case a vacancy should occur in the future. Your reader will be glad to know you still feel goodwill toward the company, and your thoughtful letter may well put you at the top of the list if another position *does* become available.

If the response to your application is favorable and you get the interview, phone or write your confirmation of the appointment time immediately. And, of course, follow whatever directions the company gives you concerning letters of recommendation.

A *very important* follow-up letter is the one you send *after the interview.* Besides expressing your gratitude for the interview, you should try to provide information which your interviewer seemed interested in, but which you didn't happen to have at your fingertips during the interview. In any case, make sure you refer specifically to something you talked about, so that your reader will know this isn't just a "form-letter thank you." If during the interview you learned something that really impressed you about the company, something that makes you all the more eager to help them achieve their goals, you should mention that.

If you put yourself in your reader's place, you will see why this follow-up letter is so very important. Imagine yourself interviewing prospective employees all day. Afterward, you have trouble even remembering which names go with which faces, and you certainly can't sort out in your mind all the pluses and minuses of each person you interviewed, even after consulting your notes. Then you get a follow-up letter from one of the persons you interviewed, and in it you get two things: (1) supporting evidence that the writer has the necessary qualifications, and (2) unmistakable assurance that the writer really wants to work for your company—the follow-up letter itself! Remember the two things the reader of an application letter wants to know? Sound familiar? If you received such a follow-up letter, would it help you decide between the writer and a similar applicant who didn't write one? You know the answer.

Matters will take care of themselves if the company offers you the job and you accept it. But what about a job offer you decide to turn down? Be diplomatic here. In writing your refusal, you can't explain what attracted you to another company—without seeming to criticize the one you are writing to. Use the "Bad-News" inductive strategy. After thanking them for the offer, explain that because you have already accepted another position, you are unable to accept theirs. Maintain goodwill; sometime in the future you may find yourself applying to them again.

Now let's consider the résumé, a copy of which you send along with each letter of application. Your résumé is a one-page summary of your educational and employment history. It contains, in abbreviated form, all a prospective employer will need to know about your background and experience in order to decide whether or not to offer you an interview. Your résumé is a word picture of you and your strengths; your application letter is a bridge between those strengths and the needs of the company you are applying to.

Although you cannot tailor the résumé to suit the requirements of each prospective employer, you can avoid many irrelevant entries if you carefully define for yourself just what *kind* of job you will be applying for. Make sure you include everything about you that qualifies you for that kind of job, and leave out whatever does not; you have only one page to work with, and you don't want that page cluttered.

As usual, it will be easiest to decide on a common-sense approach to the writing task if we turn the situation around and look at it from the reader's point of view. If you received an application letter and a résumé from someone, what would you want that résumé to contain?

First of all, you would want to have the person's complete mailing address, including Zip code, and the complete phone number, including area code, so that you could get in touch with the applicant quickly and easily. If the applicant is a student, you would want both the campus address and the permanent, or home, address.

Next, if the applicant had a very precise career objective, like wanting to become a certified public accountant, you would want to know what it is. But if the applicant says only, "I am seeking an entry-level position leading to a career in the field of accounting," you would realize the person is still uncertain about a career, and you would wish the *next* applicant has either a *specific* career objective or sense enough to omit a vague one from the résumé.

Then, you would want to see the only thing that matters to you right now: the evidence that the applicant qualifies for the job. This necessarily falls into two categories: educational background and work experience. And you expect to see the applicant put the more impressive of these categories first. If the applicant is a student, you would expect educational background first; if the applicant is currently working, you would expect work experience first.

Furthermore, in each of the categories you would expect to find the most recent, and therefore the most important, experience listed first, the next most recent listed second, and so on. That way, your first glance at the first line of the first category would tell you the applicant's major qualification for the job.

After these two important sections, you would be willing to read a little about the applicant's personal background—*if* it will help you decide whether the job and the interests of the person match. But you wouldn't mind if the applicant omitted the section on personal background altogether. You would rather base your judgment of such things on the tone of the application letter, anyway.

Next, you would want to know how you can find out more about the applicant's qualifications and how you can verify what you have already read. The names and addresses of at least three persons you can write to or call for recommendations would be nice; but if the résumé says only, "References available upon request," you understand that the applicant wants to select the most appropriate references for the particular job being applied for, and you rather like that.

Finally, you want to know how long ago the applicant compiled the résumé. You find it easier to have confidence in one of recent date.

Now let's get back to *your* side of the situation—the writing of the résumé. There are a few *do*'s and *don't*s you need to observe in order to construct a résumé that looks good, communicates clearly, and presents your qualifications in the best light.

The first thing to remember is that your résumé is a data sheet, not a letter or an essay. This means you should *list* the facts, not write them up in sentences. If you wrote sentences, they would all begin with "I," anyway, and that would be deadly. Under WORK EXPERIENCE, for example, give your reader a list of *parallel* verb phrases (see Chapter 13 for an explanation of parallelism). And be sure you use *action* verbs that give your reader specific mental pictures of what you did. For example, under EDUCATIONAL BACKGROUND do not say "Worked on the college newspaper"; say something like this instead: "Covered football, basketball, and baseball games for the college newspaper," or "Wrote a weekly sports editorial for the college newspaper," or "Interviewed a faculty member each month for a feature series in the college newspaper." Do the same for WORK EXPERIENCE. Don't say, "Spent six months on a Department of Natural Resources study of field rodents"; instead, describe the specific actions you performed, like this: "Collected and analyzed data on field rodents' foraging habits, researched other reports for corroborating information, and wrote the Department of Natural Resources's report on the six-month study."

Under EDUCATIONAL BACKGROUND list the college or university; the kind of degree; your major; and the date, or expected date, of graduation. Do not list individual courses you took, but if you participated in any work-study or other specific programs, be sure to include those. List extracurricular activities, especially if they relate to your major or if you held office in any of them, and name the offices you held. Include your grade-point average (GPA) if it is good, and mention what per cent of your college expenses you earned, if you earned a good portion of them. Be sure to include any *academic* honors or awards you won. Do not include your high school education, but list all previous colleges attended or degrees held, in *reverse* chronological order.

Under WORK EXPERIENCE you list all full-time and part-time jobs you've had, including military experience and high-school part-time work.

Again, use specific action verbs, and list your experience in *reverse* chronological order.

If you decide to include a section on your personal background and interests, follow the same verb-phrase format you used in the two earlier sections. List your interests, hobbies, or anything else you think a prospective employer might need to know in deciding whether or not you will fit in with the company and the kind of job you are applying for. But do *not* include information on sex, age, race, national origin, religion, or health.

Here is a résumé that illustrates the essential parts:

RÉSUMÉ OF WILLIAM B. APPLEWORTH
1118 Virginia Street
Maynard, WI 54308
Phone: (414) 123-4568

EDUCATIONAL BACKGROUND Jan. 1980 to the present	**MIDWEST UNIVERSITY** Will receive Bachelor of Science degree in Biology in June 1983. In upper third of class with GPA of 3.6 on 4.0 scale. GPA in major courses is 3.8. Participated on debating team in 1981 and 1982, taking Tri-State Championship in 1982. Elected to student council in 1980, 1981, and 1982, serving as president in 1982. Responsible for allocating funds as treasurer of Homecoming Committee in 1982. Earned more than half of college expenses.	**DEPERE, WI 54115**
Sept. 1979 to Jan. 1980	**MAYNARD COMMUNITY COLLEGE** Studied real estate in evening classes while working full-time as a dental-supply clerk during the day. Organized student real-estate newsletter. Served on job-placement committee. Earned all of these college expenses.	**MAYNARD, WI 57303**
WORK EXPERIENCE Jan. 1980 to the present	**GERALD'S SERVICE STATION** Tune automobile engines, change tires, and do minor body repair as part-time mechanic. Responsible for ordering supplies and keeping service-station records.	**MAYNARD, WI 53709**
June 1974 to Jan. 1980	**TOOTH FAIRY DENTAL SUPPLY CO.** As dental-supply clerk, kept records for billing, taxes, and inventory. Prepared quarterly report for manager.	**MAYNARD, WI 57304**

June 1971 *to June 1974*	*UNITED STATES ARMY* *ARTILLERY*	*FORT BLISS* *TX 87019*

As records clerk, kept copies of army regulations up to date. Attended two-week army communications school.

REFERENCES   *Personal references available upon request.*

March 1983

Once you have your résumé typed up as neatly as possible, on a single page with plenty of margins and other white space to make it eye-appealing, you can make as many good-quality photocopies of it as you need. Or, better yet, have it printed on a good grade of paper. Do *not* use any cheap means of reproducing it; you want each copy to look like an original.

When you ask someone for permission to use his or her name as a reference (And don't forget to ask!), you should give that person a copy of your résumé to use as a memory-jogger when writing a recommendation for you.

Now answer these questions about résumés: The answers are on page 229.

16. If you have been working for several years since graduating from college, would you list your work experience or your educational background first?

_____

17. If you decide to include a section on your personal background, which of the following should you not include?
(a) your hobbies
(b) your birthdate
(c) your sex
(d) your favorite reading material

_____

18. If you have served in the military, should you include that under educational background or work experience?

_____

19. Who besides a prospective employer should receive a copy of your résumé?

_____

20. Why should you list information in *reverse* chronological order in both the educational background section and the work experience section?

_____

FOR CLASS DISCUSSION

I. The purpose of this classroom exercise is to discover how well your estimate of what is important about your background corresponds with what other people (like prospective employers) think is important.

Bring to class a written description of the job you will be applying for. Beneath this description, provide a *random* list of twenty-five or thirty facts you think qualify you for that job. Keep a separate list of these same facts, arranged in order of importance.

In groups of four students each, exchange papers with each other. On another sheet of paper list the five most important facts about your class-mate's educational background and the five most important facts relating to work experience. Exchange the papers again, and repeat the process for all other members of the group.

Collect your list and your classmates' selections from it. Do your class-mates agree with each other about which items are important in your list? Do the three of them agree with your own ordering of the items?

Your classmates' selections of your qualifications may help you decide what to put into your résumé and what to leave out.

II. Discuss any shortcomings of the following application letter and suggest ways of improving it:

Dear Mr. Connors:

I would like an interview with you so I could tell you about my qualifications as a computer programmer.

My attached résumé will give you a general idea of my college studies and my work record as well as my hobbies, interests, and salary expectations. But I need to talk to you so I can explain the fringe benefits and job security I feel I would like to have in my first job. As you will see, my expectations are quite reasonable.

Professor Smythe tells me you have the same model computer that our class has been practicing on. That is why I chose your company to apply to first; I won't have to learn all about some strange computer.

I really want to become a computer programmer, so I hope you have a job opening for me.

Sincerely,

TEST YOURSELF

Indicate whether the following statements are true or false. The answers are on page 230.

1. T F   The first sentence of your first paragraph in an application letter should let your reader know you are applying for a job.

2. T F   The middle paragraphs of your application letter should emphasize and elaborate on the parts of your résumé you think relate to the specific job you are applying for.

3. T F   It is better to *state* you want an interview than to *ask* for one in the last paragraph of your application letter.

4. T F   If you address your application letter to Ms. Janice Wilson, it would be better to use "Dear Ms. Wilson:" than "Dear Jan:" for the salutation.

5. T F   If your application letter is a response to an employment ad, you should not mention the ad or the publication you saw it in until your last paragraph.

6. T F   You should write only complete sentences in your résumé.

7. T F   You should not include your age nor your birthdate in your résumé.

8. T F   You should arrange your educational background in chronological order, but your work experience in reverse chronological order.

9. T F   You do not need to include your personal background in your résumé.

10. T F   You should not state any career objective if you are the least bit uncertain about what your career objective is.

APPLY YOURSELF

If you have already written a résumé, update it. If you have no résumé, compile one.

Prepare an application letter for either an actual job or a fictitious one. Then include the application letter and a copy of your résumé in a properly addressed envelope and hand them in as your writing assignment for this chapter.

ANSWERS TO EXERCISES

1. b,e

2. c,e

3. a,d

4. a,b,c,d,e

5. b (But the others are certainly important, too.)

6. b

7. a

8. b

9. a

10. b

11. May I please arrange for an interview at your convenience, preferably a Wednesday afternoon?

12. Would it be convenient for you to see me on September 11, when I will be in your city?

13. May I please have the opportunity to learn more about Accuwhiz and to discuss with you my qualifications for the job?

14. Could I discuss my qualifications further whenever it is convenient for you?

15. Would you like me to send you my references?

16. work experience

17. b,c

18. work experience

19. You should give a copy to anyone you ask permission to use as a personal reference.

20. A prospective employer is sure to be most interested in your most recent accomplishments and experiences.

ANSWERS TO TEST YOURSELF

1. T
2. T
3. F
4. T
5. F
6. F
7. T
8. F
9. T
10. T

Part IV

Reducing Language Fog:
Advanced Techniques

11

Don't Waste Words

Don't be like the student who decided to underline all the important sentences in the textbook and discovered that every one of them was at least somewhat important. Eventually, every sentence in the book had a line under it. All the student had managed to do was make the text considerably harder to read.

In short, if you try to emphasize everything, you end up emphasizing nothing. This holds true in lesser degrees, too; the more points you emphasize, the less emphasis each point gets.

Therefore, make sure you don't dress up an idea in the form of a clause unless the idea is important enough to deserve it. A clause, as you recall, is any group of words having a subject and predicate. Try to match the degree of importance of your ideas with the degree of importance of the grammatical forms you express them in. In order to do that, you must get a clear notion of the "ranking" of the various grammatical forms.

The most important grammatical form, or structure, is the independent clause. Put your most important ideas in this kind of clause.

An independent clause is a group of words, having a subject and a predicate, and making a complete statement.

Production increased last year.
Your order is on its way.
Two members of the crew attended the meeting.

Every sentence must have at least one independent clause in it. Some sentences have more than one such clause:

Ms. Trolla authorized the investigation, and Mr. Findlap wrote the report.

233

The next most important grammatical structure is the dependent clause—a group of words that contains a subject and a predicate, but does not make a complete statement. A dependent clause can be either a subordinate clause or a relative clause.

Subordinate Clause: because the machine broke down
Relative Clause: which is obstructing traffic

Of less importance as a grammatical structure are the various kinds of phrases. A phrase is simply a group of words used as a single part of speech, but not having a subject and a predicate.

Noun Phrase: the partly opened package
Verb Phrase: shall have been counted
Prepositional Phrase: (these usually function as adjectives or adverbs):
   in the morning
   around the building
   after the meeting
Verbal Phrase   (participial, gerundive, infinitive):
   (part. or ger.) finishing the project
   (past part.) attended by the whole committee
   (infinitive) to evaluate the new data

Finally, the unit of grammar is the word. Expressing an idea in a single word tells your reader that the idea is important enough to appear, but does not deserve major emphasis—unless, of course, you place it in an emphatic position, like the very beginning or the very end of the sentence.

Therefore, we have a kind of "pecking order" among grammatical structures, and they rank this way, from most emphatic to least emphatic:

1. *independent clause*
2. *dependent clause*
3. *phrase*
4. *word*

In these next four sentences, notice the difference in emphasis placed on the location of the rug:

The rug is in my office, and I want it cleaned.
  independent clause

I want the rug which is in my office cleaned.
               dependent clause

I want the rug in my office cleaned.
            phrase

I want my office rug cleaned.
         word

You must decide how important each concept is, and then try to express it in a structure that doesn't exaggerate that importance. Only you, the writer, can decide such things. But there are a few tricks you can learn to help you "demote" a clause to a phrase when that is what you want to do. The rest of the chapter will give you practice in making such revisions, and we may even have room to try reducing some phrases to single words.

Suppose you asked several companies to send lecturers to a small convention you are hosting at your plant. What would you think if you received the following reply from one of those companies?

> *Accuwhiz Corporation*
> *422 Whitney*
> *Stearns, KS 66216*
> *June 14, 19__*

Ms. R. B. Jones
Director of Training
Bellaston Widget Company
Summit Valley, KS 67216

Dear Ms. Jones:

> *We have selected Ms. Donna Elder, who is our specialist in cost accounting, to give her lecture, which is very interesting and practical, at your convention that is scheduled for the week of July 8.*

> *We think you will be pleased with her presentation, which is entertaining and informative, and with her personality, which is warm and cheerful. Her accomplishments as a lecturer, which are numerous, and her willingness to adapt her material, which is extensive, to the particular interests which are shown by her audience, are sure to enhance your program.*

Sincerely,

Robert A. Greene
Employee Services

Surely you would wonder whether the writer of that letter could possibly be capable of judging the quality of Ms. Elder's presentation—or anyone else's. The letter is clearly abominable. Yet, not very much is wrong with it; that is, only one awkward construction appears—but it occurs eight times.

We could, for instance, improve the letter greatly by performing one simple operation on it. Let's remove all the relative pronouns (*who, which,* or *that*) followed by a form of *be.* Then our letter would read like this:

> *We have selected Ms. Donna Elder, our specialist in cost accounting, to give her very interesting and practical lecture at your convention scheduled for the week of July 8.*

We think you will be pleased with her entertaining and informative presentation and with her warm and cheerful personality. Her numerous accomplishments as a lecturer and her willingness to adapt her extensive material to the particular interests shown by her audience are sure to enhance your program.

This letter is still a bit clumsy, but you must agree that it is considerably better than it was.

You would probably never write a letter with so many relative clauses

in it as that first example has (a relative clause contains a relative pronoun—*who*, *which*, or *that*—usually referring to some noun in the main clause), yet you should recognize one very important fact about such clauses: They always imply that what they say is rather important. Therefore, if what you say in the relative clause is *not* very important, you should reduce the clause to a phrase or a single word. That is why the letter sounds so much better when we revise the relative clauses out of it. In the revision, only important ideas show up in clause structures.

Now, how do you go about reducing relative clauses to phrases or single words? Well, if the relative pronoun has some form of *be* in its predicate, the answer is simple: Just eliminate both the relative pronoun and the form of *be*. Of course, you may have to rearrange what's left in order to keep the sentence grammatical, but you will have no trouble with that.

Let's try a few. Eliminate the relative pronoun (*who, which,* or *that*) and the form of *be* in the following sentences. Rearrange the remaining parts, if necessary. The answers are on page 251.

1. We recommend consulting with Mr. James Overle, who is our district representative.

---

2. Your résumé, which is very impressive, arrived without the cover letter that is necessary.

---

3. We have been satisifed with all the terms of the contract that is expiring.

---

4. We have been satisfied with all the terms of the contract that is expiring this month.

Did those last two examples tell you anything about rearranging sentence parts after eliminating the relative pronoun and the form of *be?* Why did you have to rearrange the word order in one of them, but not in the other? Well, if after deleting the relative pronoun and the form of *be*, you have only one word from the original clause left, then you need to rearrange the word order. If you have only a few words left, then you have a choice about rearranging the word order.

Let's try a few more of these types:

5.   Last month's sales, which were surprising, are continuing at that pace.

_____

_____

6.   Last month's sales, which were completely surprising, are continuing at that pace.

_____

_____

But, notice that if you have several words left after deleting the relative pronoun and the form of *be,* you probably should leave the word order as it was in the original; it will usually read better that way:

7.   Last month's sales, which were surprising to all of us, are continuing at that pace.

_____

_____

This last example presents an interesting question: Is the revision really better than the original? You have to exercise your own judgment here. I think we gained a little conciseness and effectiveness by deleting the relative pronoun and the form of *be.* But only you, the writer, can decide how much emphasis you want to place on the idea that last month's sales were surprising to all of us. Both sentences—the original and the revision—are grammatical. All I'm suggesting here is that you use the most concise structure you can, unless you have a *good reason* to use the longer structure. Use all the words you need; just don't waste them.

Let's practice on a few more examples before we try a more complex means of achieving conciseness. Shorten the following sentences by deleting the relative pronoun and the form of *be.* The answers are on page 251.

8.   Mrs. J. Smythe, who is happy with our settlement of her claim, has increased her order for next month.

_____

_____

9. You will need to refer to the company's organization chart which is on the north wall of Ms. Slade's office.

---

10. We expect to eliminate the billing errors which are caused by the late posting of payments.

---

11. Mr. Bruce, who is our district supervisor, has told me to ask you for a list of all items which were destroyed in the fire.

---

12. Please send us only packages that are clearly labeled.

So far, we have dealt only with relative clauses containing some form of *be*. How about other kinds? Can we shorten sentences like the following one?

All employees who wish to participate should sign up now.

Yes, but it's a little more complicated, and we will usually shorten the sentence by only one word. We could revise the sentence like this:

All employees wishing to participate should sign up now.

What we've done here is to reduce the clause to a participial phrase by deleting the relative pronoun and converting the verb to a participle. We haven't made the sentence much more concise, but we have demoted the modifier from a clause to a phrase—and that makes the sentence at least seem more efficient and to the point.

Let's practice on some more of this type. The answers are on page 251.

13. Our April advertisement, which includes coupons which are redeemable after March 1, will appear in two national magazines.

---

14. Only cartons which have been inspected will have labels which are blue and white. (Note: When the relative clause has a passive-voice verb like this, you can usually delete everything in the clause up to the past participle.)

That's enough in reducing clauses to phrases, for the time being, anyway. Now let's consider another kind of tightening up you can do. Sometimes sentences get overloaded with phrases, and that can also make your meaning murky. The usual culprits are prepositional phrases. Here is a sentence from the Federal Communications Commission's rules governing Citizen's Band operation. It explains how to notify the Commission if you intend to use a CB radio for civil defense communications. At least I think it does.

In the event such use is to be a series of pre-planned tests or drills of the same or similar nature which are scheduled in advance for specific times or at certain intervals of time, the licensee may send a single notice to the Commission in Washington, D.C., and to the Engineer in Charge of the radio district in which the station is located, stating the nature of the communications to be transmitted, the duration of each such test, and the times scheduled for such use.

The writer is apparently trying to say too much in one sentence, yet the sentence's meaning doesn't seem unduly complicated. Many factors contribute to this clumsiness: passive-voice verbs and wordy relative clauses, to name only a few. But the biggest cause of wordiness here is the runaway prepositional phrase. There are sixteen (count them) in just this one sentence. Now, you cannot eliminate all prepositional phrases from your writing the way you can eliminate passive-voice verbs, but you don't need to clutter up the place with them, either. Let's try operating on that FCC sentence to see how many phrases we can reduce or eliminate. Our revision might look like this:

If such use is to be a uniform test or drill series planned for regular times or intervals, the licensee need only once notify the Commission in Washington, D.C., and the station's district Engineer in Charge, stating the test's nature, duration, and times scheduled.

We have reduced the prepositional phrases from sixteen to three, and one of them is in a proper name: Engineer in Charge. Perhaps we have gone too far; a few parts of the sentence seem to have suffered in the revising. But generally the new version is better; there are fewer words getting in our way.

Reducing prepositional phrases is not an exact science. Sometimes it involves merely turning the preposition's object into a modifier and eliminating the rest of the phrase, as we did when we changed "the rug in my office" to "my office rug." But usually we need to rethink our meaning and then choose different words, as we did when we changed "tests or drills of the same or similar nature" to "uniform tests."

Before we look at another way to economize in words, let's practice reducing some prepositional phrases to shorter modifiers.

Get rid of the wasted phrases in these sentences. The answers are on pages 251 and 252.

15. Bill Smith is negotiator for our union.

---

16. We have redesigned the form for requesting vacations.

---

17. The gross weight of the truck must not exceed limits for safety.

---

18. Prices in the catalog do not include the costs of shipping nor the charges for a rush order.

It is not always possible to reduce a prepositional phrase to a shorter modifier without changing your meaning. In this case, of course, do not make the change. The following two sentences contain some phrases you cannot reduce, but tighten up whatever ones you can.

19. The critic began her lecture on the drama by giving the audience a definition of the ridiculous.

---

20. We need an analysis of both liquids, so please send us your report of the clear by tomorrow and your report of the turgid by Thursday.

I should caution you about something at this point. You can easily overdo this phrase-reducing business if you're not careful. Don't start with a wordy sentence like "The bearings of the upper carriage of the sealer-wrapper on the conveyor end of the packaging machine in the converting room are wearing out" and try to patch it up by changing it to an even more horrible monstrosity like this: "The converting room packaging machine's conveyor end sealer-wrapper's upper carriage bearings are wearing out." Reducing phrases to shorter modifiers is a good idea, but it cannot substitute for common sense. When you find yourself writing something like "The bearings of the upper carriage of the sealer-wrapper on the. . . ." you should stop and ask yourself whether you need all that detail in order to specify exactly what you mean. If you do, then draw a picture or diagram. These are appropriate in both letters and reports. Remember, a picture is worth. . . .

Finally, there is one other thing you can do to avoid wasting words. This is the simplest, yet the most difficult, of all techniques: Cross out all the words you don't really need. It's amazing how many unnecessary words find their way into most people's rough drafts. You may find that as much as half of what you've written is really excess baggage.

The first thing to look for is redundancy. When speaking we often repeat ideas for emphasis. But remember that the reader can reread as much as necessary; therefore, say everything you need to say only once; make every word count. Especially avoid such redundant expressions as "8:00 A.M. in the morning," "return back," "basic fundamentals," "thorough and complete," "cease and desist," "aid and abet," and "delay and postpone." Many of these are clichés as well as redundancies, and both involve wasting words. We will discuss clichés in more detail in the next chapter. For now, just remember that one of the quickest ways to convince your reader you don't really know what you're writing about is to use more words than you need to. It clearly implies that you are not thinking about what each word actually means. Consider the following example and ask yourself whether you think the writer is trying to communicate or merely trying to fill up a page with words:

> *In my personal opinion I think that the refund policy of our company needs constant and continual updating and revising so that the desires and wishes of our purchasing customers who buy our products and merchandise will be better pleased and more happy to continue shopping here now and in the future. By this I mean that I think each and every time we. . . .*

The writer might simply have said, "We need to revise our refund policy to better accommodate our customers."

Of course, you can go too far in deleting words unless you are careful. You don't want your letter to read like a telegram or a newspaper headline. Nor do you want your report to read like an outline. The best way to achieve the right balance is to read the drafts aloud and ask yourself whether your letters sound friendly and to the point and whether your reports show ease and consideration for the reader. But more letters and reports suffer from wordiness than from too much terseness.

Now let's practice tightening up some sentences this way. Eliminate

242

the unnecessary words from the following sentences. The answers are on page 252.

21. If I were to classify your last shipment, I would have to say that it was truly excellent. I would classify it this way because there was no instance of color bleed-over.

_____

_____

_____

22. In the final analysis our entire workforce must practice the basic fundamentals of safety around machinery.

_____

_____

23. I will meet you at the hotel at 2:00 P.M. in the afternoon, so I can return back to my office in time to make a thorough and complete report.

_____

_____

_____

24. To explain our cost-accounting system, I must refer back to when we first began to notice a required need for one.

_____

_____

Besides avoiding redundancies, you need to recognize and eliminate other empty words in your sentences. We all have our own little pet phrases that we like to use as a substitute for thinking. And they can occasionally be useful when we write business letters; they can help to soften the letter's tone or add the warmth of personality to a message that would otherwise seem curt. But in such cases the "empty words" are not really empty after all. They do communicate our goodwill. *Please* and *thank you* are never empty words when used sincerely in a letter. It's fine to be cordial—just don't be chatty.

Most times, however, empty words are just that: words empty of real meaning. Consider the following sentence and ask yourself which words convey meaning and which words just clutter up the message:

*In my opinion I think that the level of production will probably fall
below our anticipated estimates because, as is well known, when
materials are lacking, the process of production must stop, and we ran
out of materials twice last month.*

The writer didn't need to say "in my opinion" because "I think" means
the same thing. Further, "I think" is itself superfluous because the reader
will assume that, anyway. "The level of" is unnecessary, as is "anticipated."
Can you imagine production without assuming it has some quantity or level?
Can you imagine estimates without assuming anticipation? Next, the writer
says everyone already knows that "when materials are lacking the process
of production must stop." Why state it then? Why state the obvious?

If we cross out all these unnecessary words, we will have this left:

*Production will probably fall below our estimates because we ran out
of materials twice last month.*

We have kept the meaning intact despite lopping off twenty-five words
and keeping only sixteen. Furthermore, the shorter sentence communicates
something the longer one could not: the impression that the writer is clear-
headed, direct, and businesslike.

You should now be ready for some practice in crossing out the empty
words in the following sentences. The answers are on page 252.

25. After all is said and done, we would be most grateful if you would
please use only the north exit of the parking lot until June 22.

---

26. We are returning your payment for the repairs on your camera. We
are doing this because your guarantee is still in effect.

A certain few expressions are *always* empty, or at best wordy, so try
to keep them out of your writing. Here is only a partial list; you can probably
add a few of your own:

the fact that	at the present time
that which	in the near future
is one of	in the neighborhood of
at this point in time	with reference to

Try getting rid of these empty words in the following sentences:

27. He announced the fact that he was leaving.

_____

28. The fact that he refused to sign the agreement ended the matter.

_____

29. Her letter is one of courtesy, brevity, and clarity.

_____

30. At that point in time we knew that supplies would be scarce.

_____

31. We have no alternatives at the present time.

_____

32. Your shipment will arrive in the near future.

_____

33. Sort out that which you need from that which you don't need.

_____

34. We exported in the neighborhood of five thousand mowers last year.

_____

The following sentences waste words in a variety of ways. Make whatever changes you think necessary to make each sentence concise.

35. Our sales report, which is very recent, shows that our novel new approach to advertising is working well.

_____

_____

36. Finally at last we can dismantle our old boiler, which is old and worn out, so we can install one that is more efficient.

_____

_____

37. The committee's recommendations, which are based on data of production for this year, are on the desk of the office manager.

_____

_____

_____

38. The compression ratio of 9 to 1 in this engine enables it to use fuel which is low in octane.

_____

_____

39. The plan of the mechanical engineer was very unique because of its potential for the saving of energy.

_____

_____

40. Our system of reporting requires all managers who have responsibilities in the production area to submit reports on safety on or before the tenth of the month.

_____

_____

_____

FOR CLASS DISCUSSION

1. On the chalkboard, add to the list of redundancies and other wordy expressions mentioned in this chapter. After each one write the class's suggested translation into concise English. Make a separate list of words and phrases the careful business writer should delete entirely—such expressions as "more or less," "in the amount of," and "in color" [e.g., red *in color*].

2. Bring to class three wordy sentences found in your own reading (books, newspapers, magazines, business letters). Take turns reading them aloud to the class and ask for suggestions on how to tighten them up.

TEST YOURSELF

The answers are on page 254.

Make the following sentences more concise:

1. We need to discover all the true facts about the spare-parts shipment which was lost.

2. Ms. Cooper suggested we find out that which the government requires at the present time.

3. Our X-56 model, which is new, can pack in the neighborhood of a thousand cases a day.

4. We are behind schedule because of the fact that the drive belt on the conveyor has been slipping.

5. At that point in time we bought only paint that was of high quality.

6. All employees who have been scheduled for physical examinations should check their records of immunization prior to reporting.

7. In the event that our inventory gets too low, we can do that which is necessary to increase our level of production.

8. The large cartons that are in Warehouse B can remain there until we find a place which is better for them.

9. All employees who are on salary and who wish to buy lunch tickets may do so subsequent to 1:00 P.M. on Monday.

10. In college I took some courses that were very practical, but my work experience of three years is even more practical.

APPLY YOURSELF

The paragraph below is from an actual letter written by an insurance adjuster to a client.

The situation is this: A tree fell on the client's solar-powered swimming-pool heater and destroyed it. The client had the Johnstone Company replace it for forty-four hundred dollars. Now he wants his insurance company to reimburse him for that amount. The insurance adjuster, however, has called three other solar-energy companies and found that they would have charged only about one thousand five hundred dollars to replace the heater. The adjuster explains this in earlier portions of the letter and ends with the following paragraph (the names, of course, are fictitious):

> *I again feel that I must state that I sympathize with your position concerning the estimated replacement bid on the swimming-pool heater presented by the Johnstone Company in the amount of forty-four hundred dollars. However, the fact that they have presented this bid does not negate the fact that we apparently could have facilitated replacement of the swimming-pool heater at any one of the above three described bids. If it will be of any assistance to you I would be happy to discuss these figures with the Johnstone Company; however, my numerous inquiries to them have gone unacknowledged. I do not intend to continue attempting to contact them when they fail to respond. If you can arrange for Mr. Johnstone to call me, I will be happy to refute his price in your stead.*

Assume that you are the insurance adjuster and revise the paragraph so that it is concise, but not blunt or discourteous.

ANSWERS TO EXERCISES

1. We recommend consulting with Mr. James Overle, our district representative.
OR
    We recommend consulting with our district representative, Mr. James Overle.

2. Your very impressive résumé arrived without the necessary cover letter.

3. We have been satisfied with all the terms of the expiring contract.

4. We have been satisfied with all the terms of the contract expiring this month.

5. Last month's surprising sales are continuing at that pace.

6. Last month's sales, completely surprising, are continuing at that pace.
OR
    Last month's completely surprising sales are continuing at that pace.

7. Last month's sales, surprising to all of us, are continuing at that pace.

8. Ms. J. Smythe, happy with our settlement of her claim, has increased her order for next month.
OR
    Happy with our settlement of her claim, Ms. J. Smythe has increased her order for next month.

9. You will need to refer to the company's organization chart on the north wall of Ms. Slade's office.

10. We expect to eliminate the billing errors caused by the late posting of payments.

11. Mr. Bruce, our district supervisor, has told me to ask you for a list of all items destroyed in the fire.
OR
    Our district supervisor, Mr. Bruce, has told me to ask you for a list of all items destroyed in the fire.

12. Please send us only clearly labeled packages.

13. Our April advertisement, including coupons redeemable after March 1, will appear in two national magazines.

14. Only inspected cartons will have blue and white labels.

15. Bill Smith is our union's negotiator.
OR
    Bill Smith is our union negotiator.

16. We have redesigned the vacation-request form. (Note: Hyphenate a compound adjective that precedes the noun it modifies.)

17. The truck's gross weight must not exceed safety limits.

18. Catalog prices do not include shipping costs nor rush-order charges.

19. The critic began her drama lecture by giving the audience a definition of the ridiculous.

20. (No tightening up is possible, at least not by reducing prepositional phrases.)

21. Your last shipment was truly excellent because there was no color bleed-over.

22. Our entire workforce must practice the fundamentals of safety around machinery.

23. I will meet you at the hotel at 2:00 P.M., so I can return to my office in time to make a thorough report.
(NOTE: You are also correct if you used *complete* instead of *thorough*.)

24. To explain our cost-accounting system, I must refer to when we began to notice a need for one.

25. Please use only the north exit of the parking lot until June 22.

26. We are returning your payment for the repairs on your camera because your guarantee is still in effect.

27. He announced that he was leaving.
OR
He announced he was leaving.

28. His refusal to sign the agreement ended the matter.

29. Her letter is courteous, brief, and clear.

30. We then knew that supplies would be scarce.
(NOTE: You are also correct if you placed *then* anywhere else in the sentence except after *that* or after *be*.)

31. We have no alternatives now.
(NOTE: You are also correct if you placed *now* anywhere else in the sentence except between *no* and *alternatives*.)

32. Your shipment will arrive soon.
(NOTE: You are also correct if you placed *soon* anywhere else in the sentence except between *Your* and *shipment*.)

33. Sort out what you need from what you don't need.

34. We exported about five thousand mowers last year.

35. Our very recent sales report shows that our new approach to advertising is working well.

36. Finally we can dismantle our old, worn-out boiler, so we can install a more efficient one.
(NOTE: You are also correct if you used *At last* instead of *Finally*.)

37. The committee's recommendations based on this year's production data are on the office manager's desk.

38. This engine's 9-to-1 compression ratio enables it to use low-octane fuel.

39. The mechanical engineer's plan was unique because of its energy-saving potential.

40. Our reporting system requires all managers having production-area responsibilities to submit safety reports by the tenth of the month.

ANSWERS TO TEST YOURSELF

1. We need to (or *must*) discover all the facts about the lost spare-parts shipment.

2. Ms. Cooper suggested we find out what the government now requires. (NOTE: You are also correct if you put *now* after *what* or after *requires.*)

3. Our new X-56 model can pack about a thousand cases a day.

4. We are behind schedule because the conveyor's drive belt has been slipping.

5. We then bought only high-quality paint. (NOTE: You are also correct if you put *then* before *we* or after *paint.*)

6. All employees scheduled for physical examinations should check their immunization records before reporting.

7. If our inventory gets too low, we can do what is necessary to increase our production.

8. The large cartons in Warehouse B can remain there until we find a better place for them.

9. All employees on salary (or *All salaried employees*) wishing to buy lunch tickets may do so Monday after 1:00 P.M.

10. In college I took some very practical courses, but my three-years' work experience is even more practical.

12

Use Precise Language

Earlier we discussed the importance of giving your reader vivid mental pictures. We learned, for example, that it is better to write "The mechanic installed the timer" than to write "The mechanic made the installation of the timer" because the reader can visualize someone *installing*, but cannot visualize an *installation*. This chapter is about mental pictures, too. But we will try to create those pictures by choosing more specific words, rather than by converting *-tion* or *-ment* nouns into verbs or verbals.

Novelist Joseph Conrad explained in one of his prefaces that his task "is, by the power of the written word, to make you hear, to make you feel—it is, before all, to make you see. That—and no more, and it is everything." To make the reader see—that's what *every* kind of writing is all about. The novelist does it by choosing words that call up in the reader's mind vivid mental pictures of characters and events. The business writer does it by choosing the most specific, precise words available to communicate the business message—words that also suggest images the reader can easily visualize.

Both the novelist and the business writer run into difficult obstacles when trying to paint mental pictures for their readers. Foremost is the obstacle of inertia, or simply laziness. It is much more difficult and time consuming to search for the precise word than to merely slap onto the paper the first words that come to mind. But the extra effort pays huge dividends. Hastily writing a letter that antagonizes a customer, or quickly throwing together a vague report under pressure of a deadline, is not the way to save time— or money—or goodwill—or your job. Begin early and take the time necessary to revise. Easy reading requires careful writing, and rewriting. Take time to think. You must see those mental pictures clearly yourself before you can communicate them to your reader.

Of course, you will not always have enough time to do a thorough job of revising. But you should plan your schedule to keep those "rush jobs" to a minimum. And when you do have the time, use it to practice your writing skills by looking at your draft critically from your reader's point of view. Cross out all the words that got in there only because you were trying to impress somebody, whether your reader or yourself. Never try to dazzle your reader with your vocabulary; that game never succeeds anyway. Try to cultivate a sincere respect for your reader's needs and feelings. Talk your reader's language; don't demand that your reader learn yours. Eventually your first drafts will require very little polishing because you will have been mindful of the kinds of vague expressions you tend to use and will have chosen more precise language before ever setting pencil to paper.

As you revise, you will need to watch out for these four enemies of precise language:

1. General and abstract terms
2. Clichés
3. Inflated language
4. Substandard usage

In the rest of this chapter you will learn, first of all, how to recognize these vague terms when you see them, and then how to do something about them when they show up in your writing.

ABSTRACT AND GENERAL TERMS

Abstract nouns refer to concepts, ideas, qualities. They are nouns like *responsibility, patriotism, motherhood, awareness, intention, experience, defiance.* You can usually recognize them by their endings; the seven I just listed are representative. Almost every English noun that ends in *-ty, -ism, -hood, -ness, -tion, -ience,* or *-iance* is abstract. There are others, too, like *pride, honor, belief.* But all of them refer to something other than physical objects. That means they are nearly impossible to visualize and therefore always pose at least a slight problem for your reader. Now, there is nothing wrong with using abstract terms; in fact, sometimes they are indispensable. However, once you realize that your reader will have trouble "seeing" them, you will try to keep them to a minimum and will provide enough *concrete* nouns to explain them when you do need to use them. A concrete noun is the opposite of an abstract noun; it refers to some material object your reader can easily visualize. For example, the following sentence contains only abstractions:

Our transportation requires a large capacity.

Notice how difficult it is to get a clear meaning from those words. There is nothing for the reader to visualize. But putting the same idea into concrete language enables the reader to "see" the meaning:

256

Each of our trucks must be able to carry eighteen television consoles.

Now let's get some practice recognizing abstract nouns and concrete nouns when we see them. In the following sentences classify the nouns as either abstract or concrete. The easiest way is to pretend you are an artist and then ask yourself whether you could draw a picture of what the noun means. The answers are on page 271.

1. Ms. Hartstein has considerable experience in testing program efficiency.

Ms. Hartstein _____

experience _____

efficiency _____

2. Your radio has two faulty transistors.

radio _____

transistors _____

3. Leadership requires responsibility, integrity, and decisiveness.

leadership _____

responsibility _____

integrity _____

decisiveness _____

4. The two cerebral hemispheres differ in cognitive specialization.

hemispheres _____

specialization _____

5. Attendance was poor; the lecture hall was nearly empty.

attendance _____

hall _____

Use abstractions only when you must, and then it's a good idea to follow them up with concrete examples or explanations if you think your reader might need them.

General nouns can be troublesome, too. They often give your reader mental pictures, but usually those pictures are too vague to be of any use in understanding your meaning. General nouns are ones that include several subdivisions of specific items. For example, the noun *vehicle* is more general than *truck* because *vehicle* includes cars, bicycles, trains, and other things besides trucks. The opposite of *general* is *specific*, and the more specific a noun is, the clearer the mental picture your reader will get from it. The problem is that the terms *general* and *specific* are relative. That is, almost every noun is more specific than some other nouns and more general than some others. For instance, in the following lists each noun is more general than the one below it and more specific than the one above it:

person	thing	vegetation	animal
manager	structure	tree	vertebrate
woman	building	evergreen	dog
Rita Sims	The Alamo	pine	Rover

Notice that when the noun is so specific that it refers to just one thing, we capitalize it because it is then a proper noun, by definition.

This may be very interesting, but what does it have to do with writing letters and reports? It has a great deal to do with it. Remember that the writer's responsibility is to give the reader as many vivid mental pictures as possible. In those four lists, the farther down you go, the clearer the mental picture you get. Give your reader the most specific nouns you can, without narrowing your meaning too much, of course. For instance, don't refer to your company's "product" if you are explaining how to assemble the picnic table you sell. If it's a picnic table, *call* it a picnic table. Don't report that the failure of the mechanism was caused by an obstruction after foreign matter was introduced by an external source. Say the safety engineer's hairpiece fell into the bread slicer and broke four blades, if that's what really happened.

Verbs can be general or specific, too. Be careful to specify your exact meaning by choosing the verb with the narrowest meaning that fits. For example, if you write to Mr. Smith and tell him to "contact" you if he has any questions, how will Mr. Smith know whether to write you a letter, phone you, send you a telegram, or send smoke signals? If you would like him to phone you, say so—and include your phone number so he won't have to look it up. Being specific is being considerate of your reader. Or, if you are writing a report, don't say "The new dress code has greatly affected student morale." Has the new dress code made student morale better or worse than it was? The verb *affected* gives no clue.

We'll get a little practice choosing concrete, specific terms before we go on to clichés. In the following sentences, the underlined terms are hard for the reader to visualize because they are either abstract or too general. Rewrite the sentences by substituting one of the words in the following list for each of the underlined terms. The answers are on page 271.

announce	brooms	sweepers
said	gasoline	letter
twenty-four	92 per cent	duplicator

6. Our <u>maintenance</u> <u>personnel</u> need new <u>equipment</u>.

---

7. Ms. Potter <u>indicated</u> that the <u>document</u> was missing.

---

8. The <u>machine</u> can produce <u>a</u> <u>large</u> <u>number</u> <u>of</u> copies a minute.

---

9. <u>Energy</u> costs <u>considerably</u> more than it did a year ago.

---

10. I will <u>share</u> my decision at tomorrow's meeting.

CLICHÉS

Clichés are familiar expressions like "hungry as a bear," "as scarce as hens' teeth," and "water under the bridge." The first person who ever used a particular cliché was undoubtedly imaginative and eloquent, but because the expression was so colorful and effective other people started using it, too. That killed it. For instance, I suppose whoever noticed that chickens don't like to be wet, and therefore compared a very angry person with a wet hen, showed some wit in doing so. But "mad as a wet hen" has become so overused that when we hear it or read it we automatically translate it as "very angry" and the witty comparison never occurs. Besides, most clichés are wordy, too. Always say what you mean simply and directly in business writing; if you mean someone was very angry, then say so. Using trite expressions, or clichés, does not impress—it annoys.

Almost as bad as clichés, and perhaps even more destructive of good writing because they are more frequent, are stock phrases. These are the word combinations that become never-varying units of expression. You are no doubt familiar with such phrases as "in the final analysis," "at that point in time," "in view of the fact that," "in the foreseeable future," "this is to inform you that," and "if you have any questions, please don't hesitate to call." When you read such phrases, you begin to think that the writer has a whole arsenal of rubber stamps on the desk and merely selects the proper combination to fill up the letter or report. As soon as you recognize a stock phrase, you become convinced that the writer was insincere and was not really thinking of you or of what the message really means.

Every reader hates to read clichés and stock phrases, yet those same readers will often use them when they write. Why? Laziness again. It is much easier to pull a stock phrase off the shelf than it is to think closely about the meaning and choose the precise words the meaning calls for. But if the writer would consider how much goodwill and credibility such laziness costs, the problem would take care of itself.

Sharpen your eye for recognizing clichés and stock phrases by eliminating them from the following sentences. You may have to recast some of the sentences. The answers are on page 271.

11.   It was as plain as day that we would not meet our quota.

_____

12.   Enclosed herewith is the refund as per your request.

_____

13.   I want to hit the trail as soon as the last conference is over.

_____

14.   If this contract meets with your approval, would you be so kind as to put your John Hancock on the dotted line and shoot it back to me forthwith?

_____

_____

_____

15.   I deem it advisable for you to get in touch with Bill Rogers by mail prior to the completion of your report.

_____

_____

INFLATED LANGUAGE

Effective business writing is always plain, direct, courteous, and concise. Certainly, you need to be diplomatic so that you don't antagonize your reader, but the way to do that is to stress the positive and treat your reader with respect. You must never try to intimidate by using words that sound impressive but mean very little, nor must you ever try to hide the truth by covering it with a blanket of legal-sounding, pompous terminology. Inflated language is just that—puffed-up vocabulary that makes what you say appear to be more important than it is. Its horror, besides making you sound like an arrogant stuffed-shirt, is that it enables you to convince yourself that you are saying something important when you are really saying nothing at all. One executive told me that her subordinates treated her like a mushroom: they kept her in the dark and fed her manure. She was referring, of course, to the inflated language, or gobbledegook, of their reports. You must reject the cynical attitude of the person who said that the purpose of all reports is not to communicate the truth, but to protect the writer. Don't fool yourself by thinking that reports are only "busy work" or that business letters are simply devices for letting other people know you don't want to be bothered. Both your company and your career depend on how efficiently and courteously you can communicate what your reader wants to know. And you can't do that by using inflated language.

Here are a dozen examples of the kind of language we are talking about, with their common English translations:

INFLATED TERMS	MEANINGS IN COMMON ENGLISH
ensuing	following, next
facilitator	helper, coordinator
finalization	completion
finalize	finish
impact (used as a verb)	affect
in reference to	about
option	choice
prior to	before
subsequent to	after
the fact that	that
utilization	use
utilize	use

I'm sure you could easily add to the list.

How can you recognize inflated language? First, it is generally of Latin, rather than Anglo-Saxon, origin. That doesn't help much unless you have a dictionary that includes word origins. Second, it often consists of a series of two adjectives followed by a noun, none of which has a very specific meaning. For example, using Philip S. Broughton's "Systematic Buzz-Phrase Projector,"[1] which humorously explains how to construct these inflated phrases, we can come up with the following meaningless, but impressive-sounding paragraph:

> *Our parallel management options may require total organizational flexibility unless some systemized monitored projection evolves into a compatible transitional option. If this happens, the functional logistical programming will demonstrate the total management concept of optional transitional time-phase, or else exacerbate it. But a synchronized incremental projection of the type we have been studying is certainly not compatible with our third-generation hardware. Therefore, a balanced policy contingency must clearly be kept viable alongside any*

[1] "Criteria for the Evaluation of Printed Matter," *American Journal of Public Health,* 30 (Sept. 1940), 1027–32.

optional management capability that we may desire to keep compatible with our functional policy programming. Because of this, there are two alternatives, neither of which is open to us. Consequently, we are constrained to vigorously pursue an infinite array of inactivity at this point in time. It is altogether fitting and proper that we do this, so that organizational dead heads will not have died in vain.

The real test of inflated language, however, is whether there is a simpler, clearer way to say what you mean. If there is, deflate the language and choose the simpler way.

Try deflating the inflated language in these sentences. The answers are on pages 271 and 272.

16. If we finalize the study prior to August 17, we can utilize the results in September's advertising campaign.

---

17. I have some questions in reference to your July report on whether to implement the new reporting system this month.

---

18. This new policy will impact labor negotiations.

---

19. We have only two options: modify the budget in an upward direction or terminate the project.

---

20. Please utilize ocular safety protection while utilizing the electrically powered implement.

SUBSTANDARD USAGE

Business writing demands more than just clarity. You need to make your reader confident of your carefulness, accuracy, and organization. This means you can't afford to choose grammatical structures that are fuzzy, incoherent, or downright barbaric. If your reader gets the impression that you are a grammatical purist, so much the better. The reputation of being meticulous is not a bad one to have.

In this section we will look at only a few particularly awkward and confusing word habits to avoid.

Barbarisms	*Proper English*
alot	a lot
alright	all right
and etc.	etc.
as far as. . . .	as far as . . . is concerned
can't hardly	can hardly
different than	different from
I could care less	I couldn't care less, or I don't care
in regards to	in regard to, regarding
irregardless	regardless
is when, is where	(Omit *when* or *where* when defining a term.)
less (before plurals)	fewer (before plurals)
not as . . . as	not so . . . as
reason is because	reason is that
should of, would of	should have, would have
try and	try to
very unique	unique (A thing is either unique or it isn't.)

Now do the following exercises. In working them out, try to develop a feeling for words and structures that click into place like the parts of a well-engineered watch. The answers are on page 272.

21. Mr. Robinson said he would try and complete the cost study, irregardless of his busy schedule.

———————————————————————

———————————————————————

22. His method of cost analysis is different than our old one, and his very unique tabulation system requires alot of record keeping, color coding, meter reading, and etc.

———————————————————————

———————————————————————

———————————————————————

23. A raw score is where you simply total the correct answers.

———————————————————————

———————————————————————

24.   The reason the bolts don't fit is because they are metric, but the rivets are alright to use.

_____

_____

_____

25.   I can't hardly imagine why the decision in regards to your request is taking so long; there were less requests submitted than last year, so you should of received an answer by now.

_____

_____

_____

_____

Finally, there is one kind of substandard usage so unpredictable that there are no simple ways for the writer to avoid it—except to stress careful

"The boss prides himself on having the precise word for any occasion."

proofreading. In most cases the problem arises from concentrating too much on spoken English rather than written English. Our language has many homonyms, words that sound alike even though we spell them differently. They often get tangled in our minds and result in written sentences that are sometimes meaningless, sometimes ludicrous, but always embarrassing. In our list, for example, the only explanation for using "should of" instead of "should have" is that the contraction "should've" *sounds* like "should of," and some people tend to write what they think they hear.

But there are some homonyms that are notorious for giving writers fits. What follows is necessarily a very small sampling of an endless list of possible gaffes of this kind. Correct them. The answers are on page 272.

26. He read it allowed, but I couldn't here all the words.

_____

27. Several years ago the gasoline shortage lead to public awareness of energy problems.

_____

_____

28. The breaks on the dump truck are warn out.

_____

29. Do not use letterhead stationary for inter-office memos; use memo forms or plane typing paper.

_____

_____

30. The interviewer tried to illicit some confidential information by making frequent illusions to possible construction sights.

_____

_____

_____

Now let's put it all together. These last five sentences contain general terms, abstractions, clichés, inflated language, and substandard usage. Make whatever revisions you think are necessary.

31. Less than twenty applicants shared their views with us in regards to our training program.

_____

_____

32. In the not too distant future we will have the ability to utilize our optimized billing system.

_____

_____

33. Please share with me your reactions to Ms. Peabody's recommendation.

_____

_____

34. In this day and age, with inflation rearing its ugly head, we must plan very carefully.

_____

_____

35. In the final analysis, after all is said and done, our expenditures will de-escalate.

_____

_____

FOR CLASS DISCUSSION

1. Bring to class examples of inflated language from your own reading. Choose a particularly confusing sentence and put it on the chalkboard. Ask the class for suggestions on how to deflate the language so that it is easier to understand. Keep a list of unusually pompous-sounding words and expressions that you and your classmates discover during this discussion and try to agree upon what they mean in ordinary English.

2. Discuss the validity of the following statements:
(a) I have to use big words. My boss will think I'm uneducated if I don't.
(b) In my profession, I've got to use the terms my colleagues use. They understand my sociological jargon.
(c) Stock phrases are handy. They shorten the time it takes me to write, and I'm very busy.
(d) When writing to customers I try to use legal-sounding terminology. It scares them into accepting my position.
(e) When inditing my missives I select inordinately pellucid diction so as not to give umbrage to vapid perusers who may be egregiously devoid of exegetical capabilities.
(f) Inflated language sounds very objective. I use it so I don't hurt anyone's feelings.
(g) I use clichés so I sound down-to-earth and folksy.
(h) If a janitor wants to be called a maintenance engineer, I call him or her a maintenance engineer. After all, I want people to call me a sanitation engineer, not a garbage collector.
(i) When I write, I use the same kinda words I do when I talk. Ain't that the right way to do it?
(j) I always write as plainly as I can because it takes more intelligence to explain a complicated idea in simple language than it does to explain a simple idea in complicated language. Readers who require simple language are grateful, and readers who don't require simple language are envious.

TEST YOURSELF

This chapter's quiz is more of a learning device than a test. Don't be disappointed if you miss most of the items; the main point of the chapter is that imprecise language is difficult to understand.

Revise the following sentences to remove all vague terms, inflated language, clichés, and substandard usage. The answers are on page 273.

1. Internalize the canine and externalize the feline.

2. The division manager shared some modifications in company policy with me.

3. Utilization of part-time investigative personnel will make possible the finalization of the report within the allowable time frame.

4. We can't hardly keep up with the requests for our maps of this fair city.

5. The reason we purchased the new copier is because the old one was as slow as molasses in January.

6. It has come to my attention that our bleach supplier is throwing in the towel May 5.

7. In the event that you still possess any of our old containers, kindly remit same via parcel post.

8. Do not utilize the north ramp until repairs are finalized.

9. We have at the present time finalized the painting of all our buildings exclusive of Warehouse #7.

10. The new regulations do not impact the normal interface between my department and yours.

11–15. Translate these inflated terms into common English:
(a) facilitate
(b) implement
(c) manifest
(d) optimize
(e) quantify

APPLY YOURSELF

1. Here are ten pairs of terms. In each pair underline the one that is appropriate for business writing.

    a. the reason is because—the reason is that
    b. use—utilization
    c. finish—finalize
    d. share—tell
    e. utilize—use
    f. impact (used as a verb)—affect
    g. change—modification
    h. about—in reference to
    i. prior to—before
    j. option—choice

For each term you underlined, construct a sentence that uses the term correctly. Write sentences you might include in a letter or report in your field.

2. Write a 200-word paragaph describing your duties in a job you now have or have had in the past. Be careful to avoid business jargon. Write your paragraph so that a new employee would understand it easily.

ANSWERS TO EXERCISES

1. Ms. Hartstein <u>concrete</u>
   experience <u>abstract</u>
   efficiency <u>abstract</u>

2. radio <u>concrete</u>
   transistors <u>concrete</u>

3. leadership <u>abstract</u>
   responsibility <u>abstract</u>
   integrity <u>abstract</u>
   decisiveness <u>abstract</u>

4. hemispheres <u>concrete</u>
   specialization <u>abstract</u>

5. attendance <u>abstract</u>
   hall <u>concrete</u>

6. Our sweepers need new brooms. (You are either cynical or verbally playful if you answered, "Our brooms need new sweepers.")

7. Ms. Potter said that the letter was missing.

8. The duplicator can produce twenty-four copies a minute.

9. Gasoline costs 92 per cent more than it did a year ago.

10. I will announce my decision at tomorrow's meeting.

11. It was clear that we would not meet our quota.
OR
      Clearly, we would not meet our quota.
OR
      We knew that we would not meet our quota.

12. Here is the refund you asked for.
OR
      Here is the refund you requested.
OR
      Enclosed is. . . .

13. I want to leave immediately after the last conference.

14. If you approve of this contract, please sign it and return it soon.

15. I think you should write to Bill Rogers before completing your report.

16. If we finish the study before August 17, we can use the results in September's advertising campaign.

17. I have some questions about your July report concerning whether we should start using the new reporting system this month.

18. This new policy will affect labor negotiations.

19. We have just (*or* only) two choices: increase the budget or stop the project.

20. Please wear safety glasses while using the electric sander.

21. Mr. Robinson said he would try to complete (*or* finish) the cost study, regardless of his busy schedule (*or* even though he is busy).

22. His method of cost analysis is different from our old one, and his unique tabulation system requires a lot of record keeping, color coding, meter reading, etc.

23. A raw score is simply the total of correct answers.

24. The reason the bolts don't fit is that they are metric, but the rivets are all right to use.
OR
    The bolts don't fit because they. . . .

25. I can hardly imagine why the decision regarding your request is taking so long; there were fewer requests submitted than last year, so you should have received an answer by now.

26. He read it aloud, but I couldn't hear all the words.

27. Several years ago the gasoline shortage led to public awareness of energy problems.

28. The brakes on the dump truck are worn out.

29. Do not use letterhead stationery for interoffice memos; use memo forms or plain typing paper.

30. The interviewer tried to elicit some confidential information by making frequent allusions (*or* by frequently alluding) to possible construction sites.

31. Fewer than twenty applicants told us what they thought of our training program.

32. We will soon be able to use our improved billing system.

33. Please tell me what you think of Ms. Peabody's recommendation.

34. We must plan very carefully today because of inflation.

35. Eventually our costs will decrease (*or* drop).

ANSWERS TO TEST YOURSELF

1. Let in the dog and put out the cat.

2. The division manager told me about some changes in company policy.

3. Hiring part-time investigators will enable us to complete the report on time.

4. We can hardly keep up with the requests for our city maps.

5. The reason we bought the new copier is that the old one was too slow.
OR
    We bought the new copier because the old one was too slow.

6. I have learned that our bleach supplier is going out of business.

7. If you still have any of our old containers, please send them back to us by parcel post.

8. Do not use the north ramp until repairs are complete.

9. We have now finished painting all our buildings except Warehouse #7.

10. The new regulations do not affect the normal relationship between my department and yours.

11–15. (a) make easier
        (b) put into effect, carry out
        (c) show
        (d) make best use of, use to advantage
        (e) count, describe the amount of

13

Use Parallelism and Balance

You can say a lot in a few words if you combine several statements into one. Parallelism enables you to do that. It consists of saying two, three, four, or more things at once, provided each has something in common with all the others.

Once we master the technique of using parallel structure, we will be able to get rid of a lot of wordiness. But there is a further advantage.

Forming your sentences so that they express similar ideas in parallel structures helps your reader understand concepts that could otherwise be complicated messes. This is true of all language components, from single words right on up through the organization of the outline and coordination of major parts in a formal report. The structure itself reveals relationships. Faulty parallelism does just the opposite; it gives misleading signals that confuse your reader.

First let's see how parallelism can work effectively. Consider these three sentences:

> *We can gather our data by reading books.*
> *We can gather our data by reading newspapers.*
> *We can gather our data by reading magazines.*

The first seven words are the same in each sentence. Why repeat them? Using those words only once, we get

We can gather our data by reading ⟷ books / newspapers / magazines

Smoothing this out with some punctuation and a conjunction, we get the following:

We can gather our data by reading books, newspapers, and magazines.

The three nouns ("books," "newspapers," and "magazines") are *parallel;* they all fit the *common element* (the first seven words of the sentence) in the same way.

But suppose our original three sentences were the following:

We can gather our data by reading books.
We can gather our data by conducting interviews.
We can gather our data by reading magazines.

Now only the first six words are the same in all these sentences. So we have to do our combining like this:

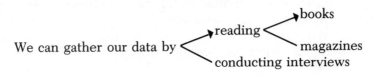

The new sentence would be the following:

We can gather our data by reading books, conducting interviews, and reading magazines.

Here we have three gerund phrases ("reading books," "conducting interviews," and "reading magazines") in parallel. But we're not finished yet. Notice that two of the three structures repeat "reading." We can further tidy up the sentence by arranging the elements this way:

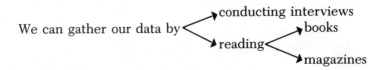

Again supplying some punctuation and a conjunction or two, we get this sentence:

We can gather our data by reading books and magazines and conducting interviews.

Or, we can rearrange the word order, like this:

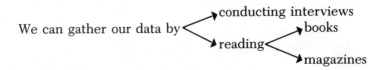

We can gather our data by conducting interviews and reading books and magazines.

Better yet, we can repeat the preposition *by:*

> *We can gather our data by conducting interviews and by reading books and magazines.*

Repeating the preposition in each parallel element insures greater clarity and often provides more flexibility in arranging word order for proper emphasis.

All of the operations we've been performing produce grammatically parallel structures. But we need to be careful not to end up with something like this:

> *We can gather our data by reading books, magazines, and interviews.*

Something obviously went wrong. The reader immediately senses that the parts don't click together right. Here's why:

$$\text{We can gather our data by reading} \underset{?}{\overset{}{\longleftrightarrow}} \begin{array}{l} \text{books} \\ \text{magazines} \\ \text{interviews} \end{array}$$

To avoid this kind of absurdity, we need to remember this rule:

Make sure every parallel item grammatically fits the common element of the sentence.

In our examples so far, the common element precedes the parallel elements. But it doesn't have to. Here it follows them:

> The treasurer's ———→
> The recording secretary's →terms of office expire soon
> The corresponding secretary's

The treasurer's, the recording secretary's, and the corresponding secretary's terms of office expire soon.

And here it encloses them:

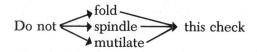

Do not fold, spindle, or mutilate this check.

Parallelism, then, makes it possible to pack several statements into one. In the examples we've used so far, we have joined three parallel elements to the common element, but you can join any number you want to. Just don't overdo it; your reader will have trouble handling more than four or five parallel elements in a single sentence. Two or three are about right.

Let's practice on a few sentences. Combine the given sentences into one. The answers are on page 296.

1. Bill Smith attended the convention.
   Martha Brown attended the convention.
   Gerald Coppersmith attended the convention.

   _____

   _____

2. Bill Smith attended the convention.
   Bill Smith attended the executive-training session afterward.

   _____

   _____

3. Martha Brown attended the convention.
   Martha Brown missed the executive-training session.
   Martha Brown missed the Saturday luncheon.

   _____

   _____

   _____

4. Gerald Coppersmith evaluated the convention.
   Gerald Coppersmith summarized the convention.

   _____

   _____

5. Bill enjoyed the convention.
   Gerald enjoyed the convention.
   Bill signed up for next year.
   Gerald signed up for next year.

   _____

   _____

   _____

   _____

FAULTY PARALLELISM

You may wonder why we're taking the long way around by repeating all those sentences. Are you supposed to write "Read the water-pressure gauge. Read the oil-flow meter." in your first draft before revising it to "Read the water-pressure gauge and the oil-flow meter"? Of course not. But there are two very good reasons for beginning our study the way we did: (1) It's important to realize that each element in parallel implies a whole statement; therefore, don't throw in parallel elements indiscriminately just to fill out a sentence. (2) The procedure we have been using will enable you to correct faulty parallelism in your first drafts. If the elements are parallel, the sentence will read grammatically when you follow any set of arrows. For example, suppose you wrote, "This shipment is as good or better than the last one." You sense that something is wrong here; the sentence just doesn't click together the way it should. Spread it out on a common-element, parallel-element diagram and you get this:

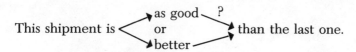

Now the error becomes evident. The upper arrows produce an ungrammatical sentence. You need to change it to read "This shipment is as good as, or better than, the last one."

Let's practice correcting faulty parallelism of this type. Use scratch paper to make "common-element, parallel-element" diagrams before revising the sentences. The answers are on page 296.

6. If you want to add or withdraw from your account, you should bring your passbook with you.

_____

_____

7. This test is an addition, not a replacement, to our regular test.

_____

_____

8. Our system is in accordance, not contrary, to government regulations.

_____

_____

9. The repair estimates are the same, or very close, to the car's total value.

---

10. Our discount rates are equal or higher than our competitors'.

Another kind of faulty parallelism you need to be aware of is that involving correlative conjunctions. These conjunctions come in pairs, like the following:

either . . . or
neither . . . nor
not only . . . but also
whether . . . or
both . . . and

The important thing to remember is this:

Whatever appears between correlative conjunctions must be parallel with what follows the second conjunction.

For instance, the following sentence has faulty parallelism because the correlatives join two different structures—a clause and a verb phrase.

> FAULTY: *Either you must pay the balance in thirty days or open a charge account.*

We can correct it either by making both elements clauses or by making them both phrases:

> *Either you must pay the balance in thirty days or you must open a charge account.*
> *OR*
> *You must either pay the balance in thirty days or open a charge account.*

First identify the correlative conjuctions, then compare what comes between them with what follows the second one; and if they don't match, change one or the other so that they do. Let's try a few. Correct the faulty parallelism in the following sentences:

280

11. Mr. Alwood neither accepted my offer nor did he reject it.

12. We don't know whether to run the test again or if we should check our computations on the last one.

13. Ms. Byron not only reorganized the stockroom, but also the shipping department.

14. By the end of June we will either have all the glue we need or it will be on order.

15. Mr. Thompson's speech was both informative and it was entertaining.

There is one kind of faulty parallelism that the common-element, parallel-element diagram won't help you to avoid. You must be careful not to combine elements that may fit together grammatically, but not smoothly. Don't mix adjectives with nouns, or infinitives with gerunds, even if each one fits the *common element* when read individually. For example, suppose you want to make the following statement:

> *The assistant manager is young.*
> *The assistant manager is energetic.*
> *The assistant manager is a conscientious person.*

After the *common element* you have two adjectives ("young" and "energetic") and a noun ("person"). If you try to make this into a single sentence, you will get faulty parallelism:

> *FAULTY: The assistant manager is young, energetic, and a conscientious person.*

You can correct the sentence by converting the last element into an adjective:

The assistant manager is young, energetic, and conscientious.

Or, suppose you wanted to make these four statements:

I like to fish.
I like camping.
I like swimming.
I like to hunt.

You would have to convert the two gerunds ("camping" and "swimming") to infinitives or the two infinitives ("to fish" and "to hunt") to gerunds before you could put them all into the same parallel structure:

I like to fish, to camp, to swim, and to hunt.
OR
I like fishing, camping, swimming, and hunting.

BALANCED STRUCTURE

So far we've looked at parallel structure mainly with an eye toward avoiding faulty constructions. But if you work at it, you can develop the knack of using parallelism to create a rhythmic, balanced sentence that achieves remarkable emphasis. *Balanced structure* is parallelism in which all the parts have the same internal structure. Usually it consists of the longer elements, like phrases and clauses. The following two sentences show the difference between mere parallelism and balance:

PARALLEL. We found that annually the controls required adjustment, the linkage needed grease every month, the motors needed daily oiling, and hourly the bolts had to be tightened.

BALANCED. We found that the controls needed adjusting every year, the linkage needed greasing every month, the motors needed oiling every day, and the bolts needed tightening every hour.

Two ways to achieve balance are to repeat key words and phrases and to follow the same sequence of parts in each parallel element. Notice the repetition and the sequencing of parts in these balanced sentences:

Our sizes will not shrink, and our colors will not fade.

We will use your new alloy if it is strong enough, cheap enough, and plentiful enough for our purposes.

"Your report, Ferret, is both good and original. Unfortunately, the part that is good is not original, and the part that is original is not good."

Place the good cartons on the conveyor, the mislabeled ones in the rack, and the damaged ones in the bin.

Of course, like all other means of emphasis, balanced structure works best when used very seldom. Don't overdo it. But occasionally, when you want to call attention to a key idea, try phrasing it in this rhythmic way. Let's try just a few exercises to make sure we can construct balanced sentences when we want to. The following are already parallel; make them balanced. The answers are on page 297.

16. We offer guided tours every Monday; on Wednesdays we process job applications; and we conduct, on Thursdays and Fridays, a lecture series.

---

17. Thank you for responding so promptly and for so completely filling out the questionnaire.

OTHER PARALLEL STRUCTURES

Every time you make a list of anything, whether in column form or not, whether two items or several hundred, you must make sure each item is parallel to all the rest. By putting the items in the same list, you are telling your reader that they are coordinate, of equal grammatical importance. This is true for both letters and reports.

If you don't keep your lists parallel, they become confusing. For example, suppose you are the manager of a large hardware store and want to explain to your sales clerks how to handle a cash refund for returned merchandise. You decide to write a memo and have a copy posted by each cash register. Let's also suppose your first draft looks like this:

When a customer wants a cash refund, you should

1. *inspect the merchandise to make sure it is from our store,*
2. *sales slip,*
3. *amount of refund,*
4. *reason for refund,*
5. *customer can redeem voucher for cash at credit desk,*
6. *merchandise then can go back in stock.*

Unless you revise this memo, your sales clerks will have trouble following your directions. In the first place, they are not all directions; some of them are merely nouns. You introduced your list by saying "you should," but not everything you included fits grammatically after this *common element.* You decide to revise, and this time it looks like this:

When a customer wants a cash refund, you should

1. *inspect the merchandise to make sure it is from our store,*
2. *check the sales slip for price paid,*

284

3. *enter amount of refund on credit voucher,*
4. *explain reason for return on credit voucher,*
5. *tell customer to redeem voucher for cash at credit desk,*
6. *put merchandise back in stock.*

Now the items in the list are parallel. Each begins with a verb telling the sales clerk what to *do*. The procedure may or may not be a good one, but at least it is now clear.

What happens when you have a list of items, some of which have lists within them? What about outlines or lengthy reports containing many divisions and subdivisions? Essentially, they are only expansions of the same structure we saw earlier in the sentence

We can gather our data by reading books and magazines and conducting interviews.

In our common-element, parallel-element diagram we explained the structure this way:

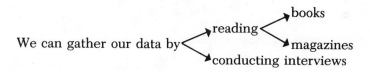

But we might just as well have put it this way:

We can gather our data by
  I. reading
     A. books
     B. magazines
  II. conducting interviews

Notice that the items with Roman numerals are parallel and the items with capital letters are parallel. If we were to subdivide "books" or "magazines," we would use Arabic numerals (1,2,3,4, and so on) for each subdivision, and lower-case letters (a,b,c,d, and so on) for the next subdivision. That's about as far as we will probably ever have to subdivide. Remember, though, that all items within a subdivision must be parallel.

Notice also that no division ever has fewer than two items in a subdivision, if it has any at all. You can't break something down into just one part. If something has only one "part," then that "part" is the thing itself. That's why we didn't list "interviews" under "conducting."

This system of Roman numerals, capital letters, and so on is appropriate only for outlines and formal reports. Business letters and informal reports usually use Arabic numerals for the major divisions and lower-case letters for subdivisions. They rarely need more than these two levels. When they do, they use Arabic numerals and lower-case letters again, but in parentheses:

    1. (First major division)
        a. (First subdivision)
           (1) (Second subdivision)
              (a) (Third subdivision)

Now practice what you've learned by correcting the errors in the following. The answers are on page 297.

18. Correct the errors in the following outline:
      Title: Security System
I. Employees
    A. Salaried
    B. Weekly Wage
    C. Hourly Wage
    D. Non-employees
        1. visitors
        2. vendors

_____

_____

_____

_____

_____

_____

_____

19. Correct the following passage taken from the body of a business letter:
    We need the following:
      a. two ramps for the loading platform
      b. one set of hinges for the following:
         1. cafeteria door
      c. extension cords
         1. two 18′ three-wire
         2. three 12′ two-wire

_____

_____

_____

_____

_____

_____

_____

20. Correct the following list taken from the body of a memo:
Before leaving the job, make sure you
　1.　put all tools away
　2.　clean up your work area
　3.　all windows should be closed
　4.　turning off the electric motors is sometimes forgotten.

_____

_____

_____

_____

Before we quit, let's flex our grammar muscles by correcting the faulty parallelism in these sentences:

21. All the radios in our last shipment were broken, scratched, and some parts were missing.

_____

_____

22. We must either increase production or we must delay some orders.

_____

_____

23. The business writer must use active-voice words, avoid inflated language, and checking for faulty parallelism is also necessary.

_____

_____

_____

24. This model is as good or better than last year's.

_____

25. Our old typewriters were quiet, dependable, and they didn't cost very much.

_____

_____

FOR CLASS DISCUSSION

1. Bring a dictionary to class. On the chalkboard, translate these sentences by Samuel Johnson (1709–1784) into modern English, but keep his sentence structure intact. Then try to come up with a few sentences of the class's own devising that follow the same patterns of parallelism and balance. Use common-element, parallel-element diagrams if you get stuck.

Although Dr. Johnson may seem out of place in a business-writing text, the old gentleman can show us a trick or two about parallelism and balanced structure.

A. *The notice which you have been pleased to take of my labours, had it been early, had been kind; but it has been delayed till I am indifferent, and cannot enjoy it; till I am solitary, and cannot impart it; till I am known, and do not want it.*

—from Letter to the Earl of Chesterfield, February, 1755.

B. *You have conferred your favours on a man who has neither alliance nor interest, who has not merited them by services, nor courted them by officiousness; you have spared him the shame of solicitation, and the anxiety of suspense.*

—from Letter to the Earl of Bute, July 20, 1762.

C. *Letters are written to the great and to the mean, to the learned and the ignorant. . . . Nothing can be more improper than ease and laxity of expression when the importance of the subject impresses solicitude or the dignity of the person exacts reverence.*

—from The Idler, No. 152.

2. Here is an army memorandum explaining how to conduct "Correspondence Quality Control Program" surveys. Boxes mark the places where Arabic numerals and lower-case letters appear in the actual memorandum. As a class, decide what number or letter should go in each box and whether it should have a period after it or parentheses around it. (HINT: Military correspondence indents only the second and third subdivisions.)

DISPOSITION FORM

For use of this form, see AR 340-15; the proponent agency is The Adjutant General's Office.

REFERENCE OR OFFICE SYMBOL	SUBJECT
	Correspondence Quality Control Program Survey

TO	FROM	DATE	CMT 1

☐ Chapter 11, AR 340-15, tasks offices with conducting annual Correspondence Quality Control Program surveys. As shown in the published schedule, your area is slated to survey communications starting next month.

☐ Preparing correspondence is one of the most expensive operations in Army administration. Mistakes may mean that improper actions are taken, By surveying correspondence periodically and finding where errors are being made, training needs and other actions can be determined to save time and produce high quality correspondence. (Individuals will not be penalized for making errors.)

☐ When you have selected your Correspondence Survey Officer (CSO), send us a copy of the appointing document. The CSO will--

☐ Review all outgoing communications.

☐ Fill out a Correspondence Correction Checksheet on each item, and:

☐ If there are no errors, keep the sheet.

☐ If there are errors, place a checkmark in the box which corresponds with the error, add any needed remarks, then:

☐ Attach the checksheet to the item and send it to the responsible person for correction, initialing of the form, and return.

☐ Review the returned corrected item.

☐ If the item is correct, withdraw the checksheet and place it with similar sheets.

☐ Collect the checksheets for about 1 month.

☐ Forward the correct communication for signature, dating, and dispatch.

☐ Tabulate the error data from the collected checksheets onto the Analysis of Correspondence Errors Worksheets (see fig 11-5 and 11-6, AR 340-15, for samples of completed worksheets). Send copies of these through program manager to the manager of the Correspondence Program.

DA ᶠᵒᴿᴹ 1 FEB 82 **2496**   REPLACES DD FORM 96, EXISTING SUPPLIES OF WHICH WILL BE ISSUED AND USED UNTIL 1 FEB 83 UNLESS SOONER EXHAUSTED.

```
SUBJECT:  Correspondence Quality Control Program Survey

☐   After the survey, this office will review the results and, with your
approval, recommend corrective action--including those shown in section II,
chapter 11, AR 340-15.

☐   Your efforts in this survey will help cut costs and improve correspondence

(Use Appropriate Authority Line)


                                        (Use Appropriate Signature Block)
```

TEST YOURSELF

Correct any faulty parallelism in the following sentences. Some sentences need no correction. The answers are on page 298.

1. Product "F" tested higher than product "H" in tensile strength, whiteness, more resilient, and retains water better.

_____

_____

2. Repairing the old clutch plate is as expensive as to buy a new one.

_____

_____

3. You must either spray the orchard or lose the harvest.

_____

4. We reviewed our records, found several errors, and been busy correcting them.

_____

_____

5. The dispatcher should complete this form, keep the yellow copy, and should submit the blue copy to the supervisor.

_____

_____

6. Please revise carefully when writing a formal report or when you have to update a form letter.

_____

_____

7. By the end of August we will have completed our tests, checked the results, and given the new data to the design department.

_____

_____

8. Insurance, transportation, and packaging costs have risen as rapidly, and in some cases more rapidly than production costs.

_____

_____

9. Our new coffee makers not only save energy, but they make excellent coffee too.

_____

_____

10. I believe Mr. Crandon is honest, reliable, tolerates other people's views, and patient when dealing with a customer.

_____

_____

_____

APPLY YOURSELF

Here are fourteen sentences that include everything you have decided to say in a paragraph of a report you are writing. Write the paragraph, using parallelism to combine as many statements into as few sentences as you think are appropriate.

1. Our supply of maple is running low.

2. Our supply of oak is running low too.

3. So is our supply of mahogany.

4. Our birch supply is running low also.

5. Prices for these woods are high right now.

6. Prices for these woods will rise even higher in the next month.

7. We should stop making bookshelves for a while.

8. We should stop making china cabinets for a while.

9. Then we will have enough wood to continue making office desks.

10. We will also have enough wood to continue making dining-room sets.

11. And we will have enough wood to continue making bedroom furniture.

12. We can do this until wood prices drop.

13. They will drop a month from now.

14. Or, they will drop two months from now.

ANSWERS TO EXERCISES

1. Bill Smith, Martha Brown, and Gerald Coppersmith attended the convention.

2. Bill Smith attended the convention and the executive-training session afterward.

3. Martha Brown attended the convention, but missed the executive-training session and the Saturday luncheon.

4. Gerald Coppersmith evaluated and summarized the convention.
OR
    Gerald Coppersmith evaluated the convention and summarized it.

5. Bill and Gerald enjoyed the convention and signed up for next year.

6. If you want to add to or withdraw from your account, you should bring your passbook with you.
OR
    If you want to add to your account or withdraw from it, you should bring your passbook with you.

7. This test is an addition to, not a replacement for, our regular test.
OR
    This test is an addition to our regular test, not a replacement for it.

8. Our system is in accordance with, not contrary to, government regulations.
OR
    Our system is in accordance with government regulations, not contrary to them.

9. The repair estimates are the same as, or very close to, the car's total value.
OR
    The repair estimates are the same as the car's total value, or very close to it.

10. Our discount rates are equal to, or higher than, our competitors'.

11. Mr. Alwood neither accepted nor rejected my offer.

12. We don't know whether to run the test again or to check our computations on the last one.

13. Ms. Byron reorganized not only the stockroom, but also the shipping deparment.

14. By the end of June either we will have all the glue we need or it will be on order.

15. Mr. Thompson's speech was both informative and entertaining.

16. We offer guided tours every Monday, process job applications every Wednesday, and conduct a lecture series every Thursday and Friday.
OR
    On Mondays we offer guided tours, on Wednesdays we process job applications, and on Thursdays and Fridays we conduct a lecture series.
(NOTE: There are several other solutions. You are correct if you made all three parallel elements follow the same pattern.)

17. Thank you for responding so promptly and for filling out the questionnaire so completely.

18. Title: Security System
    I. Employees
        A. Salaried
        B. Weekly Wage
        C. Hourly Wage
   II. Non-employees
        A. Visitors
        B. Vendors

19. We need the following:
    1. two ramps for the loading platform
    2. one set of hinges for the cafeteria door
    3. extension cords
        a. two 18′ three-wire
        b. three 12′ two-wire

20. Before leaving the job, make sure you
    1. put all tools away
    2. clean up your work area
    3. close all windows
    4. turn off the electric motors.

21. All the radios in our last shipment were broken and scratched, and some parts were missing.
OR
    All the radios in our last shipment were broken, scratched, and missing some parts.

22. We must either increase production or delay some orders.
OR
    Either we must increase production or we must delay some orders.

23. The business writer must use active-voice verbs, avoid inflated language, and check for faulty parallelism.

24. This model is as good as, or better than, last year's.

25. Our old typewriters were quiet, dependable, and inexpensive.
OR
    Our old typewriters were quiet, they were dependable, and they didn't cost very much.

ANSWERS TO TEST YOURSELF

1. Product "F" tested higher than product "H" in tensile strength, whiteness, resiliency, and water retention.

2. Repairing the old clutch plate is as expensive as buying a new one.
OR
    To repair the old clutch plate is as expensive as to buy a new one.

3. The sentence is correct.

4. We reviewed our records, found several errors, and have been busy correcting them.

5. The dispatcher should complete this form, keep the yellow copy, and submit the blue copy to the supervisor.

6. Please revise carefully when writing a formal report or when updating a form letter.
OR
    Please revise carefully when writing a formal report or updating a form letter.

7. The sentence is correct.

8. Insurance, transportation, and packaging costs have risen as rapidly as, and in some cases more rapidly than, production costs.

9. Our new coffee makers not only save energy, but make excellent coffee.

10. I believe Mr. Crandon is honest, reliable, tolerant of other people's views, and patient when dealing with a customer.

14

Maintain Continuity

When you sit down to compose a business letter or write up a report of any kind, you must never become so engrossed in your subject that you forget about your reader. It is true that your own intense interest in the content of your message and some careful organizing on your part will do much to help your reader follow your train of thought. But they are seldom enough. In fact, if you are not careful, your own enthusiasm can lead you to include some things that will only distract your reader from your central message, and your organizational plan can sometimes make you leave out a few things your reader really needs to know.

Therefore, always keep your reader in mind as you write. As you string out sentence after sentence, remember that someone is going to have to travel mentally wherever you are leading, so blaze a trail that's easy to follow. Don't make a sudden turn of direction, even within a sentence, without giving enough "detour signs" for your reader to make the turn too.

There's one simple habit you can develop for eliminating the great majority of incoherent paragraphs and contradictory statements that tend to crop up in first drafts. Before writing each new sentence, especially if you had to wait some time until it formed in your mind, put yourself in your reader's place and read all the sentences you have written so far in that paragraph. Then ask yourself what you, as the reader, would *expect* to find in the next sentence or would *like* to see there. Do the same thing each time you begin a new paragraph. Read all your previous paragraphs to yourself as if you were the reader, not the writer. Make sure the paragraph you are about to write will satisfy your reader's expectations. If it will not, perhaps you had better insert a short transition paragraph explaining why you find it necessary to change direction. In other words, give your reader a new set of expectations, and then make sure you satisfy them.

Perhaps you think all this rereading of what you have already written is very time consuming. Well, it does take a little time. But it saves hours of frustration later on. It's too late to discover your letter or report is incoherent after you have finished the whole draft. The odds against successfully revising a paragraph after you have written other paragraphs that depend on it are about the same as the odds against successfully filling an inside straight in a poker game. Don't bet on either one.

Sometimes the writer has a poor understanding of the relationships among ideas in the message. The reader then will not be able to follow a reasonable train of thought because there won't be any. More often, though, the writer will understand the relationships well enough, but faulty grammar or a careless omission of a transitional link will make the train of thought just as hard for the reader to follow as if there weren't any there.

This text cannot help you write coherently if you don't have a clear notion of what you want to say—except to advise you to do some more thinking before setting out to write. However, if your problem is faulty grammar or inadequate transitional links, you will find some ways to improve

"Here's your last paragraph: 'Regarding our phone conversation of the 14th, please confirm our order for a carload of great legs.'"

your coherence and clarity in this chapter. We will discuss first what you can do to improve the coherence of your sentences and then what you can do to help your reader follow the thought sequences of your paragraphs.

INCOHERENCE IN THE SENTENCE

It is very important that subject and verb agree with each other grammatically. If they don't, the reader can't easily connect one part of the sentence with the other. For example, if you write, "The responsibilities of the superintendent includes hiring and firing," your reader will get confused. The first part of the sentence sets up an expectation that doesn't get fulfilled. The plural noun *responsibilities* can't be the subject of the singular verb *includes,* but then the singular noun *superintendent* can't be the subject either; it is already the object of the preposition *of,* and a word can't be both subject and object at the same time.

Actually, you should have very little trouble making subjects and verbs agree if you apply the principles laid down in other parts of this text. Difficulties arise when you construct sentences that don't have the subject in the usual position immediately before the verb, and many chapters in this book try to get you to see that the normal sentence patterns—subject-verb-object, for instance—are the best ones for a business writer to use.

A few rules, however, will further help you avoid mismatching your subjects and verbs:

Objects of prepositions cannot be subjects of verbs.

Three road signs on the recently completed interstate highway have arrows pointing the wrong way.

When you use the "dummy subject" there, the true subject appears after the verb.

There are three incorrect road signs.
There is a caution sign near the ramp.
There are a package and a letter on your desk.

A relative pronoun has the same number (singular or plural) as its antecedent. (Note: If you construct your sentences the way Chapter 4 tells you to, you will have no trouble identifying the antecedents of your relative pronouns.)

He is one of many who have invested in real estate.

He is making three copies of the report that is due tomorrow.

Compound subjects joined by <u>and</u> are always plural; compound subjects joined by <u>or</u> or <u>nor</u> have the same number (singular or plural) as the last item in the series.

<u>Sharon Brown, James Dillworth, and Joan Petty</u> <u>have completed</u> their training.
Either the manager or his <u>two assistants</u> <u>have done</u> the research.
Either the two assistants or their <u>manager</u> <u>has done</u> the research.

Although collective nouns like *commitee, team,* and *faculty* can be either singular or plural, it is better to use a plural noun with them when you use them in the plural:

Grammatical but Awkward: The <u>committee</u> <u>disagree</u> with each other.
Better: <u>Members</u> of the committee <u>disagree</u> with each other.

The pronoun <u>none</u> can be either singular or plural.

<u>None</u> of us <u>is</u> sure what the new rule means.
<u>None</u> of us <u>are</u> sure what the new rule means.

Now let's try some exercises. In the following sentences, underline the correct choice in the parentheses. The answers are on page 315.

1.   One of our production departments (has, have) set a new record for consecutive hours without a lost-time injury.

2.   There (is, are) cash prizes for the best three entries.

3.   Ms. Stallings is one of those who (likes her, like their) coffee steaming hot.

4.   Neither Gerald, Marlin, nor their wives (want, wants) to attend the convention.

5.   There (is, are) two alternates arriving at 4:00 P.M.

You may run into a different sort of problem that can also make it hard for your reader to follow your train of thought. You need to be careful of pronoun reference. When you write the first part of a sentence, you put certain limitations on your pronoun choices in the rest of the sentence. That is, you must make sure you don't give your reader a singular noun in the first part of your sentence and then later refer to that noun with a plural pronoun, like this:

Faulty: When an <u>employee</u> needs a new pair of safety shoes, <u>they</u> can order them through the personnel department.

Nor should you use a singular pronoun to refer to a plural noun, like this:

Faulty: We had five hundred <u>envelopes</u> on Monday, but <u>it</u> was all gone by Friday.

Such errors are annoying to the reader and embarrassing to you, the writer.

A more serious kind of error is using a pronoun in such a way that it can have more than one antecedent. In a sentence like the following, for example, the pronoun *they* could refer either to *Adams and Holmes* or to *the night crew:*

Faulty: We suggested moving Adams and Holmes to the night crew, but they refused.

The only solution is to recast the sentence:

Adams and Holmes refused our suggestion that they move to the night crew.
OR
The night crew refused our suggestion that they take Adams and Holmes.

Now let's practice straightening out pronoun antecedents. Some of the following sentences are correct, and some are unclear because of faulty pronoun reference. Correct the ones that are unclear. The answers are on page 315.

6. He came in with his arms full of packages and set it down on my desk.

7. Each committee member made several objections, but they were all minor.

8. Each crew member buys their own tools.

9. Olson and Bailey may apply for the position as soon as it is available.

10. Olson and Bailey may not apply for the positions, even if they are available.

_____

_____

There is one other thing you can do within the sentence to help your reader follow your line of thought. You can use conjunctions and similar constructions as signposts to point the way. Conjunctions are words like *and, or, but, nor, for, yet, so, however, consequently, therefore, nevertheless, moreover,* and the like. Most of them fall into one of three general categories of meaning:

SIMILARITY	CONTRAST	CAUSALITY
and	but	so
moreover	yet	for
furthermore	however	therefore
likewise	nevertheless	consequently
similarly	on the other hand	as a result

Some of these are more powerful than others. The word *nevertheless,* for instance, carries much more emphasis—and is more important as an aid to your reader—than the "all-purpose" conjunction *and.* So choose your verbal signposts carefully, using the stronger ones sparingly and judiciously. Place them strategically, too—generally at the beginning of a clause. If you use them carefully, you can almost lead your reader by the hand to an understanding of your specific meaning.

Contrasting conjunctions are really indispensable to sentence clarity. We can show this by experimenting with a couple of sentences:

> *The advertising campaign is very successful; therefore, we will continue it for another month.*

> *Production costs have risen sharply; however, we will not have to increase our prices until next year.*

If we remove the conjunctions *therefore* and *however,* the first sentence will still make sense, but the second one won't. The contrasting conjunction *however* is necessary for revealing the relationship between the two clauses.

There is one other thing—the matter of positioning. It is true that because the longer conjunctions are actually sentence modifiers you can place them anywhere you want to in the clause. And sometimes you may want to put them at the end for emphasis. But you will be helping your reader the most if you put them at the beginning of the clause. In that position, they can alert your reader to the direction the next clause will take. Notice that in the following sentence the reader must do some mental backtracking when coming to the last word:

Production costs have risen sharply; we will not have to increase our prices until next year, however.

You don't want your reader to feel like a motorist coming upon a road sign that says, "You should have taken a right turn two miles back."

Now let's practice giving the reader adequate signposts. In the following sentences, insert an appropriate conjunction in the blank. Be sure to insert the proper punctuation, too. The answers are on page 315.

11. Certificates of deposit yield high interest rates _____ there is a severe interest penalty for early withdrawal.

12. We had to shut down the entire production line _____ we had no more packing cases.

13. We had no more packing cases _____ we had to shut down the entire production line.

14. Buying from a nearby supplier would save us shipping costs

_____ it would shorten delivery time.

15. The department has enough typing paper for the next three months

_____ it should order some before the prices increase next month.

COHERENCE IN THE PARAGRAPH

Does it strike you as unusual that we labeled the last section *Incoherence in the Sentence* and this section *Coherence in the Paragraph?* Why talk about incoherence then and coherence now? We did that because business writers seem to have most trouble *avoiding* obstacles to coherence (like faulty agreement) in their sentences and *providing* enough signposts for coherence (like transitional links) in their paragraphs.

First of all, organize your paragraphs deductively, except in Bad-News letters (See Chapter 9). That is, let the reader know at the outset of each paragraph where you are heading in that paragraph. Give your topic sentence early—either as the first or as the second sentence. Then support that topic sentence with sentences that give the details, the explanations, or the examples your reader will need in order to fully understand what the topic sentence means.

Here is a paragraph with the topic sentence at the end, rather than at the beginning where it belongs. After reading the paragraph through once, put the last sentence first and read it again. Notice how much easier it is to follow the train of thought with the topic sentence at the beginning.

I will finish my engineer training program. The contract for concrete work on the south gate will be ready for signatures. Lesson plans for instrumentation instruction will go to the printer. And my six-month quality study of production #3 will be ready for typing by the end of the month. These are the projects I will have completed by the end of July.

Also in every paragraph, be sure to provide your reader with enough repetition of your key terms to assure easy understanding. Remember that a business writer's task is a bit different from that of a novelist or an essayist. As a business writer, your primary concern is clarity. Where a novelist will use a synonym for a term that otherwise would appear too frequently, a good business writer will use the term itself. In your profession, it is better to give up a little variety in language in order to make sure your reader knows precisely what you mean. For instance, a novelist might write a paragraph like this:

The hunter, with his 30.06 held loosely aslant his chest, walked quietly through the dry leaves. The musing nimrod recalled when his parents had given him that deer rifle on his sixteenth birthday, more than seven years before. It was a beautiful weapon, one that any disciple of Orion might boast of while comparing firearms with other celebrants of this annual ritual, this yearly pursuit of hind and hart.

Now that's mighty fine writing—for a novelist. But you are not a novelist. You are a business writer. And if you were to revise that paragraph for clarity, you would get rid of those synonyms for *hunters* and *30.06 deer rifles.* Your paragraph would perhaps be less colorful, but it would be a lot easier to understand. Let's try it.

The hunter, with his 30.06 deer rifle held loosely aslant his chest, walked quietly through the dry leaves. He recalled when his parents had given him that rifle on his sixteenth birthday, more than seven years before. It was a beautiful rifle, one that any deer hunter might boast of while comparing rifles with other deer hunters.

In a way, we have spoiled the novelist's paragraph. But we have spoiled it only as a paragraph in a novel. In business writing you must always call each thing by the same name throughout your paragraph—throughout the whole letter or report, for that matter. Synonyms, while they add variety, also make your reader wonder if you're still talking about the same thing. Don't be afraid to repeat key terms whenever you need to.

Finally, the same advice we gave earlier in the chapter when talking about sentences applies to the paragraph. We saw how sentences became clearer when conjunctions (i.e., transitions) appeared at the beginning rather than at the end of the clause. You also need to provide transitions at the beginning of the paragraph and at the beginning of many of the sentences in it.

If a new paragraph is going to turn to a topic contrary to, or at least very different from, the topic of the previous paragraph, you need to explain that in the first sentence. For instance, here is the last part of one paragraph and the first part of the next one. Notice the transitional sentence at the beginning of the second paragraph.

> . . . *Besides, most students did well on the mid-term test, averaging 89 per cent in both sections. This seems to support the students' comments that the course was very easy.*
>
> *However, these test results reveal only part of the picture. On the final examination, both sections scored very poorly. Section A averaged 71 per cent and Section B averaged 68 per cent, for an overall average in both sections of . . .*

But contrasting paragraphs are not the only ones that can use a transition sentence to show the relationship between them. A paragraph which carries the same topic a step further than the one before it can benefit from a transitional sentence at the beginning too. Consider the following:

> . . . *Our Jamestown plant also manufactures electrical appliances, metering instruments, and a few garden tools. Its production has increased 12 per cent in the last year.*
>
> *However, the Jamestown plant is not the only one that has shown remarkable growth this past year. Our St. Louis plant has increased its overall production 9 per cent in that same period, mostly by doubling its output of electronic calculators and digital watches. We plan to invest even more in these lines at St. Louis because we anticipate . . .*

For another example of such a transition to open a new paragraph, look again at the first sentence of the paragraph you are now reading.

Now let's practice reorganizing a few paragraphs and relocating some of the transitions in them so that the paragraphs are easier to understand. The next five exercise items refer to the following paragraphs. I have numbered the sentences so we can refer to them later on. The answers are on page 315.

(1) Two intercoms will probably need complete refurbishing sometime in the next four months. (2) One of these may be in good enough condition to require only minor repairs, however. (3) Four wireless "beepers," on the other hand, need a few inexpensive repairs immediately. (4) As you requested, this is the summary of maintenance needed on our communication equipment.

(5) Seven calculators have broken in the last month. (6) They are less expensive to replace than they are to repair. (7) You also asked for a summary of maintenance on our pocket calculators. (8) I suggest we buy seven new ones to replace them rather than try to repair the old ones, therefore.

16. Reorganize the first paragraph and list the sequence of sentences in your new version.

_____

17. Rewrite sentence 2 so that the transition becomes more effective.

_____

_____

18. Rewrite sentence 3 so that the transition becomes more effective.

_____

_____

19. Reorganize the second paragraph and list the sequence of sentences in your new paragraph.

_____

20. Rewrite sentence 8 so that the transition becomes more effective.

_____

_____

The next five exercise items refer to this paragraph:

(1) We are well ahead of schedule on our PCB report to the Water-Pollution Control Commission. (2) Our testing laboratory has sample waste water from three of the five factories located near the river. (3) Field workers have had difficulty getting samples from the other two. (4) They expect to have them by May 1. (5) We can easily get our complete report finished by the July 1 deadline. (6) We are working on an improved definition of acceptable PCB levels.

21. Which of the following might you use as a transition at the beginning of sentence 2?
a. On the other hand
b. In fact
c. Consequently

22. Which of the following might you use as a transition at the beginning of sentence 3?
a. However
b. As a result
c. Therefore

23. Which of the following might you use as a transition at the beginning of sentence 4?

a. And

b. Therefore

c. Nevertheless

24. Which of the following might you use as a transition at the beginning of sentence 5?

a. But

b. However

c. Consequently

25. Which of the following might you use as a transition at the beginning of sentence 6?

a. In the meantime

b. Consequently

c. Yet

FOR CLASS DISCUSSION

1. Chapter 11 tells you not to waste words. Yet, the present chapter tells you to insert transitions like "on the other hand," "as a result," and "nevertheless." Do the two chapters contradict each other? Discuss.

2. Would you use more frequent transitions in a letter explaining to a customer why you cannot increase her credit limit or in a monthly report to your boss on the training status of your department? Give reasons for your answer.

3. Would you expect to find more transitions in a newspaper's account of a news story or in a textbook's explanation of a difficult concept? Bring to class samples of each kind of writing to support your answer.

TEST YOURSELF

The answers are on page 316.

Underline the correct choices:

1. For only twenty dollars more, you can have one of our deluxe models that (has, have) adjustable wheels.

2. There (was, were) several discrepancies in Ms. Alcox's account of the accident.

3. Neither the director nor her assistant (knows, know) anything about the new office assignments.

4. Both the director and her assistant (is, are) at a meeting in Toledo.

5. All employees must have (his or her, their) eyes examined each year.

6. We have had good results with our graphite lubricant; (consequently, however), I think we should try the silicone spray to see if it works even better.

7. Mr. Leroy was due back in town this Tuesday, (and, but) he has been delayed and will not arrive until Thursday.

The last three items refer to this paragraph:

(1) We have finished our eight-hour test run with the Adams Company's bottle cappers. (2) They reduced jam-ups by 30 per cent. (3) They capped five more bottles an hour than our present cappers. (4) They produced forty-nine more poorly sealed bottles than our present cappers. (5) We suggest we continue to use our present brand of cappers.

8. If you decided to begin sentence 3 with a transition, which of the following would you use?
a. However
b. Yet
c. Furthermore

9. If you decided to begin sentence 4 with a transition, which of the following would you use?
a. And
b. However
c. Besides

10. If you decided to begin sentence 5 with a transition, which of the following would you use?
a. Nevertheless
b. Therefore
c. On the other hand

313

APPLY YOURSELF

Your company is considering changing from bias-ply to radial-ply tires on its fleet of twelve cars. Your boss asked you to investigate the pros and cons of such a change and to make your recommendations early next week.

Here are the facts you have dug up:

1. Bias-ply tires cost $27.50 each.

2. Your company's cars with radials on them would use about fifty gallons of gas every thousand miles.

3. Radials cost fifty-eight dollars each.

4. Radials last about forty-five thousand miles.

5. Bias-ply tires last about twenty-two thousand miles.

6. Your company's cars with bias-ply tires on them would use about sixty gallons of gas every thousand miles.

7. Each of your company's cars averages about eighteen thousand miles of travel a year.

8. Your company trades in its cars every three years.

9. Your company has had the cars a year.

10. Whether the cars have bias-ply or radial tires makes no difference in trade-in value.

Now make your recommendation, supporting it with two paragraphs—one explaining the advantages of your recommendation and the other explaining the comparatively minor disadvantages of it. DO NOT DEVOTE ONE PARAGRAPH TO RADIAL TIRES AND THE OTHER TO BIAS-PLY TIRES.

Make sure you can provide enough transitions so that your boss can easily follow your line of reasoning.

Underline the transitions so your instructor can more easily evaluate your paragraphs.

ANSWERS TO EXERCISES

1. has

2. are

3. like their

4. want

5. are

6. He came in with his arms full of packages and set them down on my desk.

7. The sentence is correct.

8. All crew members buy their own tools.
OR
    Each crew member buys his or her own tools.

9. The sentence is correct.

10. Even if Olson and Bailey are available, they may not apply for the positions.
OR
    Even if the positions are available, Olson and Baily may not apply for them.

11. ; however, OR (; nevertheless,) (, yet) (; on the other hand,) (, but)

12. because OR (, for)

13. ; therefore, OR (; consequently,) (; as a result,) (, so)

14. ; furthermore, OR (, and) (; moreover,) (; likewise,) (; similarly,)

15. , but OR (; however,) (; nevertheless,) (; on the other hand,) (, yet)

16. 4, 1, 2, 3

17. However, one of these may be in good enough condition to require only minor repairs.

18. On the other hand, four wireless "beepers" need a few inexpensive repairs immediately.

19. 7, 5, 6, 8

20. Therefore, we should replace them rather than repair them.

21. b

22. a

23. c

24. c

25. a

ANSWERS TO TEST YOURSELF

1. have
2. were
3. knows
4. are
5. their
6. however
7. but
8. c
9. b
10. b

Part V

Reports

15

Memorandums and Periodic Reports

The purpose of all reports is to communicate information clearly and accurately. An unclear report is useless; an inaccurate report is dangerous.

Accuracy, of course, depends entirely on the writer's willingness to be both thorough and careful in gathering data for the report. This book cannot help you become more meticulous in selecting and checking your information—except to emphasize that no one can write a worthwhile report without first getting all the facts straight and thoroughly understanding them. The road to accuracy has no shortcuts.

But clarity is another matter altogether. You can learn some shortcuts that will enable you to state your intent more clearly, and they will often help you to understand your message better yourself. Unfortunately, clear reports are not merely the result of the writer's willingness to spend a lot of time in writing and revising. If you want your report to be clear, you must also learn how the reader's mind works; and then you must shape your language so that it stays out of the way. You want to keep a straight, uncluttered path between your reader's thoughts and the content of your message. You have already learned some techniques for doing this.

The earlier chapters of this book taught you how to select the most readable way of expressing your ideas from among several other possible ways that were grammatical, but hard to understand. Having studied those chapters, you would certainly never write a monstrous sentence like this:

It has been recommended by the mechanical engineer that due to the fact that the apparatus by which the cartons are sealed and which has been readjusted many times in the past has not been found to be able to maintain its alignment, it should be removed and replaced by us at this point in time with a similar apparatus that is new.

319

You would, instead, avoid passive voice, noun clutter, vague language, and inflated terminology and write this instead:

The mechanical engineer said we should install a new carton sealer because the old one will not hold an adjustment.

Both sentences are grammatical, but you have learned much more than mere grammaticality.

It is plain, then, that brushing up on your grammar is not enough, although it is a very important first step. You must try to develop a feel for the direct statement that gets the job done without any wasted motion, just as you developed a feel for what reinforces goodwill in a business letter. In fact, most of what you learned in those earlier chapters will apply to your writing of reports. The report writer, like the letter writer, must avoid the inflated, cliché-filled gobbledegook that hides its meaning in a fog of words. Writing one style rather than another is really a matter of habit, and the rest of this book will give you a chance to reinforce the good habits you now have and to learn some others that will help you write clear, informative reports.

Even though letter writing and report writing have many things in common, you should be aware of important differences between them. Here are some of the more obvious ones:

1. A letter emphasizes courtesy, observes social amenities, and exudes goodwill; a report is considerably less personal and emphasizes information and interpretation of data. *Please* and *thank you* appear in almost every business letter; they almost never appear in a report.

2. The cardinal virtue of a good business letter is its cordial, businesslike tone; the cardinal virtue of a report is its clear organization and logic.

3. A business letter should appeal to both head and heart; a report appeals only to the head.

4. Most letters are requests, announcements of decisions, or persuasive appeals to readers outside the company; most reports present or interpret information to readers within the company.

Just as when preparing to write a business letter you must make sure you have a positive attitude toward your reader, when putting together any kind of report you should always first make sure you are in the right frame of mind. Your mental attitude has a definite effect on your report's tone, clarity, persuasiveness, and overall readability. Don't think of writing your report as drudgery, as a burden you have to carry, or as an obligation you have to fulfill (it may be all of those things, but don't *think* of it that way). Think of it rather as an *opportunity* for you to call attention to something overlooked, to demonstrate your sound judgment, to circulate valuable information. If you think of your report as only so much "Mickey Mouse" paperwork that must be done because somebody requires it, your writing will definitely show that attitude.

Try to see yourself as a kind of servant or assistant to your reader. This does not imply subservience, but rather a willingness to assist, to do the necessary legwork in gathering information, to go out of your way to arrange data for your reader's convenience. Look at your material from your reader's point of view, not your own. Keep asking yourself such questions as "Will my reader want more details?" "Will my reader really want to know all this, or am I just putting it in to be impressive?" "How can I arrange my report so that what I have to say will enter my reader's mind in the most understandable sequence?" and "Have I anticipated any probable questions my reader may have after reading my report?"

The answers to these questions will immediately convince you that the act of preparing a report and the act of reading and interpreting it are just the reverse of each other.

Therefore: gather data inductively, but write your report deductively.

For example, suppose you are reporting on some equipment breakdown in your department. To write the report you will need to do the following, in order:

1. *Determine* what happened by recalling your own experience and gathering facts, figures, statistics.
2. *Interpret* this evidence so that it adds up to some kind of conclusion.
3. *State* what action you took, or somebody should take, to correct the problem.

Now, if you write it up in that order, your reader will have a very nice history of your activities, but that is not what your reader needs or wants. Your report must digest that information and rearrange it so that it will enter your reader's mind in the most understandable order. That usually means you need to start your explanation where your experience *ended;* let your reader know first where you're going and *then* explain how to get there. In this case, then, it would be better to begin by stating what action you took, or somebody should take, and then follow with the reasons (facts, data, and interpretation of them) that will convince your reader that your first statement is valid, sound, and based on good judgment. After all, when you work out a problem, you often make false starts, try solutions that don't work, and sometimes even misunderstand the problem itself at first. Why lead your reader through all this? Wouldn't *you* rather read the key idea first and then the reasons that support it, explain it, or justify it?

There is really only one situation that justifies organizing your report inductively. When you are *sure* your reader will be hostile to what you must say, you are better off saving your unwelcome conclusions, hard-to-sell recommendations, or other "bad news" until after you have shown them to be logically inevitable. But such a situation is not very common in report writing—not nearly so common as the "Bad-News" letter situation is. So, generally you should follow the rule GATHER DATA INDUCTIVELY, BUT WRITE YOUR REPORT DEDUCTIVELY—yet temper it with your own common sense.

Most companies have their own printed forms for the majority of their routine messages and short reports that circulate within the organization. Some use the heading "Interoffice Correspondence," "Interdepartmental

Memo," or simply "Memorandum." Near the top of all of them you will find places to enter at least these three items: (1) the person(s) addressed, (2) the writer, and (3) the date. Nearly all of them also include a fourth item, the subject of the message. Many also include such things as retention limit (the date after which the reader is free to throw the message away), a box labeled "Read and Out," indicating whether the reader is free to throw the message away immediately after reading it, or other boxes and blanks the writer can check or fill in to simplify filing, routing, or referencing by account numbers, etc.

Such forms are extremely flexible, and most companies use them for practically all written messages, whether to a boss, a subordinate, or a colleague. You will often find this same form used within a company for bulletin-board messages and for periodic (daily, weekly, monthly) reports all up and down the organizational structure. Some people call them "To-From-Subject-Date" messages, but we will call them simply "memorandums" (or "memos") because the name implies the message can be either a reminder of something important or new information which the reader should remember. (We will use the Anglicized plural form *memorandums*, rather than the Latin plural form *memoranda*.)

These forms are so various in use and layout that it is very hard to generalize about them beyond what we have already noted, except to say that they usually differ from an ordinary letter in three ways:

1. The writer does not sign at the bottom, but rather *initials* his or her typewritten name where it appears after "From:"
2. There is a tendency to list and enumerate, rather than to write in paragraphs, and
3. If there are two or more subdivisions of the main subject, the memorandum usually includes a heading for each.

Here are a few examples to illustrate:

Memo

Date: October 3, 1980
To: Humanities Faculty

From: Bob Van Burke *BVB*
Subject: Media Services Budget

Media Services has informed me that the 1980–81 budget in your discipline has been allocated as follows:

ENGLISH:	FILM RENTAL	MATERIALS
Jones	$212.50	$ 13.50
Smith	148.75	63.00
Kelly	170.00	112.50
staff	255.00	

If you have questions about this, call me or Linda Jamison in Media Services before our October 17 budget review.

Interdepartmental Correspondence

From:	*Gary Smith*	*Date:*	*12/14/79*
To:	*Engineering Group B*	*Retention Limit:*	*12/80*
Subject:	*Effective Writing*	*Attention:*	*D. Nolan*
			E. Ward
			F. Jamison
			L. Zimmer
			B. Mayhew
			G. Yolt

This is to confirm your participation in the Effective Writing Course and to pass on final details.

The course will run for six days—January 2, 4, 8, 10, 15, and 17. Each of you will have one hour with Professor Eglind, according to the following schedule:

> *8:00 A.M. to 9:00 A.M.—Dan Nolan*
> *9:00 A.M. to 10:00 A.M.—Erland Ward*
> *10:00 A.M. to 11:00 A.M.—Frances Jamison*
> *11:00 A.M. to 12:00 P.M.—Linda Zimmer*
> *1:00 P.M. to 2:00 P.M.—Barry Mayhew*
> *2:00 P.M. to 3:00 P.M.—Gary Yolt*

Your conferences with Dr. Eglind will be in David Lind's office in the personnel building.

The attached sheet outlines the preparation you will need to make before attending your first session.

Attachments
cc: Professor George Eglind
     1818 Barlow Street
     Monterey, CA 90901

The variety of memorandum forms is endless, of course, because each company designs its own to suit its own organizational needs. However, filling in the blanks at the top of most of them should pose no problem for you. But what about the message itself? Is there a certain style you should use in a memorandum? Should you use jargon and longer sentences than you would in a business letter? The answers to these questions depend on your purpose and your reader. You are likely to know quite a bit about your reader when you write a memorandum, and that means that if you are sure technical terminology or even jargon will give your reader no difficulty, then use it. Never forget you are writing to another human being, and your purpose is to communicate clearly.

Despite the several differences we have noted between a business letter and a memorandum, you will find that the actual message, or body, of the memorandum resembles the body of a business letter with the introductory and concluding paragraphs deleted. The "SUBJECT:" line tells what the letter is about, so there is no need for an introductory paragraph. Furthermore, your reader knows how to reach you for any necessary clarifications because you both work at the same place. Your willingness to assist goes without saying; it's part of your job. Therefore, there is no need for the customary final paragraph of a business letter.

Because the memorandum form is so flexible, serving such a variety of purposes, it would be virtually impossible to get some practice in writing all the kinds. But we can try a few typical ones. First we will put together

"He was just dictating a memo on plant safety when his stuffed swordfish fell off the wall."

324

a memorandum that makes an announcement and gives instructions. Here are some scrambled facts about a theoretical situation:

1. Employees can pick up reimbursement forms in the personnel office.

2. The employees must have their druggists record each purchase of a prescribed drug on the form.

3. Starting January 1, 1981, the group insurance will reimburse employees for the cost of prescription drugs and medication in excess of fifty dollars a year.

4. Today's date is December 1, 1980.

5. The personnel office has information on two new retirement programs.

6. Your name is Sandra Cornish, personnel director.

7. Your memo will go to all employees.

8. Your company will pay the entire cost of this additional insurance coverage.

9. At first the insurance company sent the wrong forms, but you have the right ones now.

10. An employee can turn in the completed form to the personnel office for reimbursement any time after exceeding the fifty-dollar deductible for the year.

Before writing the memo, answer these questions. The answers are on page 341.

1. Which of the following would be the best entry for the "Subject:" line?
(a) Personnel office hours
(b) Changes for next year
(c) Reimbursement for medicine and drug expense
(d) New insurance forms

2. Which numbered fact best states the key idea of the memorandum?
(a) 2
(b) 3
(c) 5
(d) 9

3. Which numbered facts include directions telling the employees what to do?
(a) 1,2,8
(b) 1,5,10
(c) 2,8,10
(d) 1,2,10

4. Which of the following numbered facts would you omit as irrelevant?
(a) 1
(b) 5
(c) 9
(d) 10

5. Your memo will consist of which of the following?
(a) numbered announcement followed by a paragraph of instructions
(b) a paragraph for the announcement followed by numbered instructions
(c) a paragraph for the announcement followed by a paragraph for the instructions
(d) a single paragraph including both the announcement and the instructions

6. Now write the memo.

To: _____   Date: _____

From: _____

Subject: _____

_____

_____

_____

_____

_____

1. _____

_____

2. _____

_____

3. _____

_____

_____

That wasn't very hard. This time we will try one a little more difficult. You will have to decide how best to present some statistics to your reader. Here is the situation:

You are Steven Giles, department manager at Lorski's Canning Factory. Your department processes and cans green beans. Today is July 6, 1981.

While comparing this past week's production figures with those of the same week a year ago, you notice that tonnage has not begun dropping off as it did last year. In fact, this week's figures resemble those of the *previous* week a year ago. This means you will still be processing large amounts of green beans for another week, yet you have scheduled four of your twelve bean-snipping machines for postseasonal maintenance next week. You decide that postponing the maintenance is the only sensible thing to do.

Only the divisional manager, Charles Toppins, can reschedule postseasonal maintenance because the cost is a budgeted item.

Here are some figures you may wish to include in your memorandum to Mr. Toppins:

Last year's tonnage for the four weeks beginning June 15 was 78 tons the first week, 143 tons the second week, 149 tons the third week, and 19 tons the fourth week. This year's tonnage from June 16 to today's date is 12 tons the first week, 79 tons the second week, and 147 tons this past week.

Before writing your memorandum, answer these questions. The answers are on page 341.

7. Did you use inductive or deductive reasoning when you compared this year's specific weekly tonnage with last year's and then decided you would need all bean snippers operating next week, therefore requiring a postponement of the maintenance?

_____

8. Which of the following will be the key idea of your memorandum, considered from your reader's point of view?
(a) This year's tonnage figures are a week behind last year's.
(b) You will need all twelve bean snippers operating next week.
(c) You must request postponement of the scheduled maintenance.

_____

9. How can you enable Mr. Toppins to see at a glance that you are likely to need all twelve bean snippers next week?

_____

_____

10. Now write the memorandum.

To: Date:
From:
Subject:

_____

_____

_____

_____

_____

_____:

(Draw your ⟶
graph here.)

Sometimes your memorandum will go to several people, and each one will need to know only part of your message. You could, of course, write a separate memorandum to each person, but that is time consuming. Moreover, you often will want each person to be at least aware of the parts that don't primarily concern him or her.

For example, the writer of the following memorandum is really writing to four departments about several different aspects of one subject. But putting everything into one message insures that each reader will understand how his or her part fits into the whole plan. Notice the headings, which you will seldom find in business letters, but which frequently appear in memorandums. Such headings do often appear, however, in letter reports. (Letter reports are simply short reports sent to someone outside the company, and therefore use the format of a business letter.) The following message uses the memorandum format because it stays within the plant:

To: Engr Dept   Date: April 23, 1980
      Constr Dept   Attention: M. Snow, Chem Engr
      Safety Div   W. Tull, Constr
      Carpentry Shop   V. Callig, Safety

From: V. Petty, Plant Mgr
Subject: Installation of Dry Chemical Storage Shelves

May 2, Site Clearance

W. Tull's team will assist M. Snow in removing chemical supplies from Building 14 to temporary storage in Building 9. Old shelves will go to Carpentry Shop for salvage. Site clearance must be complete before new shelves arrive at 3:30 P.M.

May 3–5, Construction of New Shelves

M. Tull's team will assemble the new shelves, anchor them to the walls of Building 14, and notify V. Callig when they are ready for safety inspection. V. Callig will prepare the plant safety report and the OSHA report.

May 6, Transfer of Chemicals Back to Building 14

M. Tull's team will return the chemicals to Building 14, under the supervision of M. Snow.

A rather widespread use of the memorandum form is for periodic reports. Most large companies require all managers to submit a report at regular intervals—either daily, weekly, monthly, quarterly, or annually. Quarterly and annual reports are necessarily a bit longer than the others and usually follow a formal organizational pattern, which we will discuss in another chapter. But reports covering shorter periods usually get put on memorandum forms. They seldom run to more than a page or two.

If you study a company's organizational chart, you will get a fairly good idea of how these reports circulate. Typically, a beginning manager or management trainee will report frequently—usually once a week—to his or her immediate superior. That superior will report, perhaps once a month, to the next one up on the organizational chart, and so on up the line. Such a network enables each manager and supervisor to keep informed of what is happening in his or her area of responsibility.

Copies of these reports sometimes go horizontally to other departments to keep them informed, but their most important use is to keep home offices fully aware of how well the branch offices are functioning.

Because these reports cover a specific period of time, they are necessarily status reports. But *what* do they report the status of? The writer? The routine responsibilities of the job? The special projects the writer happens to be working on? Production? Training? Morale? Actually, any or all of these and more can be fit topics for a periodic report, depending on the *reader's* needs and desires. Remember that the person you are reporting to usually must also prepare a periodic report, and the kind of information your boss must put in that report will determine the kind of information he or she will want to see in yours. There is a very practical reason for this: Your boss will want to be able to take entire sentences or even whole paragraphs out of your report and include them in the appropriate section in his or hers.

Given this situation, you can easily see how important it is for you to find out what topics your reader expects you to cover. Ask for copies of other people's reports that your boss found effective. Find out from your boss whether there are any topics that you must always include, whether there are any optional topics, and which topics he or she considers most important. For instance, a production supervisor may want production managers to begin their weekly reports with statistics on production, followed by training status, safety records, and the like.

To gather material for your periodic report, you must keep some records, or at least notes, of your job activities. It's a good idea to enter in a kind of calendar or journal the events you will want to include in your report; it's an even better idea to keep such notes on 3" x 5" notecards so you can organize them easily.

Here are a few rules or guidelines for putting together periodic reports:

1. Arrange your material by topics, NOT by time sequence. Your report should not read like a diary or a journal.
2. Organize deductively; that is, go from most important to least important.
3. Make it as easy as possible for your reader to include your material in his or her report.
4. Seek feedback from your reader on the quality of your reports.

If your department has no established organizational pattern for these reports, and if your boss says you are free to organize your report any way you like, you should use the "Accomplishments, Concerns, Plans" format. This enables you to put the good news first—as you always should—and also to acknowledge any problems while maintaining an optimistic tone. It works like this:

Under "Accomplishments" you include the things that went quite well in your department. If you set any production or sales records, or if you completed a long-term project, say so here. Don't forget to give other people credit for their help and cooperation. If you solved a problem mentioned in your previous report or if you have any other good news, this section is the place to announce it. Be specific.

Under "Concerns" you list the two or three specific things that went wrong, that you need to improve on, or that present problems for you.

Be specific, but don't make it look as if you are complaining. Don't assign blame if you can avoid it.

Under "Plans" you list your plans for the next reporting period. *Make sure you include a specific plan to attack each item you listed under "Concerns."* You may, of course, include other plans besides those aimed at your concerns.

Over a period of time you will be able to check your file copies of your own reports to see whether you have been able to carry out your plans successfully. If you have, the "Concerns" listed in one report will show up as "Accomplishments" in the next one.

Before we try writing periodic reports, let's look at some examples of them. The first two follow the "Accomplishments, Concerns, Plans" format; the last one follows an organizational pattern required by the manager to whom the writer submitted the report.

To: D. Whiting   *Date: November 8, 1980*

From: B. Everly BJE
Subject: Weekly Report

Accomplishments

The modified gearbox we installed on #3 perforator enabled us to set a production record. Case totals on all four machines totalled 5,728 for the 24-hour period from midnight 11/4/80 to midnight 11/5/80. This is 202 cases more than the previous record set on 7/3/76, for an increase of more than 3%.

There were no maintenance problems during the week, putting us well within the budget to date.

Concerns

Rejects from #4 perforator are still running high. Quality control rejected 46 unperforated cartons from this one machine during the week—more than double the number from any other machine. The new blades installed last week did not correct the problem.

Plans

I will check rotator bearing wear on #4 perforator during shutdown next Tuesday. Worn bearings could be causing the high number of rejects.

Wednesday and Thursday of next week I will complete my assertiveness training.

To: D. Whiting
From: B. Everly
Subject: Weekly Report

Date: November 15, 1980

Accomplishments

New rotator bearings on #4 perforator solved the problem of too many rejects. The worn bearings sometimes allowed the rotator to drop as much as .0013" away from the blades.

In spite of the $240 expenditure for replacing bearings, we are still within budget.

Production is still running at near record levels. Our high count for the week was Thursday's 5,712.

I have completed my assertiveness training and have already seen improvement in my contributions at weekly staff meetings.

Concerns

The modified gearbox we installed on #3 perforator last week has overheated twice. We may need to use a different kind of lubricant in it.

Plans

I will check with Spaulding Gear Co. to find out whether a different type of lubricant will solve the overheating problem on the modified gearbox.

Notice that successfully carrying out one of the plans listed on November 8, 1980, converted a November 8 concern into a November 15 accomplishment.

Finally, here is an example of a weekly report that follows an organizational pattern specified by the reader:

To: D. Smith
From: G. Allison *GBA*
Subject: Weekly Report

Date: March 11, 1979

Quality Distribution for the Week:

GRADE	MON	TUE	WED	THU	FRI	SAT	TOTAL	%
A	573	591	540	516	583	601	3,404	30
B	714	697	712	736	741	720	4,320	36
C	612	591	620	570	564	600	3,557	30
Reject	83	71	94	63	83	91	485	4

Power Usage for the Week:

	MON	TUE	WED	THU	FRI	SAT	TOTAL
kw/h	940	870	995	890	890	950	5,535

Personnel:

1. <u>Safety</u>—No lost-time injuries.
2. <u>Training</u>—Joe Merlone has completed CPR training.

Now you try one. Here is a list of scrambled facts covering the week of August 8, 1981. Examine the facts and then answer the exercise questions that follow.

1. You are C. Brownson, warehouse manager of a food processing plant.

2. The division manager to whom you report every week is J. Lawson.

3. Today's date is August 15, 1981.

4. Today you had to dispose of twenty-eight cases of breakfast cereal that got wet from a leaky roof in your warehouse. You had to remove other cases from the area so they wouldn't get wet.

5. On Wednesday you were guest speaker at a Rotary Club banquet.

6. Thursday morning you completed an inspection of the warehouse ventilating system. All equipment is in good condition.

7. You plan to attend a local management conference next Wednesday. The Chamber of Commerce is sponsoring it.

8. Next Monday you will call Acme Roofing Company for an estimate on cost of the repairs to the warehouse roof.

9. Last Friday workers installed new guard rails on your loading dock. This will lower your insurance costs by $528 a year.

10. Absenteeism was lower this week than it has been for any previous week during the year. One worker called in sick and missed an eight-hour shift. The average weekly missed time this year is 17.5 hours.

Now answer these questions. The answers are on page 342.

11. Which item is irrelevant to your report?
(a) 4
(b) 5
(c) 8
(d) 10

12. Which items will you include under "Accomplishments"?
(a) 1,5,6
(b) 4,7,9,10
(c) 6,8,10
(d) 6,9,10

13. Which item will constitute your "Concerns" section?
(a) 2
(b) 4
(c) 6
(d) 8

14. Which items will you include under "Plans"?
(a) 7,9
(b) 8,10
(c) 7,8
(d) 6,7

15. Now write the report.

To: _____   Date: _____

From: _____

Subject: _____

Accomplishments

_____

_____

_____

_____

_____

_____

_____

_____

Concerns

_____

_____

_____

Plans

_____

_____

_____

_____

FOR CLASS DISCUSSION

Assume your class is a business corporation. Your manager, otherwise known as your instructor, has decided that it might be a good idea for each class member to submit a weekly report for the remainder of the term.

The purpose of these reports would be to apprise your instructor of what you are learning, what progress you are making in developing good writing skills, whether you are keeping up with your reading assignments, and what business-writing problems you will be working on during the next week.

As a class, discuss what other specific information should go into such reports. Both instructor and students should provide input for this. List the suggestions on the chalkboard and design a format that fits the needs of both instructor and students.

Finally, after discussing whether the instructor or the students would benefit most, decide as a class whether the instructor should require these weekly reports.

TEST YOURSELF

The answers are on page 343.

Write *A* in the blank if you think the item belongs in the *Accomplishments* section of a weekly report, write *C* if you think it belongs in the *Concerns* section, write *P* if you think it belongs in the *Plans* section, and write *I* if you think the item is irrelevant.

1. ___ On Tuesday you received four customer complaints about discourteous clerks in your department.

2. ___ Next Wednesday you will attend a staff meeting to discuss a sales training program.

3. ___ You submitted a proposal for reducing energy consumption by 2 per cent.

4. ___ A fire in your department destroyed a copying machine, but injured none of the employees.

5. ___ The accountant you hired is doing a fine job in your department.

6. ___ More than 70 percent of the employees who will be retiring in the next ten years attended your "Planning for Retirement" conference and commented favorably about it.

7. ___ You need to complete an inspection of all fire extinguishers in your plant by next Thursday.

8. ___ You have decided to go camping on your vacation.

9. ___ Toxic chemicals in your plant's waste-water discharge have been rising dangerously close to legal limits.

10. ___ You will check your plant's waste-water filtration system next Monday morning.

APPLY YOURSELF

1.   Assume one of your classmates missed a class in which you discussed this chapter. She has asked you for a one-page memo listing and explaining the main topics the class covered that day. After reviewing your notes for that class, write her the memo. Use the "To: From: Subject: Date:" heading.

2.   Submit to your instructor a weekly report for the current week. Make sure you include only information that relates to your progress in learning business-writing skills. Use the "To: From: Subject: Date:" heading and the *"Accomplishments, Concerns,* and *Plans"* format.

3.   Suppose you are district manager of a pizza parlor chain. The *"Accomplishments, Concerns,* and *Plans"* format does not suit the kind of information you need from the seven local managers who report to you. Make a list of what information you need and design a format for monthly reports that will insure you get that information.

ANSWERS TO EXERCISES

1. c

2. b

3. d

4. b, c

5. b

6.

To: All Employees
From: Sandra Cornish, Personnel Director
Subject: Reimbursement for Medicine and Drugs

Starting January 1, 1981, our group insurance will reimburse employees for the cost of prescription medicine and drugs in excess of fifty dollars a year. The company will pay the entire cost of this additional coverage.

To claim this reimbursement you need to do the following:
1. Pick up a reimbursement form in the personnel office.
2. Have your druggist record each purchase of prescription medicine or drugs.
3. Turn in the completed form to the personnel office for reimbursement any time after exceeding the fifty-dollar deductible for the year.

---

7. inductive

8. c

9. Put the statistics from last year and this year on a line chart.

10.

To: Charles Toppins, Div Mgr   Date: July 6, 1981
From: Stephen Giles *SG*
Subject: Need for Postponing Scheduled Maintenance

I request postponement of postseasonal maintenance scheduled for bean snippers the week of July 13.

We will need all twelve snippers operating that week because this year's bean tonnage is a week behind last year's:

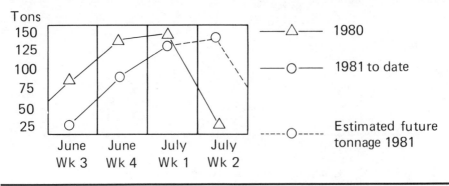

11. b

12. d

13. b

14. c

15.

To: J. Lawson   Date: August 15, 1981
From: C. Brownson *CB*
Subject: Weekly Report

Accomplishments

On Friday workers installed new guard rails on the loading dock. This will lower insurance costs by $528 a year.

Absenteeism was lower this week than it has been for any previous week during the year. One worker called in sick and missed an eight-hour shift. The average weekly missed time this year is 17.5 hours.

Thursday morning's inspection of the warehouse ventilating system found all equipment in good condition.

Concerns

Water from a leaking roof spoiled 28 cases of breakfast cereal. We disposed of these cases and removed others to prevent further spoilage.

Plans

Monday I will get an estimate from Acme Roofing Co. for repairs to the warehouse roof.

On Wednesday I will attend the Chamber of Commerce's management conference.

ANSWERS TO TEST YOURSELF

1. C
2. P
3. A
4. C
5. A
6. A
7. P
8. I
9. C
10. P

16
Special Reports

Such routine messages as memorandums and periodic reports constitute the majority of report writing that most people in commerce and industry need to do. But very frequently another kind of report becomes necessary to inform management on a specific topic or to suggest the best course of action for a decision maker to take. We will call these special reports because they satisfy special needs as those needs arise.

The two kinds of special reports are informational and analytical. An informational report presents useful information about a specific subject in as understandable a way as possible. An analytical report does that too, but it also interprets the information for the reader and suggests a course of action. You must make sure you understand before you begin whether your reader expects an informational report or an analytical report because each requires a slightly different format: An informational report includes a summary; an analytical report includes a conclusion and a recommendation or recommendations.

At first glance, you might think an informational report would be simpler to write than an analytical one. But at least in terms of organization, the analytical report is considerably easier. Because every analytical report must result in some recommended course of action, the same basic organizational plan will work for all of them. In fact, you can reduce it to a simple rule:

Organize analytical reports according to criteria.

Criteria are the standards or measuring sticks that you use for judging persons, products, services, or even ideas. *Qualifying* criteria are the standards you use to decide whether an alternative is or is not acceptable and worth considering. *Quantifying* criteria are the standards you use to decide which of the acceptable alternatives is best.

For example, suppose you need to replace your worn-out typewriter.

345

You decide that you cannot afford one that costs more than $175, that it must be portable, and that it must be electric. These are qualifying criteria; if a certain typewriter lacks any of these three characteristics, it does not even qualify for consideration. This narrows your alternatives so that you can make detailed comparisons of the few that do qualify. Once you have applied your qualifying criteria, you are ready to *begin* gathering and analyzing data for your report.

Next, you list the considerations that are most important to you. These generally will include, among other characteristics, the *degree* to which an alternative meets some of your qualifying criteria. You want to know how much less than $175 a certain typewriter costs and how lightweight and portable it is, for instance. You would also want to know how good a repair record it has, how easily you can clean it, how easily you can change ribbons, and how convenient it is to use (automatic carriage return, ease of setting tabulator, and the like). You can quantify such things and use them to compare one typewriter with another.

Now, if you organize your comparison by considering first one typewriter, then the next one, then the next one, and so on, you will hopelessly confuse yourself. You need to decide first of all which quantifying criterion (*criterion* is the singular form of *criteria*) is most important to you. Then you apply that criterion to each typewriter you are considering. Only then do you go on to the criterion that is second in importance, and apply *it* to each typewriter in turn. You do the same for each of the other quantifying criteria.

Of course, you would not write a report to yourself recommending one of the three typewriters; you could easily decide which one to buy without writing out any of your reasons. But putting reasons on paper might help you to make a more logical choice. Besides, we could use this opportunity to practice some report-writing techniques. So let's suppose you do decide to write up your considerations into an analytical report.

After applying your three qualifying criteria, you find that only three typewriters—A, B, and C—cost $175 or less, are portable, and are electric. To decide which of these machines best satisfies your needs, you must sit down and list what those needs are and express them as criteria.

Because the results of your report depend almost entirely on the validity of your criteria, you must choose those criteria very carefully. Make a tentative list and revise it as often as you need to. Remember that the criteria you eventually choose must accurately reflect what you really want in a typewriter.

After careful thought, you decide that low cost is paramount, followed by ease of maintenance, repair record, length of warranty, low weight and small size, availability of replacement ribbons, and typing convenience, in that order.

After examining data on the three typewriters, you find that all have one-year warranties, all use standard ribbons, and all are very close to the same weight and size. You therefore discard these three criteria because they will not help you make your decision.

You now have three typewriters to consider in terms of cost, ease of maintenance, repair record, and typing convenience. Your next step is to decide how you will get the necessary data to make these comparisons. You already found out the costs when you applied your qualifying criteria, and advertisements or sales brochures will provide you with lists of typing-convenience features. But what about repair record and ease of maintenance? Whenever you don't have the needed information on hand, you should consider one or more of the following means of obtaining it:

1. Use your own experience or make first-hand observations.
2. Run some tests.
3. Check printed sources.
4. Make a survey or send out questionnaires.

If you have no experience with the three typewriter models, you can ask the sales clerks to demonstrate removing the platen for cleaning, changing the ribbon, and so on, and get your ease-of-maintenance data that way. Or, you might ask some people who own any of the three models what they think of their machines in that regard.

Finding out the repair records of the three machines might pose a more difficult problem. But again you could ask owners about that. Or you could go to the library and look up a few consumer magazines to see whether any of them report the frequency of repairs for the three models you are considering.

Once you have selected your criteria and gathered your data, you are ready to write. Start with these headings:*

Introduction

Purpose
Problem
Scope
Method of Investigation

Then write a brief statement describing each of these aspects. You might do it like this:

Introduction

PURPOSE

   The purpose of this report is to recommend the best electric portable typewriter for me to buy.

PROBLEM

   My typewriter is now thirteen years old and has needed repairs twice in the last three months. The last time I had it adjusted, it began to space erratically within five weeks. I need to replace it with a new one costing no more than $175.

---

* Professor Steven E. Pauly recommends a similar format for interpreting statistics in his *Technical Report Writing Today*, 2d ed. (Boston: Houghton Mifflin Co., 1979), p. 83. The format, as given here, works well for *any* analytical report.

SCOPE

This report compares typewriters A, B, and C in terms of their cost (with trade), their ease of maintenance, their repair records, and their typing convenience.

METHOD OF INVESTIGATION

Purchase prices reflect written commitments from sales personnel; ease of maintenance data are my judgments based on sales demonstrations; frequency of repair data come from the July, 1980 issue of Consumer Concerns magazine (pp. 46–51); and typing-convenience information comes from sales brochures and from comments made by friends who own similar machines.

What you have written to this point constitutes the *Introduction* of your report. Now the rest of the report will almost write itself. All you need to do is turn to your SCOPE section, take the first criterion listed, and write a section explaining in detail how the three typewriters compare with one another when measured by that standard. Then you do the same for each of the other criteria, in turn. The body of your report will then look something like this:

COST

Typewriter B is the least expensive. As shown in the following table, two of the machines have a list price over $200; but the trade-in allowances reduce their net prices to below $175.

	LIST PRICE	TRADE-IN ALLOWANCE	NET PRICE
Typewriter A	$235.50	$65	$170.50
Typewriter B	205.95	45	160.95
Typewriter C	197.95	30	167.95

EASE OF MAINTENANCE

Typewriter C is the easiest to maintain. Both B and C have removable platens for easy cleaning, but removing B's platen requires a screwdriver. The platen on A is not removable. Changing ribbons is also easiest on C. When I asked the sales clerks to demonstrate ribbon changing, typewriter A took 5½ minutes, typewriter B took 3 minutes, and typewriter C took 2½ minutes. Also, typewriter C is the only one that permits cleaning of the type-faces without removing the cover shield.

FREQUENCY OF REPAIR

Typewriter B has by far the best repair record. According to Consumer Concerns magazine, the average number of repairs needed over a three-year period is 4.81 for A, 1.23 for B, and 3.94 for C. The typewriters in the survey averaged 36 hours of use a week; I use a typewriter approximately 20 hours a week.

TYPING CONVENIENCE

Typewriter A is slightly more convenient to use than the other two. All three machines have variable touch control and margin guides, but only A has an automatic five-space indentation key. None has a power carriage return.

Notice that each criterion section begins with a sentence that summarizes all the data presented in that section. Notice, too, that when you have many numbers to present, you can make your evidence easier to understand by putting it in a table, as in the COST section above. Finally, notice that when you present data graphically, you should describe the information in general terms *before* showing the table or graph. Keep your reader in mind; it is exasperating to try to make sense out of a table of statistics and *then* find out a half-page later what those statistics mean and why they are there.

At this point you are ready to write your conclusions and recommendations. Your conclusion should simply tie the results of the criterion sections into one paragraph, like this:

CONCLUSIONS

Although typewriter A is most convenient to use and C is the easiest to maintain, typewriter B scores a close second in both these categories. Typewriter B is the least expensive and has by far the best repair record.

RECOMMENDATION

Buy typewriter B.

You now have only a *first draft* of your analytical report; you are not yet ready to present it because not all elements are in the sequence your reader needs them in. You have to write your conclusions and recommendations last because you can't know what they are until you apply the criteria. But your reader needs to read them *first* in order to understand your supporting evidence in just one reading. Furthermore, your purpose is not to make your reader continue reading to the very end of your report. You are *not* writing a suspense novel. If your conclusions by themselves satisfy your reader and convince him or her to act on your recommendations without reading through all your supporting evidence, so much the better. You include your evidence and reasoning in case your reader *wants* to see them; but the longer your report is, the less likely any one reader will have time to read all of it. In very long reports, you will even write some parts for some readers and some parts for others. So don't feel disappointed if your reader doesn't think it necessary to read all of your analytical report. That's just the way things are. And, considering the importance of efficiency in business, you can see that that's the way things *should* be.

It is extremely important that you do not attempt to *write* your conclusions and recommendations first. If you do, you will find yourself making recommendations based on guesses and opinions rather than facts, and then later on trying to select some facts that will support those ill-founded recommendations. Your report in that case will be worse than useless—it will be misleading.

Therefore, write your conclusions and recommendations last, but place them first. After that, everything else will follow in the order you have written it.

Now do the following exercises to reinforce what you have learned. The answers are on page 367.

1. List the four major sections of an analytical report.

_____

2. List the four subdivisions of the INTRODUCTION.

_____

3. The SCOPE section of the INTRODUCTION lists the alternatives being evaluated and what else?

_____

4. Should you organize the body of the report in terms of alternatives being considered or in terms of criteria for evaluating those alternatives?

_____

5. List the sequence of the four major sections as they appear in the final draft of an analytical report.

_____

Now it's your turn to put together an analytical report. Here is the situation:

You are assistant manager of Daisy Dew Dairy Plant. Last week the plant manager, Mr. Donald DeBarth, called you into his office to discuss a problem he wants you to help him solve. Here are your notes from that meeting with Mr. DeBarth:

1. On May 8, the United States Department of Agriculture (USDA) inspected your plant and made twenty recommendations for improving operations and cleanliness. Ten of these directly referred to cracking and peeling paint in production areas.

2. The USDA will inspect Daisy Dew again in five weeks, on June 12, by which time the plant must have eliminated shortcomings found in the earlier inspection. Today's date is May 15.

3. The plant can hire Peintureur & Sons Painters to do the job, or it can hire its own employees to do the painting during slack production time and on weekends.

4. Mr. DeBarth emphasized that both the quality of the painting job

350

"Read back the reasons I've listed to document my request for a different office."

and the time it takes to do it are very important because the plant must pass USDA inspection about a month from now.

5.   Although Mr. DeBarth didn't stress cost, you know that it is always one of his major concerns.

Since last week, you have been gathering information on the painting project. Here is a list of what you did and what you found:

6.   Peintureur & Sons said they could do the entire job, including paint (super-quality) and other materials, for $14,500.

7.   You obtained the information in item 6 by asking Peintureur & Sons to examine the plant and give you a complete written estimate for the job.

8.   The humidity of the production area requires super-quality paint.

351

At least, that's what Mr. Peintureur told you when you asked him why he specified super-quality paint in his estimate.

   9. *Daisy Dew's employees' union contract calls for $5.50 an hour.*

10. *Peintureur & Sons could do the job on two weekends with their crew of 16 painters.*

11. *Daisy Dew hired its own employees to paint the plant two and a half years ago. They used 425 gallons of paint and worked 1,250 total hours to do the job. You learned this from your files.*

12. *Peintureur & Sons have done similar painting jobs for other dairies in the area. These dairies have all passed USDA inspections.*

13. *Daisy Dew would have to pay a $500 waiver fee to Amalgamated Local 446 to allow Peintureur & Sons to work in a closed shop.*

14. *Regular paint costs $6.00 a gallon, and super-quality paint costs $9.00 a gallon.*

15. *If Daisy Dew hires its own employees to do the job, 875 of the 1,250 hours would have to be overtime hours. Employees get time-and-a-half for overtime.*

16. *Peintureur & Sons gave you some brochures on the super-quality paint they use. The paint carries a five-year guarantee if applied by accredited professionals like Peintureur.*

17. *When Daisy Dew employees did the painting, poor coverage in corners and behind machinery allowed moisture to get behind the paint. Ceilings and walls in the production area began to peel about two years later.*

18. *You gathered information about other dairies by phone calls and by inspecting two of them yourself.*

19. *Several Daisy Dew employees told you they dislike having to paint, but are more than willing to do it for the overtime pay and could certainly finish the job in four weeks.*

20. *You interviewed your employees' union representative to get cost figures for hiring Daisy Dew employees to do the painting.*

(For this exercise, invent minor details, such as the names of other dairies.)
    Before you attempt your first draft of the report, answer these questions. The answers are on page 367.

  6. Which items will you include in the PROBLEM section of your report?

_____

  7. Which items will you include in the SCOPE section of your report?

_____

8. Which items will you include in the METHOD OF INVESTIGATION section?

_____

9. What are the two alternatives you are considering in the report?

_____

10. List the headings for the three criteria sections in descending order of importance.

_____

11. How much will it cost to have Peintureur & Sons paint the production area?

$ _____

12. How much will it cost to have Daisy Dew's employees paint the production area?

$ _____

13. If you prorate Peintureur & Sons' cost over the five years their paint job will last, how much will the cost be per year?

$ _____

14. If you prorate your own employees' cost over the two years their paint job will last, how much will the cost be per year?

$ _____

15. Which of the two alternatives is more cost efficient?

_____

Now you are ready to begin writing your analytical report. Reorganize the data into paragraphs under the following headings:

INTRODUCTION

PURPOSE
PROBLEM
SCOPE
METHOD OF INVESTIGATION

COST
QUALITY
TIME
CONCLUSIONS
RECOMMENDATION

When you have your first draft finished, take the CONCLUSIONS and RECOMMENDATION sections and put them at the beginning of your report. The final draft should look something like the one on pages 359–361, but *don't peek* until you have finished your own.

Before we turn to informational reports, we should note one other method of describing matters of cost. If the alternative you are considering consists of some production machinery, some time-saving equipment, or anything else that produces income for the company, you can describe its value by comparing its life expectancy with the length of time it will take to pay for itself.

For example, suppose you must now reject about 2 per cent of your product because of poor quality. These rejects cost your company $52 a day. You can buy a $25,000 electronic device that will reduce rejects to 1 per cent and will last five years. Would the device be worth buying? You can figure out its value by computing how long it would take to pay for itself. Some companies call this its "time to recover" or its "payout." If it can save your company $26 a day, it will pay for itself in about 962 days, or about 2.6 years. With a life expectancy of five years, the device would be adding $26 a day to the company's profit for the last 2.4 years of its usefulness. You could express it very simply this way:

> *With a life expectancy of five years and a payout of 2.6 years, the device would produce a net profit of $22,438 before needing replacement.*

Of course, you would need to follow this with supporting evidence and computations, preferably in tabular form.

Informational Reports

There are numerous ways to organize an informational report, depending entirely on what your reader's needs are. You could arrange your materials from most important to least important, from cause to effect, or from effect back to cause. You might use spatial order, chronological order, or some other kind of order—if that's what your reader wants.

But remember that the purpose of an informational report is strictly to communicate information; it does not include any recommendations. Your job is to present your information in the most understandable way you can.

About the only generalizations we can make about informational reports are these:

1. You must break down your overall message into clearly labeled component parts or sections.

2. Your report will always consist of at least two kinds of information: general and specific. The general amounts to a summary, and you should usually place it ahead of your discussion of the specifics.

354

Because it is practically impossible to list the many forms informational reports might take, we will have to be content with a few representative examples of some actual ones. Both of the following reports are from the same paper manufacturing company. I have changed all proper names to keep the reports anonymous, but I have kept the organizational patterns intact. Don't worry if some of the terms are unfamiliar; we are interested only in how the writers arranged their materials.

The first report is a type that occurs so frequently at this particular company that the department has reduced it to a printed form for managers to fill out. It is a preliminary informational report. I have underlined the printed parts of the form.

Preliminary Documentation of Results (Papermachine Changes)

Note: This form is not meant as a substitute for a final report. Its purpose is to document papermachine changes for future followup, in addition to sharing intermodule information on a more timely basis. This should be completed as soon as test is executed on papermachine.

DATE OF TEST   *PAPERMACHINE/CREW*
  11/18/77   *#22/XC*

OBJECTIVES OF TEST:
1. To determine the effect on parez efficiency of adding acid to the machine chest instead of to the cleaners standpipe.

2. To measure changes in bicarbonates & pH at stock pump as a result of adding acid to the machine chest.

CONCLUSIONS (Tentative):
1. Stock pump pH dropped from 6.6 to 5.9, resulting in bicarbonates change from 80 to 40.

2. Weigh sheet total tensiles increased from 770 to 823. Wet tensile did not change significantly.

3. Machine chest handsheet tensiles increased directionally from 1365 to 1480, while parez usage, refining, stock flows, and speed remained constant.

4. While we manually added acid, pH of 5.9 held stable throughout the test.

5. The test had no significant effect on machine performance.

OBSERVATIONS/COMMENTS (How well were the objectives met?):
1. While wet tensiles did not change significantly, reel total tensiles did increase more on TW than on TA. This could be a result of either parez efficiency improvement or a change in furnish tensiles. We took no samples of raw material stock.

355

2.   While machine was at sheet control limit prior to test, lower machine chest pH did not appear to have a significant effect.

3.   Difficulty with acid pump turbine delayed the base-to-conditional change comparison by about three hours.

4.   Stability of pH at stock pump while we added acid manually indicates we could lower machine chest pH to 5.5 with little risk.

DATA (Conditions that varied/validity of data):

Reel Physicals

pH	#SAMPLES	BW	TW	TA	TWET	TENSILES
6.6	10	17.8	40	36	11	1363
5.9	15	17.7	44	37	12	1490

Parez usage—50% of chart (parez solids at 7.25%).
Refiner amps—96
Speed—3890
Stock flows—Constant

Bicarbonates after stock pump:

pH	#	BICARB
6.6	1	80
6.3	1	64
6.1	1	48
5.9	2	42

FOLLOWUP Plans for Future Tests/Reports, etc.):
    Since validity of data is questionable, but directionally correct, we will run this test again, improving the validity of the results by
1.   Lowering m.c. pH to 5.5 instead of 5.9
2.   Gathering complete stock samples
3.   Increasing all sample sizes
4.   Running base samples on both sides of conditional change.

Gordon P. Schultze

Test Coordinator

The writer of this next report knew that her boss always wants to know five things about any new-product run. That is why she included the five headings she did, even if all she had to report in some sections was that everything went well.

Initial Columbine Production Run

SUMMARY   *2/5/77*

1. Number 34 Paper Machine completed its production run of Columbine tissue on November 5. The run went well, with no major problems and considerable experience gained by the crews.

2. Here is the distribution of tons and product types:

PRODUCT	GOOD TONS	SCRAP & STUB TONS
10# Med. Blue		
Crew M	112.5	48.5
Crew R	148.4	27.9
10# Dark Blue		
Crew M	95.2	33.6
Crew R	119.7	14.1
15# Dark Blue		
Crew M	30.9	12.2
Crew R	277.1	26.5

ACCOMPLISHMENTS

1. We were able to establish standards for dye bleeds, color readings, and formation. These will complete the formula card.

2. We have come a long way toward making Columbine tissue production independent of Columbine personnel. Our crews did a commendable job of insuring that we define standards objectively.

3. We were able to return all scrap and stub rolls produced during this run into the broke system. We also cut up and fed some scrap from past Columbine runs into the system.

PRODUCTION PROBLEMS

1. We lost one fabric during start-up because of problems in fabric guiding and tensioning.

2. The dye system had a few difficulties. High dye flow through the eductor caused residue build-up. This caused the dye flow to stop, and several sets of paper were marginally off color.

QUALITY CONCERNS

We encountered no major quality problems. When we lost some rolls because of holes in the sheet, we resolved these difficulties quickly by changing doctor blades or scraping the pre-dryers.

MATERIALS

We completed the run with no extra dye, and we used up all of the 97" cores.

D. Westerly

Now answer the following questions about these last two reports. The answers are on page 367.

16. The writer of the Preliminary Documentation of Results report lists and numbers the items in all sections except *Data*. The writer of the Initial Columbine Production Run report lists and numbers the items in all sections except *Quality Concerns* and *Materials*. How do you account for this?

---

17. The writer of the first report had to follow the organization built into the printed form, but the writer of the second report had no printed format to follow. Which two of the following organizational strategies did the writer of the second report use?
(a) chronological, or time, sequence
(b) from least important to most important
(c) from general to specific
(d) from most important to least important

Did the answers to exercise 17 surprise you? It *is* possible to use more than one organizational pattern at the same time—but only if they do not conflict. In this report, the writer put the SUMMARY first, thus going from general to specific. But she also arranged the other four sections from most important to least important.

18. The second report has a more conversational tone than the first. Yet both get the job done nicely. What do you think should be the dominant factor in deciding whether a somewhat conversational tone is appropriate for a report?
(a) the mood of the writer
(b) the accuracy of the data
(c) the preference of the reader
(d) whether or not the report has a printed format

19. The many technical terms in both reports show that the intended readers were probably
(a) high-level management
(b) low-level management
(c) the general public
(d) television, radio, or newspaper reporters

20. Does either report violate the two general characteristics of informational reports, namely, (1) clearly labeled component sections of the overall message, and (2) general sections preceding the specific ones?

RECOMMENDATION FOR PAINTING PRODUCTION AREAS OF DAISY DEW DAIRY PLANT

Conclusions

Hiring Peintureur & Sons to paint production areas in the Daisy Dew Dairy plant would cost, in the long run, considerably less than hiring Daisy Dew's employees to do it. Experience shows that quality suffers so badly when the plant's own employees do the painting that the production area would need painting again in about two years. Peintureur's job would last five years, and Peintureur could finish painting in two weeks, well before the USDA inspection. Plant employees would take twice that long and would not finish on time if they experienced any unforeseen delays.

Recommendation

The Daisy Dew Dairy plant should hire Peintureur & Sons to paint the production area.

Introduction

PURPOSE.   The purpose of this report is to recommend painters for doing the necessary painting in Daisy Dew's production area before the USDA inspection on June 12.

PROBLEM.   On May 8, the USDA inspected Daisy Dew Dairy and made ten recommendations that referred to cracking and peeling paint in production areas. We must repaint those areas by June 12, when the USDA will again inspect the plant.

SCOPE.   The plant can hire Peintureur & Sons to do the job, or it can hire its own employees to do the painting during slack production time and on weekends.

Criteria for deciding which of these two alternatives would be better are cost, quality of the paint job, and the time it would take to complete it.

METHOD OF INVESTIGATION.   I reviewed plant files for data on the last painting job, received brochures and a written estimate from Peintureur & Sons, phoned other dairies and inspected two of them, and then interviewed the plant's union representatives and several other plant employees.

Cost

Hiring Peintureur & Sons is more cost efficient than hiring Daisy Dew's employees to do the painting.

Although hiring our employees would initially save the plant nearly $2,000, in the long run we would save almost $18,000 by hiring Peintureur & Sons because their paint job lasts 2½ times longer.

Hiring our own employees would cost $13,106.25. Peintureur & Sons would paint the entire production area with super-quality paint for $14,500. This price includes both labor and paint. If we hire Peintureur, Amalgamated Local 446 would demand a waiver fee of $500.

Daisy Dew Employees

Paint (425 gals. super-quality @ $9.00)	$3,825.00
Labor	
Regular time (375 hrs. @ $5.50)	2,062.50
Overtime (875 hrs. @ $8.25)	7,218.75
Total	$13,106.25

Peintureur & Sons

Complete job (including paint)	$14,500.00
Amalgamated Local 446 waiver fee	500.00
Total	$15,000.00

However, because Peintureur & Sons' paint job will last five years, the cost per year is considerably less than the prorated yearly cost of having our own employees do the job, which would last only two years.

Daisy Dew Employees

$$\frac{\$13,106.25}{2 \text{ years}} = \$6,553.13$$

Peintureur & Sons

$$\frac{\$15,000.00}{5 \text{ years}} = \underline{3,000.00}$$

Yearly savings by hiring Peintureur $3,553.13

Quality

The humid atmosphere of the production area requires professional application of super-quality paint. Several other dairies in this area have contracted Peintureur & Sons to do their painting, and all are happy with the results. Lake Front Dairy reports their paint is in excellent condition after three years, and Elmira Dairy reports the same after four years. Both have hired Peintureur & Sons. My inspection of Acme and Happy Cow dairies found ceilings and walls in the production areas of both plants to

360

be in fair condition after Peintureur & Sons painted them 5½ years ago. None of these dairies has received demerits from USDA inspections.

The painting done by Daisy Dew's employees 2½ years ago held up well in the shipping and storage areas, but their faulty application of paint behind machinery in the production area allowed the humidity and surface moisture there to blister and crack the paint within six months.

Time

Peintureur & Sons could finish the job two weeks earlier than our employees could.

Daisy Dew's employees could probably finish by June 10, but this would allow for no unexpected delays in the painting schedule. Even though our employees could work 375 hours during the coming weekdays, they would need to work at least four weekends to complete the other 875 hours it would take them to do the job.

Peintureur & Sons estimate that it would take their 16 painters only two weekends to complete the painting. They assure completion by May 27. This gives us a two-week cushion in case of unforeseen delays.

FOR CLASS DISCUSSION

A. This in-class project consists of two parts:

First, assume the entire class is a committee formed to select the three or four criteria a report writer should use to determine which phonograph or tape system a discotheque should buy. Include qualifying criteria for cost, wattage output, speaker size, etc. Then establish quantifying criteria to discriminate among several models.

Second, assume the entire class is a committee formed to select the three or four criteria a report writer should use to determine which phonograph or tape system a nursing home should buy so that the people who live there can use headphones to listen to music and recorded readings of literature. Establish both qualifying and quantifying criteria that reflect the limited budget of the nursing home as well as its particular needs in a phonograph or tape system.

B. Discuss what qualifying criteria your instructor might use to decide which grading systems might be worth considering for this course. Then discuss several quantifying criteria that might help evaluate which of the acceptable systems would be best.

C. Suppose one of the quantifying criteria for evaluating several automobiles is EASE OF MAINTENANCE. Discuss ways of gathering data for applying this criterion.

D. Why is it important to write the CONCLUSIONS section and the RECOMMENDATIONS section last? Why is it important to put those two sections first in the final report?

E. Writing an analytical report like the one about painting Daisy Dew Dairy's production areas takes considerable time and effort. Does the value of such a written report justify the cost of writing it? When might it not be worthwhile to write such a report?

F. One decision maker might require an analytical report in a situation in which another decision maker might want an informational report. What are the advantages and disadvantages of each kind of report? If you were a decision maker, would you prefer to get only the information you need for deciding, or would you rather receive recommendations that you could either approve or reject? What might be the consequences of rejecting a recommendation? Is an informational report likely to contain exactly the information you need for making a decision? How could you make sure that it does?

TEST YOURSELF

The answers are on page 368.

1. What are special reports?

_____

_____

_____

2. What are the two basic types of special reports?

_____

_____

3. Explain the difference between the function of qualifying criteria and the function of quantifying criteria.

_____

_____

4. The body of an analytical report contains a major section for each:
(a) qualifying criteria
(b) quantifying criteria
(c) alternatives
(d) recommendations

5. The CONCLUSIONS section should contain the results of each major section of the
(a) Body
(b) Introduction
(c) Recommendations
(d) Method of Investigation

6. In its final form, the first major section of an informational report is usually the
(a) Purpose
(b) Body
(c) Method of Investigation
(d) Summary

7. In an analytical report, the writer should usually organize the criteria sections comprising the body in which of the following kinds of order?
(a) from least important to most important
(b) in chronological order
(c) from most important to least important
(d) in any order

8. In an analytical report, the SCOPE section must contain which of the following?
(a) problem and method of investigation
(b) alternatives and criteria
(c) criteria and purpose
(d) method of investigation and recommendations

9. Which of the following are not part of an informational report?
(a) Summary
(b) Specific Data
(c) Recommendations
(d) Conclusions

10. Which of the following is not part of an analytical report?
(a) Summary
(b) Specific Data
(c) Recommendations
(d) Conclusions

APPLY YOURSELF

1. You are assistant director of employee services at Accuwhiz Widget Manufacturing Company. Your plant has five cafeterias for employees. Each cafeteria contains twenty-four frozen-food vending machines and four microwave ovens.

In recent weeks several employees have complained that half of the microwaves have been out of order more often than they have been working. Last week your boss, Mr. Nolan Nerff, told you that the company needs to do something about the problem soon because workers' morale is deteriorating and lately some have returned late from lunch after having to stand in line to use the few microwaves that work. Mr. Nerff wants you to recommend the best microwave ovens, under $200 each, to replace the ten that keep breaking down.

Since the employees use the ovens only for thawing and warming sandwiches, hamburgers, and hot dogs, any microwave that features various heating levels, cooking probes, or digital readouts would be inappropriate.

During the past week you have checked the repair records on your microwave ovens that you will be replacing, received literature explaining specifications and warranties from three manufacturers of microwave ovens, and gathered test data from current issues of *Consumers' Reports* and *Consumers' Research* magazines. You know that Mr. Nerff considers cost and safety primary factors in making any decision. You also know Accuwhiz has been trying to reduce its energy consumption for public-relations purposes as well as for economy and conservation. Also very important are repair records and length of warranty on the microwaves you will be considering.

Now you have a collection of the following data, not listed here in any particular order:

A. The commercial-utility models of the three local appliance distributors carry the following unit prices, in purchases of eight or more:

Acme model S-219	$179.50
Newcastle model LX14	185.00
Whiz-Ding model 2	138.50

B. Newcastle also has a model (LY18) that is identical to its LX14 model, but has three temperature ranges and costs $198.50 in purchases of eight or more.

C. All brands carry a three-year warranty.

D. The microwaves in your cafeterias are all Acme brand. They are five years old, and they carried three-year warranties when Accuwhiz bought them.

E. Although all brands emit less than one milliwatt of radiation when new, the Newcastle models emit three milliwatts after five years, and the Whiz-Ding model emits four milliwatts after five years. The Acme emits only one milliwatt of radiation after five years. The Bureau of Radiological Health has established five milliwatts of radiation leakage as the maximum allowable for safety.

F. The Acme model consumes 450 watts of electricity, the Newcastle model LX14 and model LY18 both consume 650 watts, and the Whiz-Ding model consumes 425 watts.

G. According to *Consumers' Reports* magazine, the Acme model's average life expectancy is 4.2 years, the Newcastle model LX14's is 5 years, the Newcastle model LY18's is 4.5 years, and the Whiz-Ding model's is 3.1 years.

H. According to your own calculations, all four models consume approximately the same amount of energy because the lower wattage units take longer to heat the food.

I. Each of the appliance distributors will give you a $50 trade-in allowance for each of the microwaves you are replacing.

J. Repairs on the Acme model average $38 per year, on the Newcastle LX14 the average is $36, on the Newcastle LY18 the average is $42, and on the Whiz-Ding model the average is $74.

K. The model you will be replacing has cost you an average of $92 per year for repairs.

Apply your qualifying criteria. Then write your analytical report to Mr. Nerff. Present your data graphically where appropriate.

2. Suppose that yesterday Mr. Nerff transferred to one of your plants in another city. His replacement, Mr. James Terry, called you into his office today and told you that he prefers to examine his options himself before making a decision. Therefore, you must change your report from analytical to informational. Write your informational report to Mr. Terry, using the data given in the previous writing assignment.

ANSWERS TO EXERCISES

1. Introduction, Body or Discussion, Conclusions, Recommendations

2. Purpose, Problem, Scope, Method of Investigation

3. The criteria for evaluating the alternatives

4. In terms of criteria for evaluating the alternatives

5. Conclusions, Recommendations, Introduction, Body or Discussion

6. 1,2

7. 3,4,5

8. 7,8,11,16,18,19,20

9. (1) Have employees do the painting. (2) Hire Peintureur & Sons.

10. Cost, Quality, Time

11. $15,000.00

12. $13,106.25

13. $3,000.00

14. $6,553.13

15. Hiring Peintureur & Sons to do the painting

16. The writer needs to list and number data only when there are two or more items comprising the section. The writer must not use a "1." unless there is at least a "2." after it.

17. c,d

18. c

19. b

20. No.

ANSWERS TO TEST YOURSELF

1. Special reports are those written to satisfy special needs as they arise.

2. Analytical reports and informational reports.

3. Qualifying criteria are standards for deciding whether an alternative is acceptable and worth considering; quantifying criteria are standards for deciding which acceptable alternative is best.

4. b

5. a

6. d

7. c

8. b

9. c,d

10. a

17

Formal Reports

Major projects and in-depth studies require more than short special reports for thorough treatment; they require formal reports.

In essence, formal reports are the same as special reports—except for two major differences. Most noticeably, they contain some additional parts: preliminaries and end material. Preliminaries are such things as title page, letter of transmittal, table of contents, table of illustrations, and so on. End material consists of such things as appendixes and bibliographies. But the body of a formal report—that is, the part that appears between the preliminaries and the end material—should follow exactly the same organizational pattern any other analytical or informational report would follow.

Besides these additional parts, the only difference between a formal report and a special report is that the formal report usually documents supporting evidence, enabling the reader to verify the accuracy of the data and to weigh its importance by considering how up to date it is.

Let's consider documentation first. Formal reports generally are on much more important and complex subjects than ordinary special reports are. Furthermore, the reader of your formal report is less likely to know you personally or be able to ask you for details left out of the report. Typical are the reports architects make to their clients, or prospective clients, and the reports of studies made by commissions, task forces, government agencies, medical research teams, and the like. In practically every case, the writer knows that many people will eventually read the report, or at least some parts of it. Therefore, it is important that the report be thorough, that it contain all the information each reader could want to know. When you write a formal report, then, you must include the answers to whatever questions several readers might have, while at the same time preventing such details from distracting the reader who does not need them or want them.

There are two ways of handling this problem, and both of them involve removing the detailed references from the body of the text and putting them someplace else, either at the bottom of the page or among the end material.

FOOTNOTE-BIBLIOGRAPHY SYSTEM

If you want references at the bottom of the page, do it like this: When you go to the library to dig up source material, make sure you take some blank note cards with you. Go directly to the reference librarian and ask what specialized encyclopedias or other reference books the library holds in the field you are writing on. Turn to the bibliographies included in the encyclopedias and make a list of books relevant to your specific subject. Next, go to the periodical indexes and do the same there. You should end up with a fairly long list of books and articles relating to your topic. Your library will not have all of them, of course. To find out which ones *are* immediately available, go to the card catalog and check your list against what you find there. Usually, you will run across some recent acquisitions that you don't have on your list. These are most valuable to you.

Make out a bibliography card for each book; include the author, the title, the publisher, and the place and date of publication. Also include the call number so you can find the book in the stacks. Your bibliography card should look like this, but in longhand, of course:

651.75
L64w

Lindauer, J. S. Writing in Business. New York: The Macmillan Company, 1971.

(Contains glossary of grammatical and rhetorical practices)

If there are some sources you really need but your library doesn't have, ask the librarian about the possibility of getting them through interlibrary loan.

Now dig out the books and *carefully* quote significant and usable passages on note cards, *one passage to a card!* Include quotation marks, and be sure you list author, title, and page numbers on each note card. Take more information than you need; it's easier to discard some later than it is to hunt for the book again if you forget to include page references, for instance. Your note cards should look like this:

Lindauer stresses the importance of explaining why as well as telling how in writing directives:

"You may wonder why it is necessary to report any more . . . than the facts of the new procedure; the reader is an employee who should simply do his job as he is told. Nevertheless, some people prefer the way they are used to doing things, especially when new ways require more effort. Thus, they have to know why, or they will not pay attention."

—J. S. Lindauer, Writing in Business, p. 174.

Later on, when you write your report, you may decide to paraphrase Lindauer instead of quote directly. But you cannot decide to quote the passage directly if you have only a paraphrase of it on your note card.

The reason you put only one passage on a note card is that you will then be able to shuffle your stack of notes into the sequence demanded by the organization of your report.

In your final draft, you must footnote every reference to a particular source, whether you quote verbatim or only paraphrase. Number your footnotes consecutively throughout your report and put them at the bottom of the page the reference appears on. This does complicate typing because the typist needs to guess how much room to leave at the bottom of each page for footnotes. But it saves your reader the inconvenience of flipping to the back of your report to find them.

Here are some sample footnotes referring to books:

[1] *Dorothy Rubin, The Vital Arts—Reading and Writing (New York: Macmillan Publishing Co., Inc., 1979), p. 45.*
[2] *Kenneth W. Houp and Thomas E. Pearsall, Reporting Technical Information, 5th ed. (Encino, California: Glencoe Publishing Co., Inc., 1980), pp. 219–220.*
[3] *Rubin, p. 48.*

Notice that you need to give complete information only for the first reference to a particular source; listing only the author and the page reference is sufficient for subsequent references to that same source. But if somewhere else in your report you refer to another book by Rubin, footnote 3, above, would then look like this: "[3] Rubin, *Vital Arts*, p. 48."

These next footnotes refer to periodicals (a magazine, a journal, and a newspaper, in that order):

[4] *"American Housing: From Dream to Nightmare," Consumers' Research, June 1980, p. 9.*
[5] *Donald Greene, "Periodical Publications in Post-Restoration and Eighteenth-Century Studies," The Scriblerian, Vol. XI, No. 2 (Spring, 1979): 87.*
[6] *"Editorial," New York Times, 14 July 1980, p. 17.*

Here are the same references as they would appear in a bibliography. Notice the alphabetizing by last names, the punctuation, and the absence of page references, except to indicate inclusive pages of articles in periodicals:

"American Housing: From Dream to Nightmare." Consumers' Research, June 1980, pp. 9–15.
"Editorial." New York Times, 14 July 1980, pp. 17–18.
Greene, Donald. "Periodical Publications in Post-Restoration and Eighteenth-Century Studies." The Scriblerian, Vol. XI, No. 2 (Spring, 1979): 87–91.

Houp, Kenneth W., and Thomas E. Pearsall. *Reporting Technical Information*, 5th ed. Encino, California: Glencoe Publishing Co., Inc., 1980.

Rubin, Dorothy. *The Vital Arts—Reading and Writing*. New York: Macmillan Publishing Co., Inc., 1979.

You should triple space between the body of the text and the footnotes at the bottom of a page. Single space within footnotes and bibliography entries, and double space between them.

Now it's your turn to try some. Rearrange the following data into either footnote form or bibliography form, as the directions indicate. The answers are on page 395.

1. Write a footnote that includes the following information:

The title of the book is *Effective Business Communications;* the page you are quoting from is 194; the publisher is McGraw-Hill Book Company; the place of publication is New York; the authors are Herta A. Murphy and Charles E. Peck; the book is the second edition; although this is the seventh footnote in your report, it is the first time you refer to this book; and the publication date is 1976.

_____

_____

_____

2. The fourteenth footnote in your report refers to page 204 of Murphy and Peck's book. You refer to no other books by Murphy and Peck in your report. Write footnote fourteen.

_____

3. Rearrange the following data into a footnote reference:

The magazine is *Saturday Review;* the author is Edwin McDowell; the page number of the reference is 69; the issue of the magazine is October, 1980; and the title of the article is "Is the First Novel Boom a Bust?" Although this is the third footnote in your report, it is the first time you refer to this article.

_____

_____

_____

4. Arrange the Murphy and Peck source as a bibliography entry.

_____

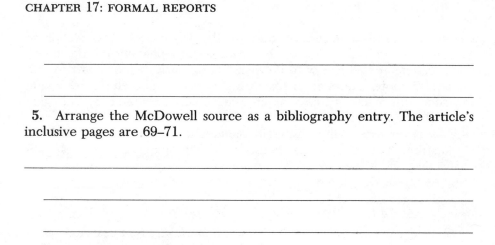

5. Arrange the McDowell source as a bibliography entry. The article's inclusive pages are 69–71.

AUTHOR-DATE, REFERENCES-CITED SYSTEM

Documenting with footnotes and bibliographies, although at one time by far the most common system and still the one preferred by some people, has recently given way, especially in the sciences, to a much more streamlined method. Known as the author-date, references-cited system, it is now acceptable in all research reporting for business. It makes the necessary information available to the reader, but it does not clutter up the text's pages with such information as publisher, place of publication, and so on, since all of that shows up at the end of the report anyway.

Using this system, the writer includes in parentheses, right in the text of the report, any of the following information the text itself does not give: author's last name, date of publication, and page references (if the writer is referring to specific passages). For example, these three sentences from three different reports use the author-date, references-cited system:

> *Houp and Pearsall (1980: 71–72) quote paragraphs from a medical school's health letter to explain methods of presenting background material.*
>
> *A recent text (Rubin, 1979) integrates workbook exercises with explanatory paragraphs so that the student can apply the theory immediately after reading about it.*
>
> *A more recent study (Stevens and Garcia, 1980: 31–32) argues for an increase of critical literature on the discipline of journalism history.*

In place of the usual bibliography at the end of the report, writers using this method include a section headed *References Cited.* The list includes all the sources the writer referred to in the text, arranged alphabetically by authors' last names. This serves, then, as both bibliography and footnotes, except that traditional bibliographies also may include books not referred to in the text.

In reading the report, the reader learns author, date, and page references immediately, and, if necessary, turns to the *References Cited* section to get the publication data. Since the entries are in alphabetical order there, this is easier for the reader to do than paging back in the report to find the first footnote reference to a source. The system also eliminates giving the same information twice: once in a first footnote reference, and again in a bibliographical entry.

The writer uses slightly different punctuation in the *References Cited* section from the usual punctuation used in bibliographies. Compare capitalization and underlining as well as commas and sequence of elements in these examples with the ones given earlier as bibliography entries:

> *Editorial, 14 July 1980, New York Times, pp.17–18.*
>
> *Greene, Donald, Spring 1979, Periodical publications in post-restoration and eighteenth-century studies, The Scriblerian, v.11, no.2, pp. 87–91.*
>
> *Rubin, Dorothy, 1980, The vital arts—reading and writing: New York, Macmillan.*

Using this system requires no changes in the way you go about digging up your material in the library, except that your note cards and bibliography cards should reflect the kind of punctuation you will be using in the *References Cited* section of your report.

Now try using the author-date, references-cited system of documenting. The following three exercises give you footnoted sentences from the body of a report, followed by the corresponding footnote itself. First convert the documentation from footnote-bibliography to author-date, references-cited form. Then write the entry you would use for that source in your *References Cited* section. The answers are on page 395.

6. Footnote-Bibliography:

Text: Who receives the death penalty? This question has no definite answer, except that it depends on the seriousness of the crime and the status of the offender.[5]

Footnote: [5] Elinor Lander Horwitz, Capital Punishment, U.S.A. (Philadelphia: J. B. Lippincott Co., 1933), p. 15.

Author-Date, References-Cited:

Text:

_____

_____

_____

References Cited: _____

_____

7. Footnote-Bibliography:

Text: According to one authority, "The mood and the temper of the people with regard to the treatment of the crime and the criminals is one of the unfailing tests of the civilization of any country."[4]

Footnote: [4] James V. Bennett, I Chose Prison (New York: Alfred A. Knopf, 1970), p. 158.

Author-Date, References-Cited:

Text: _____

_____

_____

_____

References Cited: _____

_____

8. Footnote-Bibliography:

Text: Allen Nevins believed that Roosevelt was to blame for the failure of the 1933 London Conference.[17]

Footnote: [17] Allen Nevins, The New Deal and World Affairs (New York: Yale Press, 1950), p. 76.

Author-Date, References-Cited:

Text: _____

_____

References Cited: _____

_____

For these next two exercises, convert the bibliography entry into a *References Cited* entry.

9. Burns, James. The Lion and the Fox. New York: Harcourt, Brace, Inc., 1956.

_____

_____

10. Bronson, Margaret. American History for Today. Boston: Ginn and Company, 1970.

_____

_____

PRELIMINARIES AND END MATERIAL

The formal report differs from a short special report in another way besides the documenting of evidence. Because not all readers will want to read the whole report, and because the length and complexity of the subject may make it difficult for them to use the report efficiently, it is necessary to add some sections to help those readers. Adding a table of contents and a synopsis at the beginning and a bibliography, some appendixes, or an index at the end will do that. It is also necessary to make the report identifiable at a glance and to give potential readers a context for reading the report—a context that includes the genesis and intended use of the report. A title fly, title page, letter of authorization, and letter of transmittal will do that.

First of all, the company you work for may well have a standard format that all formal reports identified with that company must follow. If so, by all means use that format. But if you are free to design your own report, the following comments will help you put together one that meets the tests of clarity and common sense.

"Nobody does a formal report like Mr. Cranston."

The most important thing to remember when designing your report and selecting its components is that a formal report, like a machine, should have no unnecessary parts. Every section must have a clear function.

A few of these sections will always be necessary, simply because of the nature of formal reports. For example, the length of the report and its consequent sectioning of internal parts make a table of contents indispensable.

Here is a list of preliminary sections and end-material sections, with the optional ones in parentheses. You would probably never use all of them in the same report, but the ones you do use should appear in this sequence:

Preliminary Sections	Title Page (Letter of Authorization) Letter of Transmittal Table of Contents (Table of Illustrations) Abstract
Body	Essentially, an analytical or informational special report, with full documentation of evidence
End Material	Bibliography or References Cited Appendix (Index)

Title Page

The title page must contain these four items: (1) title of the report, (2) name, office, and firm of the person receiving the report, (3) name, office, and firm (or department, if report is intra-firm) of the writer of the report, and (4) the date. Center these four items on the title page and space them evenly from top to bottom.

Choose a title carefully. Try to answer the *who, what, when, where, why,* and *how* of your report in fewer than twenty words. For instance, ENVIRONMENTAL EFFECT OF SEWERAGE PLANT EFFLUENT ON REPRODUCTION OF COLIFORM BACTERIA IN THE FOX RIVER DURING SUMMER AND AUTUMN would be a good title for a formal report. But EFFLUENT AND BACTERIA would be too vague, and A SEASONAL ASSAY OF COLIFORM BACTERIA IN THE FOX RIVER WITH RESPECT TO ENVIRONMENTAL FACTORS AND REPRODUCTIVE ABILITY MADE BY COMPARING SAMPLES FROM TWO TEST SITES ABOVE THE SEWERAGE PLANT EFFLUENT AND ONE SITE BELOW IT FROM JULY TO NOVEMBER would be too long and detailed for a title.

Letter of Authorization

If someone has asked you in writing to make the report, include a copy of that authorization immediately after the title page. This is not necessary, but it can serve as a reminder to all concerned of what the exact purpose of your report is.

Letter of Transmittal

If you are submitting your report to someone within the organization, use your company's memorandum form (To:, From:, Subject:, Date:) to direct your report to that person. If you are submitting your report to someone outside the organization, use letterhead stationery. Make sure your letter or memorandum mentions the title of your report, refers to the reader's request for the report, contains some general commentary on the report's purpose and coverage, and acknowledges cooperation you received in gathering your information. Use the date on your title page in dating this letter or memorandum.

Table of Contents

Include only headings used in your report. Capitalize and punctuate them just as they appear in the body, and make sure the page numbers are accurate. Use lower case Roman numerals (i,ii,iii,iv) for the pages of the preliminary material; use Arabic numerals (1,2,3) for all other pages, starting with the first page of the body. Count the title page, but do not put any number on it; that means you will never use the Roman numeral *i*. Center all page numbers at the bottoms of the pages. Do not include in the Table of Contents any material that precedes the Table of Contents.

Table of Illustrations

Use this section only if you think the illustrations might be useful beyond the purposes of your report. If you intend them strictly as elaborations of statements you make in the text, do not include a Table of Illustrations, but in that case be especially careful of where you place them. They should appear immediately after whatever it is they illustrate, so that your reader will not have to hunt for them.

Abstract

The abstract is, in some respects, the most important section of all. It is a one- or two-page condensation of your entire report, and it is the *only* part that some of your readers will ever choose to see. To save time and expense, most large corporations distribute report abstracts throughout the organization so that people can decide for themselves whether they need to see a copy of the entire report. If your abstract very cogently and convincingly explains your report in a nutshell, you have accomplished your purpose and saved many people valuable reading time in the process. Because the abstract is so important, you should take special care in its wording. Be concise, but make sure you include the report's purpose, the conclusions and recommendations (or the summary, if the report is informational), and the main evidence supporting them. In other words, give your reader a one-page statement of the *purpose,* the *evidence,* and the *bottom line* of your report if you can. This may take two pages, but if you write more than five hundred words for this, you are defeating the purpose of the abstract.

Bibliography or References Cited

If you use the Footnote-Bibliography system, the Bibliography section may contain more sources than just the ones you cited in the text. This can be useful to a reader who wants to gain a wide background on the subject of your report. But include such sources only if you think some readers will really want them.

If you use the Author-Date, References-Cited system, include only the sources you actually cited in the text.

Appendix

The Appendix section enables you to make your report extremely flexible in its usefulness. In general, write the body of your report for an *uninformed* reader, and put technical details in the Appendix. This way, top management can easily understand the text of your report because your reasoning in it is free of technical terminology and complex data.

Index

You may include an index similar to ones found in most textbooks if you think it will be useful. But it is very seldom worthwhile unless the report is extremely large.

Begin each section of the preliminaries and of the end material on a new page, but begin each section of the body immediately after the previous one.

Now, to reinforce your understanding of the preliminaries and end material of a formal report, answer the following questions. The answers are on page 395.

11. What preliminary sections should all formal reports contain?

---

12. What other sections may the preliminaries contain, but only if they serve a functional purpose?

---

13. What end-material sections should all formal reports contain?

_____

14. What other section may the end material contain, if there is a need for it?

_____

15. Which section of a formal report gets the widest readership?

_____

"I dread doing these annual reports."

The following fictitious example illustrates the preliminary and end-material sections necessary in a formal report. I have omitted the body of the report itself because it would be simply a documented version of an analytical or informational report, and we have already studied those.

380

EFFECT OF SEWERAGE PLANT EFFLUENT

ON REPRODUCTION OF COLIFORM BAC-

TERIA IN THE GREEN RIVER DURING

SUMMER AND AUTUMN

Prepared for

Mr. Thomas P. Lylen
Superintendent
Municipal Sewerage Plant
Fox Bay, VT 79826

by

R. Skelton Howard
Director
Howard Laboratories
Eau Claire, WI 56799

December 3, 19XX

(Howard Laboratories Letterhead)

December 3, 19XX

Mr. Thomas P. Lylen
Superintendent
Municipal Sewerage Plant
Fox Bay, VT 79826

Dear Mr. Lylen:

Here is the report you asked me to make for you in
your letter of April 13, 19XX. You said you needed
specific data on the extent to which your plant's effluent
affected the environment, in particular the numbers of
coliform bacteria in the Green River.

Effect of Sewerage Plant Effluent on Reproduction
of Coliform Bacteria in the Green River During Summer and
Autumn thoroughly measures that effect. New techniques
in developing control cultures enabled us to describe the
effects of sewerage-plant effluent much more accurately
than was possible in the past.

I think you will find the report useful in planning
your new filtration system. For instance, the "Appendix"
contains data from all three sites. This should help you
decide what filtration capacity you will need in your new
system.

Your employees gave our team excellent cooperation
throughout the study. Please extend my thanks to them,
especially to Ms. Jaynelle Roberts for her help in checking
sample identifications. The accuracy of our report depended
on that.

My staff and I enjoyed working on this for you, and
we would be happy to assist you in any way we can to derive
the most benefit from the findings presented here.

Sincerely,

R. Skelton Howard

R. Skelton Howard
Director

RSH/rl

TABLE OF CONTENTS

iii

ABSTRACT

The purpose of this report is to measure the effect of Fox Bay's Sewerage Plant effluent on coliform bacteria numbers in the Green River. Water samples taken from three river sites--one above the Hidetown dam, one 200 feet upstream of the plant's discharge pipe, and one 200 feet downstream of the plant's discharge pipe--show a considerable increase in coliform bacteria downstream of the pipe. Although the maximum number found is within EPA standards, it is evident that the plant's present filtration system is just barely able to keep the bacteria within limits.

All sampling took place between July 11 and November 22, 19XX, a period when coliform bacteria numbers are naturally at their highest. The filtration system is therefore more than adequate during the winter and spring months, when the bacteria count is naturally quite low.

The thirty-seven page body of the report would appear between the previous page and the following one.

REFERENCES CITED

Bigger, J.W., 1937, The growth of coliform bacilli in water, Journal of Pathological Bacteriology, 44:167-211.

Butterfield, C.T., 1933, Observations on changes in numbers of bacteria in polluted water, Sewage Works Journal, 5, 4, 600 (July 1933).

Collins, V.G., 1960, The distribution and ecology of gram-negative organisms other than enterobacteriaceae in lakes, Journal of Applied Bacteriology, 23:510-514.

Hendricks, C.W., 1971, Enteric Bacterial degradation of stream detritus, U.S. Environmental Protection Agency, 16050 EQS, 12/71.

Kittrell, F.W., and S.A. Furfari, 1963, Observations of coliform bacteria in streams, Water Pollution Control Federal Journal, 35:1361-1385.

Morrison, S.M., and J.F. Fair, 1966, Influence of environment on stream microbial dynamics, Hydrology Paper No. 13, Colorado State University, Fort Collins, Colorado.

------- 1967, Recovery of bacterial pathogens from high-quality surface water, Water Resources Research, V. 3:799-803.

Petersen, N.J., and J.R. Boring, 1960, A study of coliform densities and escherichia serotypes in two mountain streams, American Journal of Hydrology, 71:134-140.

Taylor, E.W., 1958, The examination of waters and water supplies, 7th ed.: London, J. & A. Churchill, Ltd.

38

APPENDIX
    The next three pages contain sample data, in tabular form, for each of the three sites.

DATE	TEMP. C	D. O.	Ortho Phosphate	Nitrite Nitrogen	Free Chloride	Coliform per 100 ml	Salmonella per 100 ml
7-11	28	7	2.1	--	175	25,800	20
7-19	27	7	1.38	--	75	TNC	36
7-27	29	6	1.4	--	105	58,500	632
8-4	25.5	6	5.9	.025	120	85,000	343
8-17	25.5	4	1.21	.04	150	170,000	224
8-23	23	6	1.0	.089	65	31,000	440
9-8	25	4	.95	.035	95	52,000	380
9-23	18	7	.7	.065	35	43,000	293
10-14	14.5	10	.85	.12	95	89,100	213
10-29	10	8	--	.07	40	41,000	236
11-22	1.5	11	1.15	.01	40	29,000	98

Environmental and bacteriological data from Site 1.
All physical data are expressed in mg/l.

40

DATE	TEMP. C	D. O.	Ortho Phosphate	Nitrite Nitrogen	Free Chloride	Coliform per 100 ml	Salmonella number per 100 ml
7-11	23	10	.32	--	25	25,600	12
7-19	26	10	.93	--	25	TNC	12
7-27	28	8	.8	--	35	47,500	30
8-4	24.5	8	3.2	.015	30	57,000	232
8-17	24.5	5	.6	.02	25	63,000	124
8-23	23	6	1.4	.039	40	36,000	446
9-9	24	7	.7	.015	30	40,000	133
9-23	16.5	10	.425	.015	25	36,000	160
10-14	13	12	.18	.018	25	38,000	142
10-29	9.5	10	--	.02	25	37,000	136
11-22	1.0	11	1.45	.01	30	24,000	96

Environmental and bacteriological data from Site 2.
All physical data are expressed in mg/l.

41

DATE	TEMP. °C	D. O.	Ortho Phosphate	Nitrite Nitrogen	Free Chloride	Coliform per 100 ml	Salmonella number per 100 ml
7-11	23.5	11	.23	---	15	19,000	0
7-19	26.5	8	.58	---	15	19,000	28
7-27	27	8	.58	---	20	11,000	92
8-4	25.5	11	.25	.005	20	15,000	108
8-17	26	8	.7	.01	20	17,000	72
8-23	24	7	.55	.019	25	15,000	66
9-8	24	6	.9	.005	20	14,000	20
9-23	15.5	11	.5	.005	30	10,000	26
10-14	11	12	.1	.01	17.5	32,000	20
10-29	9.5	10	---	.009	15	31,000	13
11-22	1.0	11	1.01	.005	30	17,000	8

Environmental and bacteriological data from Site 3.
All physical data are expressed in mg/l.

42

FOR CLASS DISCUSSION

1. In spite of what you learned in this chapter, in the real world there do exist many lengthy reports that contain preliminary and end-material sections, but that have no documentation whatsoever. What subjects might not require any documentation? Is an undocumented report of this type likely to be analytical or informational? Would an architect's formal proposal for a new building need documentation? Would a formal report tracing recent trends in labor negotiations require documentation?

2. Discuss the following advice to writers of formal reports: "You should write the preliminary sections in the *reverse* order of their actual appearance in the finished report."

3. Describe some specific situations that might induce the writer of a formal report to include
(a)   a letter of authorization
(b)   a table of illustrations
(c)   an index

TEST YOURSELF

The answers are on page 396.

Matching

1. ( ) footnote-bibliography

2. ( ) Abstract

3. ( ) Letter of Authorization

4. ( ) Letter of Transmittal

5. ( ) Index

6. ( ) Body

7. ( ) Title Page

8. ( ) Author-date, references-cited

9. ( ) Appendix

10. ( ) Lower case Roman Numerals

a. documented special report

b. not written by report writer

c. traditional system of documentation

d. last section of preliminaries

e. optional section in end material

f. first page of entire report

g. pagination of preliminaries

h. section for technical details

i. memorandum or letterhead stationery

j. modern system of documentation

APPLY YOURSELF

You are Daniel Shelby, research assistant at Accuwhiz Publishing Company. Today you received the following memorandum from the senior editor, Ms. Eleanor Elzevir:

NOTE: Insert your major field of study in the blanks.

Memorandum

To: Dan Shelby   Date: November 15, 19XX
From: E. Elzevir
Subject: Textbook Market in _____

I need to know some details about our competitors' textbook offerings

in _____ because I will be making some decisions soon on whether or not to increase our college textbook titles in that field.

Specifically, I have to have a clear idea as to whether the trend is toward or away from general courses in that subject. I also need to know whether our competitors offer workbooks or books of readings as supplements to their basic texts and whether those basic texts use a programmed format. It would also help if you could find out the average number of pages and the average price for a hardcover text designed for general or introductory courses in the field.

I will need your report by December 20.

Write the formal report you would submit to Ms. Elzevir. Get your data from the library, from questionnaires, from interviews, or from any combination of these.

ANSWERS TO EXERCISES

1. [7] Herta A. Murphy and Charles E. Peck, *Effective Business Communications*, 2d ed. (New York: McGraw-Hill Book Co., 1976), p. 194.

2. [14] Murphy and Peck, p. 204.

3. [3] Edwin McDowell, "Is the First Novel Boom a Bust?" *Saturday Review*, October 1980, p. 69.

4. Murphy, Herta A. and Charles E. Peck. *Effective Business Communications*, 2d ed. New York: McGraw-Hill Book Co., 1976.

5. McDowell, Edwin. "Is the First Novel Boom a Bust?" *Saturday Review*, October 1980, pp. 69–71.

6. Text: Who receives the death penalty? This question has no definite answer, except that it depends on the seriousness of the crime and the status of the offender (Horwitz, 1973: 15).
   References Cited:
   Horwitz, Elinor Lander, 1973, Capital punishment, U.S.A.: Philadelphia, Lippincott.

7. Text: According to one authority (Bennett, 1970: 158), "The mood . . . country."
   References Cited:
   Bennett, James V., 1970, I chose prison: New York, Knopf.

8. Text: Allen Nevins (1950: 76) believed that Roosevelt was to blame for the failure of the 1933 London Conference.
   References Cited:
   Nevins, Allen, 1950, The new deal in world affairs: New York, Yale.

9. Burns, James, 1956, The lion and the fox: New York, Harcourt Brace.

10. Bronson, Margaret, 1970, American history for today: Boston, Ginn and Company.

11. Title Page, Letter of Transmittal, Table of Contents, and Abstract

12. Letter of Authorization and Table of Illustrations

13. Bibliography (or References Cited) and Appendix

14. Index

15. Abstract

ANSWERS TO TEST YOURSELF

1. c
2. d
3. b
4. i
5. e
6. a
7. f
8. j
9. h
10. g

18
Oral Reports

As a member of a business organization, you will have to use your speaking skills as well as your writing skills. In fact, you may find yourself making more oral reports than written ones.

You may have to conduct training sessions in your area of expertise. Frequently your boss will ask you for an oral presentation that explains the status of a project you are working on. When you have completed a project, you may need to report its results orally first and then in writing. Sometimes you will want to call a meeting of your subordinates so that you can make an oral explanation of new policies or procedures; that way you will get immediate feedback and will be able to clarify your meaning on the spot. Perhaps you will need to make a committee report at a general meeting. Maybe you will have to conduct a sales-campaign kickoff. Or you might present an advertising campaign proposal orally to a prospective client. You might even find yourself invited to speak to outside groups as a lecturer at their meetings or conventions.

All these speaking assignments have much in common with business-writing assignments. You must have a clear idea of your purpose, you must see things from your audience's point of view, you must know your subject thoroughly, and you must organize your material so that it enters your audience's minds in the most understandable sequence.

Therefore, the first steps in preparing an oral report are exactly the same as the first steps in preparing a written one. That is, you gather your material and organize it the same way for both: good news deductively and bad news inductively. But after those steps, the differences are very great.

When you write a report, you have no options as to mode of presentation; the written word is the written word. But when you report orally, there are four possible modes you could choose from:

1. IMPROMPTU. An impromptu speech is one made without specific

preparation. The speaker relies on his or her general knowledge of the subject and attempts to "wing it." Usually, impromptu speeches are very weak in accuracy and organization. DO NOT USE THIS MODE FOR ORAL REPORTS.

2. MEMORIZED. A memorized speech is one delivered totally from memory. Such speeches are inflexible; they prevent the speaker from adapting to the needs of the audience and seldom sound sincere or convincing. And the speaker could easily ruin the speech by having a brief memory lapse. DO NOT USE THIS MODE FOR ORAL REPORTS.

3. WRITTEN. A written speech is one composed ahead of time and read word for word from the paper. Such speeches have mostly the same shortcomings as memorized speeches do. But when precise details and exact wording are very important, you may need to use this mode. If you do use it, be careful to make your delivery sound like normal speech; i.e., do not pronounce the word *a* to rhyme with *day,* and do not pronounce *the* to rhyme with *me,* except when it precedes a vowel sound. **Do Not Use This Mode Unless You Have To.**

4. EXTEMPORANEOUS. An extemporaneous speech is one organized very carefully beforehand and delivered from an outline or from note cards. It is extremely flexible in that the speaker can spend more time or less time on any of the sections to suit the audience's needs. **Use This Mode for Oral Reports Whenever You Can.**

Suppose you have gathered your material, selected your main points and organized them on the basis of your purpose and your audience's needs, and chosen your mode of delivery. From this point on, you must keep in

"A funny thing happened on my way over here. . . ."

mind the most important difference between a written report and an oral one: In a written report the *reader* controls the pace, but in an oral report the *speaker* controls the pace.

The reader of a written report can go back to reread earlier sentences, spend considerable time studying complex tables, charts, and verbal explanations, read the report piecemeal at several sittings, and even skip over the less important sections. The audience listening to an oral report can do none of that.

The speaker delivering an oral report determines how much information *all* of the audience must hear, how quickly they will have to absorb it, and how long they will have to listen to it. When you give an oral report, then, you must exercise your control over pace so considerately that no one in the audience will feel the need to reread, to pore over complex explanations in order to digest them, or to skip over the parts that pertain to somebody else. How can you do this? Mainly by simplifying your points, by speaking slowly and pausing sufficiently for your statements to sink in, and by using enough repetition to keep your organization clear every step of the way. But there are other ways too. Maintain good eye contact with your audience so that you can respond to puzzled looks, slouching bodies, or signs of inattention. But most of all, plan your presentation so that it will not outlast the attention span of your audience. Keep it down to about twenty minutes, or a half hour at the most. After that, nobody will be listening, anyway. And by all means plan to use some audiovisual aids, or at least visual aids. Graphics are very important in a written report, but they are practically indispensable to a good oral report.

Because preparing an oral report is the same as preparing a written one up to and including the outline stage, we need to consider here only the four main steps you should follow once you have completed the outline: (1) prepare your visual aids, (2) plan your opening and closing remarks, (3) rehearse your speech, and (4) deliver your speech in a cordial tone that invites goodwill.

PREPARE YOUR VISUAL AIDS

Effectively using visuals to illustrate your speech involves two considerations: the illustrations themselves and the equipment needed to present them. Let's discuss some of the more common types of equipment.

The chalkboard, or blackboard, is perhaps the best all-round visual tool. It is very inexpensive to use, yet has remarkable flexibility. You can write or draw on it before your speech, cover it with a shade or screen of some kind, and reveal the material at the appropriate time in your presentation. You can erase material you no longer need, so it will not distract your audience during the rest of your speech. You can even keep your major points visible while you illustrate the particular subdivisions of each one— if the chalkboard is large enough, of course.

The only shortcomings of a chalkboard are that it is difficult to write on while facing your audience, and it is also difficult to make lines heavy enough so people more than thirty feet away can see them clearly. But a little experience in using the chalkboard can greatly minimize these shortcomings.

The overhead projector enables you to face your audience while presenting your visual material on a screen or large, light-colored wall. It has the added advantage of putting you in complete control of your audience's attention. With a plain sheet of paper you can mask everything on a transparency except the thing you are talking about; with a grease pencil you can point to, or underline, the parts you want to stress; and with a flip of the switch you can remove the image altogether and reestablish eye contact with your audience. You can use it with the room lights on if you wish your audience to take notes, or you can use it with the room lights off if you want to make the image more vivid and eliminate all visual distractions for your audience. You can use translucent, colored inks on the transparencies to make easy-to-understand, multicolored graphics. You can use the same transparency several times during your presentation, and this can be a big help when you summarize at the end. You can even prepare several transparency overlays so that you can show contrasts, gradual developments or progressions, and the like. And you can use the same transparencies time and time again if you need to deliver the same speech to several groups of people.

The major shortcomings of the overhead projector are that, unless you want to use it as a chalkboard by writing on the projector stage with a grease pencil, you need to spend some time and money making your transparencies in advance. You also need electricity, of course, and a spare bulb to replace the one that is sure to burn out in the middle of your presentation.

It will also take some experience to learn how to walk around the machine towards your audience without tripping over the power cord. I know whereof I speak.

Opaque projectors are less flexible than overhead projectors in their use, but they have the advantage of requiring no preparation other than getting a screen and the machine itself to the site of your oral report. You can project the actual material onto the screen; you do not have to make transparencies or slides beforehand. Opaque projectors do require a very dark room for a satisfactory screen image, so your audience will be unable to take notes while the image is on the screen. But if you have multicolored bar graphs, colored illustrations, or even colored photographs to show your audience, you may find the opaque projector just right for your needs.

Again, learn how to change the bulb, and watch out for the cord.

Flip charts are large pads of blank paper (about a yard square) attached at the top so you can flip one sheet over at a time. The pad rests on a portable easel that allows you to locate your visual material in the best place for viewing by your audience. You can use a flip chart much the same way you use a chalkboard, except that you use a felt marker instead of a piece of chalk. But, unlike a chalkboard, the flip chart allows you to return to an earlier graphic quickly and easily. A further advantage, one it shares with the overhead projector, is that you can conveniently prepare some or all of your graphics in advance while you prepare your speech, without having to copy them out on the chalkboard during your delivery. This can save valuable minutes of your presentation time, and it avoids the distractions of writing and erasing while you are talking. By leaving the first sheet of the flip chart blank, you can also quickly flip all sheets forward and remove all your graphics from sight so they don't distract your audience. This corresponds to turning off the switch of an overhead projector.

A flip chart, then, combines a few advantages of the chalkboard and the overhead projector. And it eliminates some of their disadvantages. You can prepare pages of your flip chart more easily and at less cost than you can prepare transparencies, and you can show and conceal graphics much more quickly than you can on a chalkboard. An additional advantage of a flip chart is that you can tear off the sheets of paper as you fill them up and tape them on the wall in front of your audience for easy comparisons, references to cumulative effects, and the like.

It is also possible to trip over the leg of a flipchart easel.

Posters are similar to flip charts except that they enable you to do a much neater job in drawing graphics beforehand. But they are not very suitable for writing on during your presentation, except for such things as connecting dots on a line chart or putting a check mark after topics as you cover them. You can use posters very effectively in conjunction with other visual-aid tools like flip charts or chalkboards to keep certain graphics in your audience's view throughout your presentation. Place them on the chalk tray of a blackboard or on easels of their own.

Duplicating machines and copiers, although not actually used *during* your presentation, are important tools for making visual aids that can enhance and clarify your oral report. If the purpose of your speech is to explain a policy or a procedure, for example, it may be much easier for your audience to understand your message if each person has a copy of the policy or procedure you are explaining, especially if the material is rather complex or detailed. The greatest advantage, however, is that each member of your audience will have a personal copy to refer to long after your presentation is over.

But there are some serious drawbacks to using this kind of visual aid, too. First of all, you need to be careful about timing. If you distribute copies at the beginning of your presentation, your audience will be looking at their copies when you want them to be listening to you. If you distribute copies right before you intend to discuss them, the distribution process itself is distracting and invites some members of your audience to visit with each other. At any rate, distributing copies during your speech always interrupts the continuity of your presentation. Furthermore, your audience is not likely to take notes if you give them duplicated copies of your message, even if only in outline form. And people remember what they write down much better than what they merely see or hear—even if they never look at their notes again afterwards. Because of this, some speakers distribute copies of outlines and graphics only after the presentation is over, but audiences usually resent being tricked into taking notes this way.

In general, then, you should observe these two rules about handing out copies during your speech:

1. *Never distribute copies before you intend to cover that material in your speech.*

2. *Distribute only copies of complex charts, tables, or lists that are too detailed to show clearly on an overhead projector or other means of graphic presentation.*

Now we will consider some characterisitcs of good graphic illustrations themselves. They should be (1) easily visible, (2) simple and clear, and (3) manageable.

Visibility is crucial. A mock-up or model that is too small for everyone to see, or a chart with tiny lettering, is worse than no visual aid at all. And passing it around the room does not help; then it turns into a conversation piece for a constantly changing segment of your audience. Make sure even those in the back can clearly see the object you are displaying, or don't display it. Everything you expect your audience to read—except for distributed copies, of course—must have lettering large enough so those in the very back of the room can easily make it out. A good rule of thumb is that lettering size should be about one inch for every twenty-five feet of distance to the back of the audience. Use both capitals and lower case letters, and leave plenty of white space around the words on posters and flip charts to make them easy to read. Overhead projectors and opaque projectors must be far enough from the screen to make the image clearly legible. Make sure all projectors are in sharp focus.

All visual aids—whether charts, tables, graphs, or lettering—must be simple. Do not try to give all the details. Present only main divisions or topics in your visuals; present the subheadings and details in your oral development of them. Too much detail in a chart, for instance, clutters and confuses rather than clarifies. A written report can easily contain four or five main divisions without confusing the reader, but a visual aid for a speech should seldom have more than three or four main parts—whether they are topics listed on a poster, columns or rows of figures on an overhead-projector transparency, or diagrams on a chalkboard. Each new element you add to a figure complicates its message in a geometric progression. Keep it simple.

A good visual aid must be manageable. This doesn't mean only that it must be lightweight and portable instead of awkward and cumbersome. Its timing must be manageable too. You should be able to direct your audience's attention to it and away from it very easily. Whatever you intend to show, keep it out of sight until you get to the appropriate part of your presentation. Then show it, discuss it, and refer to it. But then immediately get it out of sight again so your audience can mentally move on to your next topic with you.

Models, mock-ups, and distributed copies of anything are very difficult to manage; flip-chart visuals and overhead-projector transparencies are very easy to manage.

Before we go on to planning your opening and closing remarks, answer these questions about what you have learned so far. The answers are on page 415.

1. What are the four modes of making an oral presentation?

_____

2. Which of the four modes should you generally use for making oral reports?

_____

3. Preparing an oral report and preparing a written report are the same up to and including what stage?

_____

4. What four steps follow the outline stage in the preparation of an oral report?

1. _____

2. _____

3. _____

4. _____

5. If you had to give the same oral presentation a large number of times to many different audiences, which types of visual aids do you think you would use?

PLAN YOUR OPENING AND CLOSING REMARKS

As noted earlier, the body or content of your oral report should be the same as it would be if you were making a written report. That includes the organization of the content, too. But an oral report is not a written report. And nowhere do the two kinds differ more than in their beginnings and endings. Think of these as gradually inclined ramps that enable your audience to ease up onto your topic and to ease themselves back down again into their everyday worlds where the knowledge they have just acquired or the arguments they have just heard will make a difference in their lives.

Opening remarks in an oral report should do two things: break the ice and stimulate interest in the content of your report. If the occasion is to be somewhat formal, someone will introduce you to the audience and acquaint them with your background and credentials. Be sure to thank the person who introduced you, and then greet the audience warmly. Immediately put your listeners at ease by relating yourself to them as cordially and humanly as possible. Stress what you have in common with them, explain why you are happy for the opportunity to speak to them, mention whatever good things you have heard about them. Whatever you do, make sure it is *positive;* if you get them feeling good about themselves, they will feel good about you—and that is essential.

If your oral report is very informal, like a twenty-minute oral presentation to your boss and a few other people who already know you and have an interest in your topic, you will need no introduction and can break the ice merely by saying something like this: "I know how important this budget proposal is to all of you, so I will get right down to what we are here for."

After breaking the ice by putting your audience at ease, you must prepare them for the business at hand. Again your strategy differs from what it would be in a written report. Because your audience cannot flip back to something you said earlier, it's a good idea to follow the age-old advice: Tell them what you're going to tell them; tell them; and then tell them what you told them. Your opening remarks, then, should include a capsule summary of what you are going to tell your audience. Once you have done that, go right into your report. For a twenty-minute speech, your opening remarks should take no more than a minute or two. They should never take more than five minutes, no matter how long your speech is.

Closing remarks should be brief, too. Once you say the welcome words "In conclusion . . ." or "In summary . . ." make sure you stop talking within a minute or two. After devoting a sentence or two to telling your audience

"Tell them what you're going to tell them, tell them, then tell them what you told them; tell them what you're going to tell them, tell them, then tell them what you told them; tell them what you're going to tell them, tell them, then tell them what you told them. Got it?"

what you have told them, you should help them down the off-ramp by relating your message to their lives. What does your report mean *to them?* If your message is persuasive, your call to action belongs here. State precisely what it is you are asking them to do. If your report is primarily informative, relate your central point to your audience's work responsibilities, their future planning, their everyday lives.

It's a good idea to include a question-and-answer period at the end of your speech, if you can. In answering questions from the audience, make sure you repeat all questions so everyone knows what you are answering, and always treat every question as if it were the best one you ever heard. It is very easy to talk down to an audience when answering questions because, after all, you certainly know more about the subject than your listeners do—otherwise you wouldn't be giving the speech in the first place. But *never* answer sarcastically. If you do, you may win a point, but you will surely lose an audience. If someone asks a question you cannot answer, say so; but promise to find the answer and report it later. Then make sure you do that. If necessary, get the person's name and address so you can

405

mail the answer. A little effort of this kind wins an enormous amount of goodwill.

If you decide to use a story as part of either your opening or closing remarks, be sure it is an anecdote, not merely a funny story; it must clearly relate to your subject or, better yet, stress some important point you make in your presentation. If it doesn't do that, leave it out.

Now answer the following questions about openings and closings. The answers are on page 415.

6. What are the two functions that opening remarks must perform?

_____

7. Why must opening remarks contain only *positive* statements about the audience?

_____

8. On the basis of this advice to speakers: "Tell them what you're going to tell them; tell them; and then tell them what you told them," which of the following would be a better quality in an oral report than it would be in a written report?
(a) evidence
(b) correct grammar
(c) repetition
(d) sound logic

_____

9. Your closing remarks should both summarize and
(a) include an unrelated joke.
(b) discourage questions from the audience.
(c) emphasize your background and credentials.
(d) relate your message to your listeners' lives.

_____

10. What should you do if, during a question-and-answer period, someone asks you a question you cannot answer?

_____

_____

REHEARSE YOUR SPEECH

You can never anticipate the snags you will run into in making an oral presentation nor be able to estimate how much time it will take you to give it unless you rehearse the whole thing. You might have some friends listen to it or you might tape record it and listen to it yourself, but in either case you should give your presentation a dry run in a room approximately the size of the one you will be using.

Practice everything, including your use of visual aids and your responses to probable questions from the audience. You might discover you have to speak louder and slower than you had thought. You might find that some of your transparencies are illegible on the projection screen or that your posters don't show up very well to someone sitting in the back of the room. It is better to find out such things while you can still do something about them.

Use a tape recorder especially if you will be reading your speech. When playing it back, listen carefully to discover whether your voice sounds conversational. It should not *sound* as if you are reading your sentences, even though you *are* reading them. Don't read too rapidly; if your speech is double-space typewritten (as it *should* be, and not in all capitals either), you should read at about the rate of three pages in five minutes.

If your speech will be extemporaneous, you will still be able to rearrange your material if you have your notes on note cards rather than on one sheet of paper. During or after your rehearsal, you can cue your notes to your visual aids so that you show your visuals at just the time your audience will need to see them.

The most important thing a rehearsal will do, however, is give you confidence in your subject and in your ability to present it clearly. This will go a long way toward relieving the inevitable stage fright you will feel when facing an audience, especially a large audience. But that doesn't mean you should rehearse only speeches you will make to large groups. You should rehearse *every* oral report you give, just to make sure you have your act together.

DELIVER YOUR SPEECH IN A CORDIAL TONE THAT INVITES GOODWILL

Tone, in this context, does not refer to voice pitch or resonance, but rather to the voice signals that reveal the speaker's attitude toward the subject and toward the audience. It has the same meaning as in a sentence like this: "I didn't like the tone of his voice when he said that." It is practically impossible to make your voice tone show an attitude that you don't really have. Therefore, the only way to deliver your speech in a cordial tone is to have a sincerely cordial attitude toward your audience. But even if you could speak in a tone contrary to your real feelings, your body language, vibes, or whatever else you want to call it would reveal your true attitude anyway. You must look at everything from your audience's point of view and sincerely try to help them receive your message. Only then will you get their goodwill, and only with their goodwill can you communicate successfully.

But what about that inevitable stage fright? Won't that distort your tone and make you seem stiff, tight, overly formal, and stodgy even when you have a very cordial attitude toward your listeners? Probably not. Unlike your true feelings toward your audience, your stage fright always seems hardly noticeable to other people. What you experience as stage fright is mostly adrenalin that actually makes you more alert and able to do a better job than you otherwise could.

Besides having a positive attitude toward your audience, however, there are a few other things you can do to improve your delivery.

The most important thing to do is to maintain eye contact with the people you are talking to. This is vital. It is the only way you can convince your audience you are talking *to* them and not *at* them. Without eye contact you cannot establish any kind of rapport with your audience, and you certainly cannot make sure they understand what you are saying. If the group is large, generally maintain eye contact with persons sitting toward the back of the room; those sitting in front will think you are looking at them too. But the reverse is not true.

The next most important thing you can do is to use facial expressions. In general, this will take care of itself if you maintain good eye contact. But sometimes you will have to practice in front of a mirror to avoid looking like The Great Stone Face. Nobody can listen very long to what appears to be a clothing-store mannikin wired for sound. Don't be afraid to smile when it seems appropriate to do so.

Pay special attention to your posture. Don't slouch or drape yourself over the lectern. Stand up straight.

When speaking in a large room to a large audience, make sure you open your mouth wider than you normally do in pronouncing your words. Besides helping you to slow down and articulate more carefully, this will help your voice to carry to the back of the room. Even if you use a microphone and don't need the extra voice volume, or even if you are speaking to a small group in a small room, you should open your mouth a bit wider than usual so that you can articulate crisply.

Don't overstress. When you put too much emphasis on stressed syllables, you invariably will swallow the unstressed ones. Vary your pitch, loudness, and rate of delivery, of course, but don't forget that overstressing the stressed syllables is just as bad as speaking in a monotone. You can try the experiment yourself: Try overstressing the primary stresses in the words of a sentence aloud. You will find that in order to make the stressed syllables more dominant, you will involuntarily decrease the loudness of the unstressed ones until they become practically inaudible.

Do not stress pronouns. Instead, stress the main verbs of your sentences. To convince yourself that this is good advice, listen to other people's normal conversation.

Finally, during your rehearsal, ask your friends to watch for any distracting mannerisms you may have. Such habits as putting all your weight on one foot, or fiddling with your watch, or rocking back and forth from your toes to your heels tend to keep your audience from concentrating on what you are saying. The problem here is that only other people can help you with this. If you knew your behavior distracted or annoyed others, you wouldn't have those habits and mannerisms in the first place. They are unconscious, and that is why they are so hard to eliminate. The easy way to get rid of a habit is, of course, to replace it with a new one. But new habits can soon become annoying to your listeners, too. The very best remedy is to concentrate very hard on your subject and your audience. Put everything else out of your mind. That way, whatever mannerisms you have will go unnoticed because your listeners will be concentrating on your message, not on you.

Now answer these questions about tone and delivery. The answers are on page 415.

11. Having a sincerely cordial attitude toward your audience is the only way to achieve
(a) the proper tone.
(b) audience goodwill.
(c) both of the above.
(d) none of the above.

12. Why is it good to experience some stage fright?
(a) You always appear more frightened than you are.
(b) The extra adrenalin helps you to relax.
(c) Both of the above.
(d) None of the above.

13. The best way to convince your audience you are talking *to* them, not *at* them, is to
(a) maintain eye contact.
(b) speak in a monotone.
(c) keep your own attention on your visual aids.
(d) none of the above.

14. It will be easier to use meaningful facial expressions if you
(a) memorize your speech.
(b) maintain eye contact.
(c) use an opaque projector.
(d) none of the above.

15. The very best remedy for annoying habits and mannerisms is to
(a) replace them with new habits.
(b) concentrate on your subject and your audience.
(c) rock back and forth from your toes to your heels.
(d) concentrate on your own clothing.

FOR CLASS DISCUSSION

A. Some speakers prefer to plan their opening and closing remarks a few minutes before actually delivering their speeches. What are the advantages of doing it this way? What are the dangers?

B. The ancient Greeks identified three elements as essential to good public speaking: (1) *ethos*, or the *character* of the speaker; (2) *logos*, or the *content* of the message; and (3) *pathos*, or the emotional appeal and *enthusiasm* of the delivery. Do these apply to giving oral reports?

C. Why are visual aids practically indispensable to an effective oral report?

D. Why are impromptu speeches and memorized speeches generally inappropriate for oral reports? Are there any business situations in which they would be appropriate?

TEST YOURSELF

Fill in the blanks. The answers are on page 416.

1. The _____ mode is appropriate for most oral reports in business.

2. When precise details and exact wording are very important for an oral report, the speaker should choose the _____ _____ mode.

3. In a business letter the _____ controls the pace.

4. The size of the lettering on posters should be about one inch for each _____ feet of distance between the poster and the back of the room.

5. All graphic illustrations should be (1) easily visible, (2) _____ _____, and (3) manageable.

6. The opening remarks in an oral report should break the ice and _____.

7. If your message is persuasive, your call to action belongs in your _____ remarks.

8. After you outline your material, your next four steps in making an oral report are (1) prepare your visual aids, (2) _____ _____, (3) rehearse your speech, and (4) deliver your speech in a cordial tone that invites goodwill.

9. The _____ mode makes it very difficult for the speaker to maintain good eye contact.

10. The best way to improve your use of facial expressions is to _____.

APPLY YOURSELF

A. Beginning with the outline of one of the reports you wrote for this course, construct some visual material, prepare your opening and closing remarks, rehearse the report as a ten-minute speech, and deliver your oral report to the class. Reserve the last two minutes of your allotted time for a question-and-answer period.

B. Present a four-minute speech to the rest of the class on one of the following topics:
(1)   Preparing Visuals for Oral Reports
(2)   Opening and Closing Remarks
(3)   Rehearsing an Oral Report with Tape Recorder and Mirror
(4)   Improving Your Speaking Skills
   Be sure your speech appeals to the eye as well as to the ear. Use visual aids, demonstrate your meaning by role playing, or have a classmate act out, as part of your presentation, such things as annoying mannerisms in a speaker and effective opening and closing remarks.

C. Prepare a three-minute *written* speech, practice delivering it, and present it to the class. Have your classmates evaluate your ability to make your voice sound conversational and your ability to maintain eye contact.

ANSWERS TO EXERCISES

1. impromptu, memorized, written, extemporaneous

2. extemporaneous

3. outline

4. (1) prepare visual aids, (2) plan opening and closing remarks, (3) rehearse the speech, and (4) deliver the speech in a cordial tone that invites goodwill

5. overhead-projector transparencies or posters

6. break the ice and stimulate interest in the content of the report

7. so the audience will feel good about themselves—and about the speaker

8. c

9. d

10. Admit you can't answer the question and promise to find out and report later, and then do it.

11. c (or a,b,c)

12. d

13. a

14. b

15. b

ANSWERS TO TEST YOURSELF

1. extemporaneous
2. written
3. reader
4. 25
5. simple and clear
6. stimulate interest in the content of the report
7. closing
8. plan your opening and closing remarks
9. written
10. maintain good eye contact

Part VI
Review of the Basics

19

Write Complete Sentences

The writer has two very important advantages over the speaker. First, writing allows careful thought, planning, and organization of the message. Perhaps you have noticed that when answering essay examinations you often discover, when time is nearly up and after you have been writing for hours, that finally you get a clear insight into the problem and wish you could begin all over. Such late insights are normal, and the business writer can use them to advantage, when not rushed to get the letter or report finished. The wise writer puts ideas on paper immediately, then rearranges and polishes their expression *after* the insight comes. (One look at the rough draft of this chapter would convince you of the importance of sorting out and revising before submitting the message to the reader.) When we speak extemporaneously, we do not have this advantage.

Second, writing provides a permanent record that the reader can read, re-read, and digest as quickly or slowly as necessary. Words on paper are permanent, legal documents. Such messages can be useful and influential for years. Moreover, they can influence more people than even our celebrated modern electronic media. This statement sounds extravagant until we consider the impact on civilization made by such pieces of written communication as the Bible, Shakespeare's plays, and our own Declaration of Independence and Constitution. Furthermore, when our readers get our ideas on paper those readers can study our meaning very carefully, re-read previous sentences, and weigh the significance of every word, every mark of punctuation. When we speak, our listeners cannot do this.

But these advantages are not free. It takes a lot of care and effort for the writer to capitalize on them.

For one thing, all writers—but especially business writers—must be careful to shape their messages into complete sentences. This is not so important for speakers because when we speak we accompany our words with voice inflections, facial expressions, and sometimes gestures that help us to clarify

419

our meaning. Even a chuckle, a grunt, or an unusually long pause can convey messages to a listener. But the writer does not have these aids; all the reader has to work with are the words on the page.

Therefore: *write only complete sentences.*

If you read the following aloud, it will sound like good English:

Our sales campaign cannot begin before March 15. Which is three weeks too late for adequate television exposure.

The listener can hardly notice the difference between dropping the voice for a period and dropping the voice for a comma. In fact, the following sentence would probably sound the same to a listener:

Our sales campaign cannot begin before March 15, which is three weeks too late for adequate television exposure.

But the *reader* of the two examples would certainly notice a big difference between them and would probably regard the writer of the first one as practically illiterate. Yet, the only real difference between the two is that the first one gives the reader the wrong punctuation and capitalization signals. When we read, we expect a capital letter at the beginning and a period at the end of a group of words to mean that those words add up to a complete statement.

You might wonder why "which is three weeks too late for adequate television exposure" does not constitute a sentence, while "This is three weeks too late for adequate television exposure" does. We need to distinguish between relative pronouns and demonstrative pronouns in order to see why. Relative pronouns—*who, whom, whose, which,* and *that*—need to have an antecedent (the thing they refer to) in the *same* sentence they appear in.

I have read your 　report　 *, which I think is very accurate.*

Demonstrative pronouns—*this, that, these,* and *those*—can have antecedents in the previous sentence.

They offered us 　a sedan and a station wagon　 *. These are the only cars available this month.*

In fact, an entire previous sentence can be the antecedent of a demonstrative pronoun.

I worked until eleven o'clock last night　. That is why I am so tired this morning.

Now, in order to discuss this difference between relative pronouns and demonstrative pronouns in a practical way, we will have to simplify a bit. First, we will refer only to declarative sentences (sentences that make a statement). Second, because only four of the relative pronouns—*who, whom, whose,* and *which*—are likely to give us any trouble in avoiding sentence fragments, we will ignore the relative pronoun *that* for the time being.

Now we can make the blanket rule: never begin a declarative sentence with who, whom, whose, or which.

The easiest way to correct a fragment beginning with one of these words is to change the preceding period to a comma and reduce the capital letter to lower case. However, you can do this only if the relative pronoun refers to the last noun of the preceding sentence.

EXERCISES

Let's practice revising a few. The answers are on page 437.

1. Here is next year's budget. Which reflects increasing energy costs.

_____

_____

Try this one:

2. I submitted my cost estimates to Ms. Mayer. Who will forward them to you.

_____

_____

And now try this:

3. I received this report from Mr. Lyttelton. Whom we have recently assigned to our Atlanta office.

_____

_____

Try one more:

4. You should talk to Mr. Morrow. Whose knowledge of the project is very extensive.

_____

_____

Of course, there are other ways to correct the relative-clause fragment. Instead of attaching the relative clause to the previous sentence, we might choose to make it into a sentence by itself. In the last example, for instance, we might have revised the passage this way:

> _You should talk to Mr. Morrow. His knowledge of the project is very extensive._

You should notice, however, that this revision has a different emphasis from the earlier one.

One more way we could correct the relative-clause fragment would be to convert it into the second half of a compound sentence:

You should talk to Mr. Morrow; his knowledge of the project is very extensive.

Again, you should notice a slight change in emphasis.

Which revision is best? Any one of them might be. It all depends on where you want to place the emphasis. This, in turn, depends on what precisely you are trying to say. If you want to stress the idea that your reader ought to talk to Mr. Morrow, and only want to mention the reason as a kind of afterthought, the first way is best:

You should talk to Mr. Morrow, whose knowledge of the subject is very extensive.

If you want to stress the reason as a kind of explanation of why you are telling your reader to talk to Mr. Morrow, the third revision is best:

You should talk to Mr. Morrow; his knowledge of the project is very extensive.

Here the semicolon binds the two clauses together, clearly suggesting that the second explains or justifies the first. But it also suggests that both clauses are nearly equal in importance.

The second revision, of course, makes two separate statements. In this kind of revision, the relationship between the two clauses almost seems to disappear, and each clause receives about equal emphasis. You would revise this way if you were trying to stress the second clause as much as possible.

The one thing you must not do is just let the relative clause float there. You must anchor it with a complete meaning of its own, or you must hook it onto some other sentence so it doesn't drift away into meaninglessness.

One other thing you need to remember is that you can't simply attach the relative clause to the previous sentence unless the last noun of that sentence is the antecedent of the relative pronoun. For instance, in the following example "Which" refers to the whole preceding sentence, not to the last noun of that sentence:

My order got mixed in with Mr. Dalrymple's. Which is why he received my shipment.

Here "Which" does not refer to Mr. Dalrymple, so we need to find another way to correct the fragment. We could change the relative pronoun to a demonstrative pronoun:

My order got mixed in with Mr. Dalrymple's. That is why he received my shipment.

Or, we could reconstruct the whole thing:

Mr. Dalrymple received my shipment because my order got mixed in with his.

Now let's try to eliminate a different kind of sentence fragment. There are certain words called subordinators that change an independent clause into a subordinate clause. Here are some of those subordinators:

if, when, although, because, that, before, after, while, though, whenever . . .

You can probably think of others. Whenever we put one of these subordinators in front of a sentence, that whole sentence becomes a single part of speech—either a noun, an adverb, or an adjective. For instance, if we put *if* in front of the sentence *We allow no price increases*, the whole sentence becomes a fragment:

If we allow no price increases

We no longer have a sentence; the whole thing has become just an adverb—with nothing to modify. To correct this, we must attach it to an independent clause, like this:

If we allow no price increases, our profit margin will disappear.

Or, of course, we could tag the fragment onto the end of an independent clause, rather than at the beginning:

Our profit margin will disappear if we allow no price increases.

(Notice that when the subordinate clause comes at the end rather than at the beginning, it usually does not require a comma to separate it from the rest of the sentence.)

Now we can make another rule: make sure every subordinate clause has an independent clause in the same sentence to support it.

5. Practice what you have learned by eliminating fragments from the following paragraph. The answer is on page 437.

This is Part III of the Abrams Report. Which you asked me to send you as soon as we finished it. The third paragraph explains the steps we took in determining the best site for the warehouse. Because you said you wanted detailed explanations of the procedures we followed. We used guidelines given us by Attorney F. E. Cassidy. Whom we have engaged as legal counsel. He comes to us highly recommended. Although his expertise is in another branch of the profession.

_____

_____

_____

_____

_____

_____

_____

_____

_____

_____

You might have constructed the second and fourth sentences like this:

The third paragraph explains the steps we took in determining the best site for the warehouse because you said you wanted detailed explanations of the procedures we followed.

And

He comes to us highly recommended although his expertise is in another branch of the profession.

But then *all* the sentences in the paragraph would end with a modifying clause. It is better to break up that kind of monotony.

So far we have looked at fragments that are really only dependent clauses—either relative or subordinate. Now let's look at a third kind that isn't a clause at all. These fragments lack either a subject, a predicate, or both.

Consider the following:

1. Before July 21.
2. The shipment having left our plant.
3. After analyzing the request for employee sickness benefits can go into effect July 1.

The first fragment, *Before July 21,* lacks a subject and a predicate. It is simply a prepositional phrase of the type some advertisers use to catch the reader's attention. No doubt you have seen sales letters or magazine advertisements that read this way. It's the sort of thing one often finds in junk mail in which the writer tries very hard to be informal: "Be sure to order your set of fluorescent dentures today. Before July 21." This kind of fragment makes the writer sound very enthusiastic, almost breathless, and encourages the reader to feel enthusiastic, too. Therefore, it may be appropriate for some kinds of advertising, but if carried too far, it sounds sophomoric. It certainly has no place in any other kind of business writing.

The second example, *The shipment having left our plant,* lacks a predicate. The noun *shipment* could serve as a subject of a sentence, but *having left our plant* is only a participial phrase modifying that noun. To change this fragment into a sentence, we would have to (a) convert *having* to a verb, or (b) add a whole new verb to serve as the predicate:

(a) *The shipment has left our plant.*
(b) *The shipment, having left our plant, should arrive soon.*

The third example, *After analyzing the request for employee sickness benefits can go into effect July 1,* lacks a subject. Apparently the writer wants *employee sickness benefits* to do double duty, both as object of the preposition *for* and as subject of the verb *can go.* But no term can serve more than one function in a sentence at a time. The best way to correct such a fragment is to provide the predicate with a new subject of its own:

After analyzing the need for employee sickness benefits, we can put them into effect July 1.

This is not a very good sentence; it seems to promise putting the benefits into effect while at the same time suggesting such a decision will depend on the results of the analysis. Yet, the writer is now in a position to sharpen the clarity of the sentence because it *is* now a sentence, not a fragment.

Notice that each of these fragments lacks some essential part of a sentence. We can now add this rule:

Make sure every declarative sentence contains a subject and a predicate.

The first thing to do when you come across a "sentence" that doesn't look right in your rough draft is to try underlining the subject with a single line and the predicate with a double line, just to make sure you have included all the necessary parts. Let's try a few.

Underline the subject once and the predicate twice. Remember that a term cannot be both subject and object at the same time. Some of them may lack either a subject or a predicate. The answers are on page 437.

6. The Affirmative Action core group will meet in Room 214.

_____

_____

7. The carton sealer dripping glue on the address labels.

_____

_____

8. There is no predicate, so revise the sentence.

_____

_____

9. On the second page of the outline is incomplete.

_____

_____

10. There is no subject, so revise the sentence.

_____

_____

11. I want to talk to you. About the contract deadline.

_____

_____

12. There is neither subject nor predicate for the second "sentence." Correct the problem.

_____

_____

Remember earlier we specified that we are considering only declarative sentences in this section on fragments. You need to know something about other kinds of sentences so that you don't confuse yourself by trying to find subjects and predicates where they don't belong. Although nearly all sentences in business writing are declarative, you may occasionally need to write interrogative, imperative, and even exclamatory sentences. Here are some examples of each:

Interrogative

Who compiled the information on the Browning account?
Whom do you suggest I contact?
Which department won the safety award?
Whose approval does this require?

(Notice that who, whom, whose, or which can begin an interrogative sentence, but when used this way they are interrogative, not relative, pronouns.)

Imperative

Fold the long flap so that it covers the contents.
Remove the packing slip carefully.
Keep the green copy for your files.

(Each of these sentences implies the word <u>you</u> as subject for the verb.)

Exclamatory

Congratulations on your new position here at Acme Sales.
How nice of you to write me on this occasion.
Welcome to our growing list of subscribers.

(Notice that although these sentences are exclamations they end with a period rather than with an exclamation mark, which would also be acceptable. This low-key approach is generally more effective.)

Let's summarize the ways to avoid sentence fragments.

1. Never begin a declarative sentence with who, whom, whose, or which.

2. Make sure every subordinate clause has an independent clause in the sentence to support it.

3. Make sure every declarative sentence contains a subject and a predicate.

Now try the following exercises. Revise each of the "sentences" that are only fragments. If no revision is necessary, go on to the next example. The answers are on pages 437 and 438.

13. Two of the packages arrived without shipping labels. Which must have fallen off in transit.

_____

_____

_____

14. Please sign and return the contract. If you agree with the provisions.

_____

_____

_____

15. We will meet at 2:30 P.M. In the conference room.

_____

_____

16. Indicate your preference in the space provided.

_____

_____

17. After the mechanic adjusted the dwell and timing on the engine could burn regular gas.

_____

_____

_____

18. We have tours beginning on June 4 and July 8. Which date do you prefer?

_____

_____

_____

19. I recommend the June tour. Which includes a bus trip to our Oaktown plant.

_____

_____

_____

20. Congratulations on exceeding your sales quota.

_____

_____

21. After considering your proposal and discussing it with Mr. Benson because of his concern for safety hazards on the assembly line.

---

22. Thank you for telling us how you like your new Bettco toaster.

Each of the following paragraphs contains two sentence fragments. Identify the fragments and revise them so that the paragraphs read smoothly.

23. I am happy to send you our hunting and fishing catalogue. Which you requested. Be sure to notice our reduced prices on outdoor cooking equipment featured on pages 29 to 36. And you can save an additional 10 per cent. If you order before July 1.

---

24. Machine #4 produced 5,758 cases this week. This breaks the old record of 5,752 set the week of August 10 last year. When we had a larger crew. Now that we have redesigned the cartons seldom clog the conveyor.

_____

_____

_____

_____

25.   Here is a list of the magazine articles you asked for. In your letter of October 17. I am sure you will find them useful. Because they are more recent than the ones you told me you have.

_____

_____

_____

_____

_____

26.   Because the cartons fell apart means they had very little glue along the seams. Which is why the freight company refuses to pay for the damage. (You can't repair the first "sentence" very easily. In such cases, rethink the idea and construct a new sentence.)

_____

_____

_____

27.   About your advertisement in last week's *Journal.* Your third "sentence" is not a sentence at all. Just a fragment. I thought you'd like to know. (It seems a shame to correct this gem; it takes all the fun out of the message. But try it, anyway.)

_____

_____

_____

_____

Correct whatever needs correcting in these last three items:

28. Which plan do you prefer?

_____

29. Our delivery fleet consists of seven trucks. Two of which are more than five years old.

_____

_____

_____

30. However I can arrange for a press conference on recent improvements in our air-pollution abatement system which we installed two years ago and updated last year.

_____

_____

_____

_____

_____

FOR CLASS DISCUSSION

Here is an actual letter written by a large corporation's employee publications manager, who edits the company magazine, *The Plumber's Helper*. Imagine yourself receiving this letter; then in class discuss its strengths and weaknesses in terms of clarity, organization, and sentence structure. Suggest ways of improving its effectiveness.

(I have slightly altered the letter to insure anonymity and to highlight the main points of this chapter.)

Acme Plumbing International
72 Joliet Place
Cambridge, MA 00228
Executive Offices

January 11, 1980

Mr. LeRoy Delphin
402 Willow Avenue
Cambridge, MA 02214

Dear LeRoy:

We are very pleased that you have agreed to be one of the judges for our Plumber's Helper Employee Photo Contest. Which we are sure you will enjoy.

In addition to you, Bill Stanley, chief photographer for the Cambridge Gazette, will participate in the judging.

We will have all the entries ready for your inspection at 10:00 A.M., Friday, January 18. As I promised, I've attached a map. To help you find our building in the industrial park. Allow yourself 30–45 minutes to get here from the downtown area.

Mr. LeRoy Delphin
January 11, 1980
Page two

Following judging, which we anticipate taking 1–1½ hours. It will be our pleasure to take you to lunch at a nearby restaurant. Also, in appreciation of your time, we will be providing you with a $50 honorarium.

Thank you again. For agreeing to be one of our judges. We are looking forward to seeing you on the 18th.

Sincerely,

Eugene Silveren
Manager, Employee Publications

EAS/ef

TEST YOURSELF

Get rid of all the sentence fragments by turning them into grammatical sentences. The answers are on page 439.

1. The ZYX 5000 computer is easy to program. If you read the manual carefully.

2. On the last page of the report contains some surprising information.

3. If you wish to visit our bakery, I will arrange for a guided tour. Which I'm sure you will enjoy.

4. The second page of your letter was missing. Which is the reason I am writing to you for the prices again.

5. We need to reduce production costs. Although we were within budget for the last quarter.

6. I will be happy to discuss your project with you. As soon as I return from Toronto.

7. Thank you for participating in our safety campaign.

8. Because Ms. Sumner has a speaking engagement next Tuesday at 4:00 P.M. is the reason why she cannot meet you at the airport.

9. I wrote to Mr. Billings and asked him for a copy of the contract. But he said he had not received one either. Which is delaying the start of our project.

10. Your letter of January 23, asking for an extension on your loan and not arriving at my office until February 25.

APPLY YOURSELF

Correct the sentence fragments in the following letter and insert a paragraph of your own where one is missing. Your paragraph should be about forty to fifty words long and should contain no sentence fragments. Invent whatever content you think would be appropriate.

2001 Oakhill Drive
Denver, CO 80229
August 14, 19—

Ms. Della Brownlow
Customer Relations
Acme Products Co.
3028 Dearborn Ave.
Chicago, IL 60606

Dear Ms. Brownlow:

I am returning the collapsible lawn chair. Which I bought through your catalogue.

Your advertisement says, "Satisfaction is guaranteed." But I am not satisfied with this chair. Let me tell you what happened.

(Insert your paragraph here.)

Therefore, I would like my money back. As soon as possible.

Sincerely,

Ms. Sally Sloan

ANSWERS TO EXERCISES

1. Here is next year's budget, which reflects increasing energy costs.

2. I submitted my cost estimates to Ms. Mayer, who will forward them to you.

3. I received this report from Mr. Lyttelton, whom we have recently assigned to our Atlanta office.

4. You should talk to Mr. Morrow, whose knowledge of the project is very extensive.

5. This is Part III of the Abrams Report, which you asked me to send you as soon as we finished it. Because you said you wanted detailed explanations of the procedures we followed, the third paragraph explains the steps we took in determining the best site for the warehouse. We used guidelines given us by Attorney F. E. Cassidy, whom we have engaged as legal counsel. Although his expertise is in another branch of the profession, he comes to us highly recommended.

6. The Affirmative Action core group will meet

7. The carton sealer

8. The carton sealer drips glue on the address labels.

9. is

10. On the second page the outline is incomplete.
OR
On the second page of the outline the information is incomplete.

11. I want

12. I want to talk to you about the contract deadline.

13. Two of the packages arrived without shipping labels, which must have fallen off in transit.

14. Please sign and return the contract if you agree with the provisions.

15. We will meet at 2:30 P.M. in the conference room.

16. No revision is necessary.

17. After the mechanic adjusted the dwell and timing on the engine, it could burn regular gas.
OR
After the mechanic adjusted the dwell and timing, the engine could burn regular gas.

18. No revision is necessary.

19. I recommend the June 4 tour, which includes a bus trip to our Oaktown plant.

20. No revision is necessary.

21. After considering your proposal, I discussed it with Mr. Benson because of his concern for safety hazards on the assembly line.

22. No revision is necessary.

23. I am happy to send you our hunting and fishing catalogue which you requested. Be sure to notice our reduced prices on outdoor cooking equipment featured on pages 29 to 36. And, if you order before July 1, you can save an additional 10 percent.

24. Machine #4 produced 5,758 cases this week. This breaks the old record of 5,752 set the week of August 10 last year when we had a larger crew. Now that we have redesigned the cartons, they seldom clog the conveyor.

25. Here is a list of the magazine articles you asked for in your letter of October 17. Because they are more recent than the ones you told me you have, I am sure you will find them useful.

> (You are also correct if you put the "Because . . ." clause at the end of the sentence. But putting it at the beginning allows the final emphasis to fall on the independent clause.)

26. The cartons fell apart because they had very little glue along the seams. This is why the freight company refuses to pay for the damage.

27. In your advertisement in last week's *Journal,* your third "sentence" is not a sentence at all. It's just a fragment. I thought you'd like to know.

28. No revision is necessary.

29. Our delivery fleet consists of seven trucks, two of which are more than five years old.

30. (Just put a comma after "However." This changes the word from a subordinator that means "in whatever way" to a sentence modifier that means "on the other hand.")

ANSWERS TO TEST YOURSELF

1. The ZYX 5000 computer is easy to program if you read the manual carefully.

2. On the last page of the report is some surprising information.
OR
    The last page of the report contains some surprising information.

3. If you wish to visit our bakery, I will arrange for a guided tour, which I'm sure you will enjoy.

4. The second page of your letter is missing. That is the reason I am writing to you for the prices again.
OR
    I am writing to you for the prices again because the second page of your letter was missing.

5. We need to reduce production costs although we were within budget for the last quarter.
OR
    Although we were within budget for the last quarter, we need to reduce production costs.

6. I will be happy to discuss your project with you as soon as I return from Toronto.
OR
    As soon as I return from Toronto, I will be happy to discuss your project with you.

7. No revision is necessary.

8. Because Ms. Sumner has a speaking engagement next Tuesday at 4:00 P.M., she cannot meet you at the airport.
OR
    Ms. Sumner's speaking engagement next Tuesday at 4:00 P.M. is the reason she cannot meet you at the airport.
OR
    Ms. Sumner cannot meet you at the airport because she has a speaking engagement next Thursday at 4:00 P.M.

9. I wrote to Mr. Billings and asked him for a copy of the contract. But he said he had not received one either. This is delaying the start of our project. (Note: You are also correct if you joined the first two sentences like this: ". . . contract, but . . .")

10. Your letter of January 23, asking for an extension on your loan, did not arrive at my office until February 25.

20

Punctuate with Care

A young boy returned a large book on turtles to the library's circulation desk the day after he had checked it out. When the librarian asked him why he was returning it so soon, he explained:

"This book tells me more about turtles than I want to know."

This chapter will not tell you more about punctuation than you want to know. As a business writer, your writing will almost always be expository or persuasive; therefore, you will have little need to know the niceties of punctuating dialogue in a narrative, for instance. For the purposes of this chapter, we will stick to just those marks of punctuation that tend to give ulcers to many business writers—and their readers—when the punctuation error results in costly misunderstandings.

Before we start discussing them, though, perhaps we had better consider what punctuation is in general. Punctuation is to the writer what voice inflection is to the speaker: both help convey meaning by showing how the words of the message relate to each other. Looked at another way, the various marks of punctuation are signals of meaning every bit as much as the words themselves are. A period at the end of a sentence, for instance, says to the reader, "You have just finished reading a complete statement." Readers interpret the period to mean this, of course, because their experience has shown them that writers of English generally seem to imply that meaning when they use periods.

When you write a report or a business letter, you want your message to be as clear as it can be. Punctuation clues to your meaning depend on your reader's experience of what the various marks of punctuation usually mean. Therefore, the more conventional your punctuation is, the better. The creative writer, when constructing a story or a poem, can afford to be unconventional by punctuating in unusual ways to make the work more "personal" or to shock the reader into attention. But *you* cannot afford to be unorthodox. Your punctuation must not call attention to itself; it must not make your reader see more than one possibility in what you mean. It must point clearly to the word relationships that you intend.

Unclear or misleading punctuation in business writing results mainly from misuse of the following punctuation marks:

1. apostrophe
2. colon
3. semicolon
4. comma

THE APOSTROPHE

The apostrophe has several uses, but we will consider only the troublesome ones—showing possession and indicating plural.

Possessive

To make a noun possessive, always add 's unless the noun is plural and ends in s.

If the noun is a plural ending in s, then add only the apostrophe after the final s.

Do not use the apostrophe or 's to indicate the possessive of the following pronouns: I, we, you, he, she, it, they, who. All other pronouns form their possessives the same way nouns do.

Let's practice applying these rules. The answers are on page 463.

1. Change the following to possessive:
person
manager
report

—————————————

—————————————

—————————————

2. Change these to possessive:
men
women
workers

—————————————

—————————————

—————————————

442

3. Try these:
dress
dresses
one

_____

_____

_____

4. Here comes a curve ball. Watch out.
Mr. Jones
Ms. Wondrash
Mr. Prentiss

_____

_____

_____

Did you miss that last one? Don't feel bad. Actually, according to some grammarians, "Mr. Prentiss' " would also be correct. Some texts argue that proper names of more than one syllable, and ending in *s*, form the possessive by adding only the apostrophe. This perhaps does make the word a little easier to pronounce. But really, since *both* forms ("Mr. Prentiss' " and "Mr. Prentiss's") are correct, common sense dictates using the *'s* because it keeps the rule a lot simpler. Therefore, don't criticize someone for writing "Mr. Prentiss'." Just do it the other way yourself. If you follow the simple rule of always indicating the possessive of all nouns by adding *'s* unless the word is plural and ends in *s*, you will always be right.

Now, let's try applying the third rule.

5. What is the possessive form of the following?
I
he
we

_____

_____

_____

6. What is the possessive form of the following?

they

it

who

_____

_____

_____

Notice that these possessive forms do not use apostrophes.

Some of these words do use the apostrophe, but not to show possession.

7. What do the following words mean?

he's

it's

who's

_____

_____

_____

There's another thing you should remember about these forms. They give your writing a markedly informal tone; that is, they tend to make your writing sound a lot like conversation. That's why I've used them throughout this textbook myself. For some kinds of business writing, such as letters to people with whom you are on a first-name basis, this is exactly what you want. But for most reports and for certain kinds of letters—those that demand a more businesslike, objective tone—you should not use contractions. It's important to be able to control the tone of voice your reader "hears" when reading your writing. Using contractions or not using them is a major technique in controlling that tone.

Now then, getting back to apostrophes, we have said that they also can serve to indicate plural. The one thing to remember here is that numbers, letters, and words form their plurals this way *only* when you use them *as* numbers, letters, and words—that is, when you italicize (underline) them.

> *Your list has two 3's in it.*
> *I think the advertising slogan has too many m's close together.*
> *This sentence has so many or's in it I can't figure out its meaning.*

Notice that the underlining does not extend to the *'s*.

THE COLON

Earlier we said that a period tells the reader, "You have just finished reading a complete statement." The colon "talks" to your reader that way too. It says, "You have just read a general statement, and you are now going to read a detailed list or explanation of what that statement means." Because your reader will assume that is what the colon means, you should use it only after a complete statement.

> ***Use a colon as sentence punctuation only if a complete statement precedes it and a list or specification follows it.***

For instance, do *not* use it like this:

> *I objected to his using such terms as: fraud, dishonesty, and criminal.*

There is no complete statement before the colon here. You can correct the sentence merely by dropping out the colon.

> *I objected to his using such terms as fraud, dishonesty, and criminal.*

Or, you can convert the first part of the sentence into a statement, like this:

> *I objected to his using such terms as the following: fraud, dishonesty, and criminal.*

Some writers have trouble deciding whether to use a colon or a semicolon between two independent clauses. Only the particular kind of relationship between the two clauses can provide an answer. Consider these sentences:

> *You may tour our plant any weekday morning; we are always glad to visit with our good customers.*
> *The first shipment was damaged; the second one arrived late.*
> *He explained why he was late: he had a flat tire and cut his hand while changing it.*
> *This applicant has two important qualifications: she writes well and her college grades are excellent.*

Notice that the colon seems to hint to the reader "You are about to read a specification, a listing, of what you just finished reading."
Now you try some.
Place either a semicolon or a colon between the independent clauses in the following sentences. The answers are on page 463.

8. First you must turn off the power then you must check every fuse in the line.

_____

_____

_____

9. The safety campaign has only one purpose we want to reduce lost-time injuries.

_____

_____

_____

There is one other thing you should notice about colons and semicolons. They both must have an independent clause before them, but only the semicolon requires an independent clause after it. You can put words, phrases, dependent clauses, or independent clauses after a colon. For instance, in the last example we could change the sentence like this:

> The safety campaign has only one purpose: to reduce lost-time injuries.

We could even have just a list of nouns after a colon:

> The following items were missing from the kit: nuts, bolts, washers, and endcaps.

Or we could have just a single word after a colon:

> He gave only one reason for the accident: carelessness.

Of course, we use colons other places too. For example, we put them after salutations and between hours and minutes. But here we are considering only colons within a sentence. Remember, I promised not to tell you in this chapter any more about punctuation than you wanted to know.

Now lets's get some practice in using the colon.

Which of the following sentences contains a _misused_ colon?

10. (a) Our sleeveless sweaters come in four pastel colors: blue, green, yellow, and violet.

(b) Our sleeveless sweaters come in: blue, green, yellow, and violet.

11. (a) I cannot understand this report: It seems disorganized.
    (b) The report makes a very important point: Our security needs improvement.

——————

12. (a) Our options are: repair the old boiler or replace it with a rebuilt one.
    (b) We have two options: Repair the old boiler or replace it with a rebuilt one.

——————

13. (a) We need to increase our inventory of the following items: wrenches, hammers, hacksaws, and chisels.
    (b) Wrenches, hammers, hacksaws, and chisels: these are the items we need to increase our inventory of.

——————

THE SEMICOLON

You have already learned some things about the semicolon from our discussion of colons. You know, for instance, that semicolons require an independent clause before them and after them, too. You also know that the semicolon tells the reader something about the relationship between the independent clauses that it both separates and joins. But its message to the reader is not so specific as the colon's. About all it says is "You have just read an independent clause, and you are about to read an independent clause that relates to it closely enough to be in the same sentence with it."

If we consider the comma as a very weak divider between two equal parts, and the period as a very strong divider between two equal parts, then we can see the semicolon as a half-way kind of punctuation to divide two equal parts.

However, when we put a coordinating conjunction (*and, or, but, nor, for, yet,* or *so*) between the clauses, we have no need for the semicolon.

He wanted to leave, yet he stayed.

Use a semicolon between independent clauses not joined by and, or, but, nor, for, yet, or so.

Let's look at some examples. In the following sentences, one clause explains the other:

The changes we made on Line 4 seem to be working; production is up 7 per cent over last month's.

447

Do not calibrate the meter before aligning the circuit; aligning affects calibration.

Mr. Johnson has approved your request; therefore, you need not send the information I asked for.

In the following sentences, the two clauses have a similar structure:

When she joined our department, we were disorganized; by the time she left, we had become efficient.

On Mondays, Wednesdays, and Fridays I am in my office; on Tuesdays and Thursdays I am on the road.

In all of these examples we could have used a period instead of a semicolon, but the semicolon suggests a closer relationship between the two clauses than writing them as separate sentences would show.

There is one other use for the semicolon that is just the opposite of what we have seen so far. Up to now we have used the semicolon when we could have used a period, but wanted something a little weaker than that. Sometimes, however, where we would ordinarily use a comma we may need punctuation a little stronger than a comma. Suppose we write a sentence with three or more elements in series.

Our new tracking system will eliminate delays, reduce the number of misplaced items, and provide a record for tax purposes.

Commas are enough to do the separating here. But suppose we have a series of three or more items *within* one of these elements. Then we need something stronger than commas to separate the major divisions.

Our new tracking system will eliminate delays; reduce the number of misplaced dresses, hats, coats, and boots; and provide a record for tax purposes.

Even one comma within an item in a series requires us to use semicolons between the items. For example, notice the punctuation in this sentence:

I have received a memorandum explaining our policies on retirement; on sick leave; and on lost-time injuries, whether work related or not.

This brings us to the second rule for the semicolon:

Use semicolons to separate items in series if there are any commas within the items.

The semicolon, then, is both a very weak period and a very strong comma. Maybe that is why it looks like a combination of the two.

Which of the following sentences contain *misused* semicolons? The answers are on page 463.

14. (a) We will send four managers to New York; including the two who asked for the assignment.

(b) We will send four managers to New York; these include the two who asked for the assignment.

---

15. (a) The night crew produced 412 cases; the day crew produced only 340.

(b) We need to order more stationery; typewriter ribbons; and desk calendars.

---

16. (a) We need to order more stationery, both white and buff; typewriter ribbons; and desk calendars.

(b) Ms. Belton sent your request to me; because her department processes only orders for merchandise.

---

17. (a) After studying the situation carefully; Mr. Nolter decided to buy from another vendor.

(b) Mr. Nolter studied the situation carefully; then he decided to buy from another vendor.

THE COMMA

The comma is perhaps the most frequently used—and most frequently abused—mark of punctuation we have. Its uses are so varied that we cannot always be sure exactly what it says about word relationships. But your reader ought to feel confident that you have a good reason for every one you use.

Of the comma's many uses there are four that can be particularly troublesome to the business writer:

1. to separate items in a series
2. to separate two independent clauses joined by a conjunction
3. to separate introductory adverb clauses from the rest of the sentence
4. to separate parenthetical material from the rest of the sentence.

And there are three places where you must never use just a single comma:

1. between the subject and its verb
2. between the verb and its complement (direct object, predicate noun, or predicate adjective)
3. between a preposition and its object

For example, the following sentences violate one or the other of these rules:

> **Wrong:** *Our new pen and pencil set with its gold-leaf casing and ruby pocket clip, is very attractive.*
> (Here the comma wrongly separates the subject <u>set</u> from its verb <u>is</u>.)
> **Wrong:** *The gatekeeper announced in a firm voice, that no visitors had entered since noon.*
> (Here the comma wrongly separates the verb <u>announced</u> from its complement, a direct object, the noun clause <u>that no visitors had entered since noon</u>.)
> **Wrong:** *We need a new fence around, the visitors' parking lot.*
> (Here the comma wrongly separates the preposition <u>around</u> from its object <u>lot</u>.)

Of course, you may sometimes put commas in these places—but only in pairs to separate something parenthetical. For instance, in the first two examples above, you could place commas like this:

> *Our new pen and pencil set, with its gold-leaf casing and ruby pocket clip, is very attractive.*

> *The gatekeeper announced, in a firm voice, that no visitors had entered since noon.*

Now, how about commas to separate items in series? To avoid having your reader misread your message, you should stick to the following rule:

> **Use the serial comma. (The serial comma appears before the word <u>and</u> or <u>or</u> in a list of three or more items.)**

It is true that most newspapers and popular magazines do not use the serial comma. But your writing must be as precise and clear as you can make it. You do not want your reader to consider the last two items of a series as if they were a single unit if you don't intend them to be. But not using the serial comma can sometimes invite such a misreading.

Suppose you write the following:

> *We stock a variety of pennants: green, orange, brown, blue, white.*

Would this be grammatical?

Certainly. You don't *need* to use the word *and* in a series at all. The Greeks called this structure "asyndeton," and it is grammatical in English.

Now suppose you write the sentence like this:

> *We stock a variety of pennants: green, orange, brown, blue and white.*

How can your reader tell whether there are five kinds of pennants or only four? Without the serial comma your reader has no way of knowing whether you intend the last two items in the series as one item or two.

Therefore, if you want *blue* and *white* as separate choices, write it this way:

We stock a variety of pennants: green, orange, brown, blue, and white.

If you intend *blue and white* as a unit, write it this way:

We stock a variety of pennants: green, orange, blue and white, and brown.

Remember that this use of the comma applies only to a series of three or more items. Do not use any comma if the series has only two items in it.

To practice applying this rule, put punctuation where it belongs in the following sentences: The answers are on pages 463 and 464.

18. We ordered two stencil brushes two ink pots one stencil-making kit and three bottles of solvent.

_____

_____

_____

19. We received only one stencil brush and two ink pots.

_____

_____

20. We still did not receive the following one stencil brush one stencil-making kit three bottles of solvent.

_____

_____

_____

21. Please let us know which of the following colors you want on your warm-up jackets blue and gold red and white blue and white or green and gold.

_____

_____

_____

Now let's consider a particularly troublesome use of the comma. Some writers tend to use a comma to separate two independent clauses. Unless there is a coordinating conjunction after that comma, the reader's eye skips along from the first clause right into the second, and the reader's mind registers "Items in a series!" Don't mislead your reader this way; it's very annoying. Therefore, be sure to follow this rule:

Do not use a comma to separate two independent clauses unless you also use one of these conjunctions after the comma: _and, or, but, nor, for, yet, so._

It's a good idea to memorize these conjunctions. They are the only ones in the English language that permit joining two independent clauses with a comma. Without one of them, you end up with a "comma splice," a serious and confusing kind of punctuation fault.

Actually, there are four ways you can join two independent clauses:
1. a colon

He gave me a brief explanation: The rope was too short.

2. a semicolon

This new brochure is very attractive; it certainly catches the eye.

3. a semicolon and a long coordinating conjunction (e.g., *however, moreover, therefore, nevertheless, consequently*) followed by a comma

The parts arrived only yesterday; however, we can still meet the assembly deadline.

4. a comma followed by *and, or, but, nor, for, yet,* or *so*

The parts arrived only yesterday, but we can still meet the assembly deadline.

(But use a semicolon before one of these conjunctions if there is another comma nearby in the sentence.)

Be careful to avoid the comma splice. Do not join two independent clauses this way:

Wrong: *Our replacement hinges are very durable, we make them of stainless steel.*

Even worse is to join two independent clauses without even a comma between them. This kind of run-on sentence greatly confuses your reader:

Wrong: *This is the only book on the topic I can recommend the others are too difficult to understand.*

Write it like this:

Correct: *This is the only book on the topic I can recommend; the others are too difficult to understand.*

Another important comma rule that can help you to keep your meaning clear is this:

Put a comma after an adverb clause that begins a sentence.

This rule will keep you from writing confusing statements like this one:

Soon after we started the machine began to vibrate.

The writer probably meant this:

Soon after we started, the machine began to vibrate.

The normal place for an adverb clause is at the end of the sentence. In that position it usually requires no comma.

He asked for Thursday off because he has a dental appointment.

But if you put the adverb clause at the beginning, you need to put a comma after it.

Because he has a dental appointment, he asked for Thursday off.

Finally, we will consider one more use of the comma. To help your reader mentally separate the essential parts of your sentence from the nice-to-know-but-not-crucial parts, you need to give comma signals. The following rule is therefore an important one:

Use commas to separate appositives, nonrestrictive clauses and phrases, and any other parenthetical material from the rest of the sentence.

We need to define a few terms before we can talk about this rule. An appositive is a noun meaning the same as the noun immediately before it.

Ms. Phyllis Van Doote, plant safety director, will give a slide presentation on fire hazards.

A nonrestrictive clause or phrase is one that does not limit (restrict) the meaning of the word it modifies.

He gave a gift to all the employees, who had worked hard.

Notice that if we omit "who had worked hard," the sentence will retain its essential meaning. *All* the employees received gifts.

But suppose we want to say that only the hard-working employees received gifts and that the others did not. Then we would not use the comma; we would make the clause restrictive.

He gave a gift to all the employees who had worked hard.

In general, when in doubt whether a phrase or clause is parenthetical, you should try reading the sentence without it. If the sentence still has essentially the same meaning, the phrase or clause is parenthetical, and you should use commas to separate it from the rest of the sentence.

454

If the parenthetical material has one or more commas within it, then use dashes instead of commas to make the main separation.

Four employees—Bill, Sue, Jim, and Dan—received service awards last month.

Put commas where they belong in the following sentences. The answers are on page 464.

22. Our special mending tape will adhere to metal wood glass leather and cloth.

_____

_____

23. Last month's production is disappointing but because we have solved the jamming problem we expect to reach our goal by the end of the month.

_____

_____

_____

24. Because our plant will close for maintenance next week we need to complete the energy test by this Friday.

_____

_____

_____

25. Mr. Jessup's proposal which is the most thorough one I have seen in a long time can save us $4,000 a year.

_____

_____

_____

26. After Ms. Finch left on her vacation these two letters for her arrived.

_____

_____

27. These two letters for Ms. Finch arrived after she left on her vacation.

_____

_____

Now let's try a few sentences that require a variety of punctuation marks. But, before we do, it would be a good idea to summarize the main rules so we don't forget them. Look them over and then try the last few exercises.

> *To make a noun possessive, always add 's unless the noun is a plural and ends in s.*
>
> *Use 's to indicate plural for underlined numbers, letters, and words.*
>
> *Use a colon as sentence punctuation only if a complete statement precedes it and a list or specification follows it.*
>
> *Use a semicolon between independent clauses not joined by and, or, but, nor, for, yet, or so.*
>
> *Use the serial comma.*
>
> *Do not use a comma to separate two independent clauses unless you also use one of these conjunctions after the comma: and, or, but, nor, for, yet, so.*
>
> *Put a comma after an adverb clause that begins a sentence.*
>
> *Use commas to separate appositives, nonrestrictive clauses and phrases, and any other parenthetical material from the rest of the sentence.*

28. Mr. Kress list included the following mens hats womens shoes and boys shirts trousers and jackets.

_____

_____

_____

29. Six managers Jill Bayer Tom Wills Ann Ryekamp Lew Smith Alice Schwartz and Tom Allison attended the convention however only Tom Allison submitted a travel voucher.

_____

_____

_____

_____

_____

30. Your typewritten messages are hard to read because your typewriters e [plural] look like o [plural] nevertheless I can make out most of what you asked for.

_____

_____

_____

_____

Finally, we need to say a few words concerning the writing of numbers.

NUMBERS

You should follow whatever convention your company prefers for writing numbers. But in the absence of any such preference, these very general rules can be useful:

1. In business letters, write out any number that begins a sentence or that you can express in one or two words, e.g. fifty-three, ninety, four hundred. Use figures for other numbers.

2. In reports, write out numbers from one to nine, inclusive, and also any number that begins a sentence. Use figures for other numbers.

FOR CLASS DISCUSSION

Here is the actual text of an insurance executive's letter to one of his agents. Comment on the letter's tone, clarity, and readability. What can you discover about the writer from the diction (word choices)? How does the letter's punctuation affect your attitude toward the writer? Discuss the letter's good qualities and bad qualities in class.

(Letterhead)

(date)

(Inside address)

(Reference data)

Dear _____ :

We fooled around with these people long enough, if they are going to try and get cute with us; I think what we better do is refer it to Attorney's in the area for Subrogation. I want someone to start suit on the claim immediately; I don't want any fooling around.

If you can't find anyone locally that will do it; let me know and we'll make some arrangements.

Very truly yours,

(Signature block)

TEST YOURSELF

Punctuate the following sentences correctly. Do not break any of them into two separate sentences. The answers are on page 465.

1. We would like to help you find the information about insurance coverage purchase date and model year but we have no data on Mr. Nayliss car.

2. After you have completed your investigation please report your findings to Ms. Simpson the area coordinator.

3. You have so many ands in the sentences that your meaning is not clear therefore I am returning the draft for revision.

4. Don't try to rush it will only increase the risk of injury.

5. These sweaters come in only three sizes small medium and large.

6. We have branch offices in the following cities Boston Massachusetts Cleveland Ohio Boise Idaho and Escanaba Michigan.

7. Four members of the council John Holt Bill Molin Sue Danielsen and Jim Huff signed the report.

8. The newly elected officers are Mr. T. Holm Ms. F. Barry and Ms. M. Duval.

9. We have not been able to get the necessary loan consequently we must withdraw our offer.

10. Our accident rate is declining yet we are still above the national norm.

APPLY YOURSELF

Your assistant, who edits the company's monthly newsletter for employees, has asked you for some punctuation guidelines so that the publication can have a consistent style. Write the section you will give him on use of the semicolon.

Be sure to give clear examples of every point you make. Your reader will need to use what you have written as a reference, so present your material in whatever way you think will be most convenient to use. Try to use fewer than 150 words.

ANSWERS TO EXERCISES

1. person's
    manager's
    report's

2. men's
    women's
    workers'

3. dress's
    dresses'
    one's

4. Mr. Jones's
    Ms. Wondrash's
    Mr. Prentiss's

5. my
    his
    our

6. their
    its
    whose

7. he is (*or* he has)
    it is (*or* it has)
    who is (*or* who has)

8. power; then

9. purpose: we

10. B

11. A

12. A

13. B

14. A

15. B

16. B

17. A

18. We ordered two stencil brushes, two ink pots, one stencil-making kit, and three bottles of solvent.

19. No commas are necessary; there are only two items in series.

20. We still did not receive the following: one stencil brush, one stencil-making kit, three bottles of solvent.
(Did you remember to use the colon here?)

21. Please let us know which of the following colors you want on your warm-up jackets: blue and gold, red and white, blue and white, or green and gold.

22. Our special mending tape will adhere to metal, wood, glass, leather, and cloth.

23. Last month's production is disappointing, but because we have solved the jamming problem we expect to reach our goal by the end of the month. (A comma after *problem* is optional, not necessary; the adverb clause does not begin the sentence.)

24. Because our plant will close for maintenance next week, we need to complete the energy test by this Friday.

25. Mr. Jessup's proposal, which is the most thorough one I have seen in a long time, can save us $4,000 a year.

26. After Ms. Finch left on her vacation, these two letters for her arrived.

27. No comma is necessary; the adverbial clause is in its normal position at the end.

28. Mr. Kress's list included the following: men's hats; women's shoes; and boys' shirts, trousers, and jackets.

29. Six managers—Jill Bayer, Tom Wills, Ann Ryekamp, Lew Smith, Alice Schwartz, and Tom Allison—attended the convention; however, only Tom Allison submitted a travel voucher.

30. Your typewritten messages are hard to read because your typewriter's *e*'s look like *o*'s; nevertheless, I can make out most of what you asked for.

ANSWERS TO TEST YOURSELF

1. We would like to help you find the information about insurance coverage, purchase date, and model year; but we have no information on Mr. Nayliss's car.

2. After you have completed your investigation, please report your findings to Ms. Simpson, the area coordinator.

3. You have so many *and*'s in the sentences that your meaning is not clear; therefore, I am returning the draft for revision.

4. Don't try to rush; it will only increase the risk of injury.

5. These sweaters come in only three sizes: small, medium, and large.
   OR
   These sweaters come in only three sizes—small, medium, and large.

6. We have branch offices in the following cities: Boston, Massachusetts; Cleveland, Ohio; Boise, Idaho; and Escanaba, Michigan.

7. Four members of the council—John Holt, Bill Molin, Sue Danielsen, and Jim Huff—signed the report.

8. The newly elected officers are Mr. T. Holm, Ms. F. Barry, and Ms. M. Duval.

9. We have not been able to get the necessary loan; consequently, we must withdraw our offer.

10. Our accident rate is declining, yet we are still above the national norm.

Correction Symbols

agr	Faulty agreement between subject and predicate (p. 301).
ant	Antecedent not clear (pp. 75, 302).
awk	Awkward phrasing.
cs	Comma splice (p. 452).
def	Define word or term.
defl	Deflate the inflated language (p. 260).
dm	Dangling or misplaced modifier (pp. 69, 73–75).
ev	Give supporting evidence.
ew	Empty words (pp. 243–44).
frag	Sentence fragment (Chapter 19).
i	Illogical.
ir	Irrelevant.
nc	Noun clutter (Chapter 2).
o	Omit the encircled word or words.
pa	Use a more positive approach (p. 116).
pl	Faulty parallelism (p. 276).
pw	Poorly worded.
r	Faulty repetition.
red	Redundant (p. 242).
ros	Run-on sentence (p. 452).
sp	Spelling error.
su	Substandard usage (pp. 262–63).
sx	Sexist language (Chapter 5).
tns	Error in verb tense.
tr	Transition needed (pp. 306–307).
tri	Trite expression, cliché, or stock phrase (p. 259).
v	Vague; use specific language (p. 258).
vo	Avoid the passive voice (Chapter 3).
w	Wordy (Chapter 11).
ww	Wrong word (Chapter 12).
¶	Begin a new paragraph here.
no ¶	Do not begin a new paragraph here.
?	Is this accurate?

Index